ROUSSEAU

A STUDY OF HIS THOUGHT

emile   P77

ROUSSEAU

A STUDY OF HIS THOUGHT

by

J. H. BROOME

Lecturer in French
University of Keele

LONDON

EDWARD ARNOLD (PUBLISHERS) LTD

© J. H. Broome 1963

First Published 1963

PRINTED IN GREAT BRITAIN BY
ROBERT CUNNINGHAM & SONS LTD
ALVA, SCOTLAND

Preface

*

FROM whatever point of view he is considered, Jean-Jacques Rousseau must be accounted one of the outstanding figures of the eighteenth century. His influence, good or bad, is still discernible in literature, philosophy, religion, politics and education; but his actual doctrine has become somewhat obscured by the haze of controversy and the sheer mass of erudite criticism with which it is now surrounded.

Rousseau himself is responsible for much of the confusion, because of the frequent ambiguity of his expression, and also because of his deliberate cultivation of paradox; but there are other obstacles to understanding for which he can hardly be blamed. One of these is the fact that the more popular presentations of him tend, naturally, to exploit the curiosity-value of his life, and consider his works separately in the intervals of biographical narrative; another is that serious discussions of his thought are apt to be highly specialized. It so happens that Rousseau comes up for attention in a number of different academic disciplines, and is, in consequence, studied more often in the parts than in the whole. This, again, is understandable, in view of the scope and density of his writings, but the results are unfortunate, to say the least. For example, the student of French literature may encounter the *Nouvelle Héloïse* in the history of the novel—and will probably hasten on to something more digestible; the student of education will note *Emile* as a source of some modern attitudes, but is unlikely to become familiar with more than the first sections; those concerned with history, politics and philosophy may be called upon to study the *Contrat Social* in various contexts, involving, perhaps, Plato or Hobbes or Locke, but disregarding Rousseau's other writings; and it is rarely that he is set specifically against the religious background, although this may well be the way to make most sense of him. As for the general reader in search of human interest, he may try the *Confessions*, as the record of an unusual and disturbing personality, but is less likely to tackle the *Dialogues*, or to understand the significance of the *Rêveries*.

The aim of this book is to counteract this dismembering of Rousseau, by providing for the student and the general reader alike a perspective

v

in which it may be possible to grasp the close relationships which exist between the principal writings. It is not a biography, but an exposition of the main lines of his thought, in both its public and private aspects, and as it develops in those works which are most likely to be encountered in practice. A few relevant biographical details are mentioned in the text, but otherwise, the scheme of historical reference is reduced to a separate chronological outline. In general, the texts are discussed in chronological order, because this is also a logical order; the exception is the *Nouvelle Héloïse*, the examination of which is deferred slightly for reasons of convenience.

In addition to offering concise expositions of the movement of ideas in individual texts, this study raises the more important problems of criticism and interpretation, not necessarily to provide simple answers, but to show why Rousseau's work is still alive, and why he has been the subject of so much controversy. It is in no sense a thesis; but it does rest on the belief that Rousseau's doctrine is, if not convincing, at least comprehensible and even inevitable in the historical context in which it evolved; and that it is coherent, provided that it is viewed as a whole, with a sense of its dynamic quality and some sympathy towards the transcendental elements in it.

Contents

C'est un grand et beau spectacle de voir l'homme sortir en quelque manière du néant par ses propres efforts; dissiper, par les lumières de sa raison, les ténèbres dans lesquels la nature l'avait enveloppé; s'élever au-dessus de lui-même; s'élancer par l'esprit jusque dans les régions célestes; parcourir à pas de géant, ainsi que le soleil, la vaste étendue de l'univers; et, ce qui est encore plus grand et plus difficile, rentrer en soi pour y étudier l'homme et connaître sa nature, ses devoirs, et sa fin.

Discours sur les sciences et les arts

CHAPTER I

Background

*

ONE of the most constant impressions which the writings of Rousseau have left with succeeding generations is that of a man in revolt. Because of this, his works cannot be satisfactorily expounded or discussed without a brief preliminary account of the order of life and thought against which he was reacting, and of various factors, historical, personal and philosophical, which can provide some general explanations of his attitude.

The historical background to his work is, on a broad view, European rather than national; but it must be recognized from the outset that in this respect his status is somewhat exceptional. Although he wrote in French and belongs to the literature and the intellectual life of France, he was a native of the independent city of Geneva, which he left at an early age, and where he was unable to integrate himself again, although he tried to do so. Much of his thinking, particularly on politics and religion, is conditioned by the atmosphere of his native city; but on the other hand, his philosophy is largely a reaction against a form of civilization of which the France of the seventeenth and eighteenth centuries is in many ways the epitome. The Genevan influence is relevant, on the whole, to his constructive thought, but his critical attitude can be understood most easily in relation to the Parisian society which he encountered in the middle decades of the eighteenth century, and to the political, social and cultural evolution of France during the previous hundred years.

We must, therefore, go back at least to the age of Louis XIV, when France, following policies of reconstruction after the upheavals caused by the Renaissance, the Reformation and certain aristocratic resistances, had emerged as a nation-state with an absolute monarchy functioning, ostensibly, on the basis of the political theory of Divine Right. This was the *Grand Siècle*, when France appears to have achieved an outward and temporary equilibrium between traditional values and the progressive forces of humanism; and to have found expression for it in art, and in the neo-classical literature associated with names such as Racine, Molière, La Fontaine or Boileau.

This era, symbolized by the Versailles of Louis XIV, is, on the surface, a period of conformity. Since the mid-century disturbances of the Frondes, the central political authority is firmly established and working through an efficient bureaucracy; the atmosphere is not conducive to bold enterprises in political philosophy; and the association of the regime with the ideal of a wholly Catholic France means that religious devia- tions are met with strong measures, as the treatment of Protestants and Jansenists shows well enough. The structure of French society itself, though not absolutely rigid, reveals the stratification to be expected in such an age, and the upper divisions of the hierarchy are themselves subdivided, partly in accordance with military, legal or ecclesiastical functions, or, slightly lower down the scale, with a wider range of pro- fessional activities. The mass of the population is, of course, not arti- culate or politically conscious; but on the whole, the France of Louis XIV displays to the world a façade which remains imposing even when it is admitted that the unity and homogeneity which used to be attributed to the age are more or less a myth. The cultural achievements, at least, are real and authentic, and the social ideal of urbanity, enshrined in the formula *honnête homme*, will retain much of its force and influence well into the following century.

It is, however, not to be expected that a system with so many impli- cations of repression or rigidity, and depending so much upon the personality of the monarch, could, however genuine his gifts, establish a permanence or remain unaffected by movements outside the frontiers, and covert resistance within them. The early years of Louis XIV may have been times of expansion and success, greeted with appropriate enthusiasm, but cracks which had never really been filled in begin to reappear in the façade at least as early as 1680. They are associated partly with economic stresses and the financial burden of Louis's less rewarding military adventures, partly with specific and dubious policies such as the persecution of the Protestants, leading to the revocation of the Edict of Nantes in 1685; and partly with the resurgence of a spirit of criticism, never very obtrusive but always present throughout the century. This spirit derives mainly from Renaissance humanism, and can be traced constantly in the writings of certain freethinkers or *libertins*. It is also associated with the particular brand of rational and scientific enquiry to be found in the philosophy of Descartes; and in a way, it is one of the achievements of seventeenth-century France, that it managed to canalize or contain for so long the critical implications of Descartes's methodic doubt.

The reviving spirit of criticism in France gains considerable strength during the last two decades of the century, and is expressed in various ways, some innocuous, some more potent. Objection to cultural traditionalism, for example, finds an outlet in the famous literary controversy over the relative merits of the Ancients and the Moderns, destined to flare up at intervals throughout the following century and inspire new approaches to aesthetic problems. What lies behind it, is a critical relativism and a belief in progress, expressing itself in a 'safe' sector of intellectual life. Other currents of opposition, however, begin to appear in the more dangerous areas of religion, philosophy and even politics. They can be detected occasionally in recognized Classical spirits such as Fénelon or La Bruyère; but are more commonly associated with lesser-known figures like Fontenelle, Saint-Evremond (exiled in England), and Pierre Bayle who, as the author of a famous *Historical and Critical Dictionary* and one of the founders of serious French journalism, is acknowledged to be a major source of the ammunition discharged in all directions by Voltaire and the later *philosophes*. Bayle, officially a Protestant, wrote mostly in Holland, where he had established himself at the time of the Huguenot exodus; but his career is a pointer to the new factor in the intellectual life of France at the turn of the century: namely, the sudden increase in the importance of foreign influences, especially those of northern Europe, which for a time tend to replace those of the classical civilizations. The Protestant exiles have a great deal to do with this, as journalists, propagandists and publishers, operating from Holland, England, Germany and Switzerland, including, of course, Rousseau's native city. From a literary point of view, their work is undistinguished, but it is largely through their efforts as translators and commentators that French writers of Rousseau's generation are able to familiarize themselves with the theories of Dutch and German jurists, or the currents of English philosophy and political thought, including the work of Bacon, Hobbes and Locke.

The effect of these influences is to give a greater impetus to the liberal tendencies of French thought during the first decades of the eighteenth century; to promote a cautious but far-reaching political criticism of the regime, exemplified by the *Lettres Persanes* of Montesquieu in 1721, or the *Lettres Philosophiques* of Voltaire, a decade later; and to favour the spread of Deism, or natural religion, in the face of the orthodox Catholic establishment of France and the corresponding Protestant systems entrenched, for example, in Calvinist Geneva. The desire for reform becomes increasingly widespread, and the Enlightenment, with its optimism and its belief in rational progress, gathers momentum in France as elsewhere. It is a period, in short, of intellectual liberation, leading to a form of criticism which is, likewise, predominantly intellectual in character. Rousseau himself will in due course be profoundly influenced by this resurgent humanism, like all the French writers of his century; and in the long run, can even be said to have pushed far ahead of most of them, at least in many ways. Yet this does not explain why he appears as a rebel and as a man apart, pursuing an individual line which will lead him ultimately to break with the band of Encyclopedists led and organized by Diderot, and to stand out in bitter opposition to Voltaire. Some of this discord can, no doubt, be accounted for by incompatibilities of temperament, or particular circumstances of a more or less personal nature, but it is clear that there is some fundamental difference in the *kind* of critical spirit discernible in the main body of the *philosophes*—Voltaire, Diderot, d'Alembert, Holbach, Helvétius and the rest—compared with the attitude of Rousseau. One fact which helps to explain the difference, is that the main group are criticizing *within* a society in which they are, after all, tolerably well integrated, whereas Rousseau is not. And to understand his peculiar and special dislike of this civilization, we must look a little more closely at the social scene in France after the conclusion, in 1715, of the long era of Louis XIV.

The last years of that age were accompanied by a certain gloom and frustration, caused partly by the burden of the War of the Spanish Succession, and partly by the monarch's return to a spirit of devoutness. It is not surprising that his death was felt to some extent as the departure of an incubus, and that the regency of the Duke of Orleans which followed, should appear as a period of social as well as intellectual liberation. Its atmosphere contains a curious blend of optimism and cynicism, and it sets the tone for the succeeding decades, covering the first part of the reign of Louis XV and the years preceding Rousseau's arrival in Paris. After the seventeenth century, it is an age of relative social fluidity, an age of speculation witnessing the rise of the commercial class, and especially that of the great financiers, profiting from the fiscal arrangements of the Old Regime, and the iniquitous system of tax-farming. It is true, of course, that this minority have, in their own time and since, been made convenient scapegoats, but the emergence of the financier as a stock figure in eighteenth-century satire is not without

significance as a testimony to the possibilities of extreme economic inequality in this period. Money does become more important as a
criterion of social esteem, and the ideal of urbanity is accompanied increasingly by standards of luxury which Rousseau is by no means alone
in condemning as a threat to traditional moral values. Materialism in
the social sense is a prelude to the philosophic materialism which he will
attack in the Encyclopedists; and it is an aspect of life concerning which
the century seems to have a divided conscience. On the whole, however,
the thinkers, in France as elsewhere, are inclined to put up with the in-
conveniences of luxury and console themselves with the doctrine of
Mandeville and others, to the effect that private vices may be public
virtues. Excessive luxury is scandalous, no doubt, but it provides employment, makes life more comfortable even for artists and intellectuals,
and accords well enough with the hedonism of the age—or at least with
the simpler forms of it.

> J'aime le luxe, et même la mollesse. . . .

So says the still optimistic Voltaire in *Le Mondain* of 1736, and he speaks
for many; because, after all, the century has its charm, and for some at
least, life is agreeable and tolerably amusing. There is good conversation
in the salons of Paris; there are the intimate supper-parties; there are the
theatres, and the society of the opera-girls, and all the amusements of the
capital. There is also, of course, rural depopulation and poverty, and
the fact that merit is not necessarily the surest way to advancement;
there is a dubious legal system, arbitrary imprisonment, religious intolerance. There is, in fact, plenty to criticize, and a multitude of
observers in the cafés and elsewhere, producing a vast and ephemeral
critical literature. There is, moreover, a censorship, and this in a way
adds to the pleasure of criticism by the encouragement of deviousness
and ingenuity.

Life in the France of the mid-eighteenth century has its drawbacks,
therefore, but it also has its compensations, especially in the capital;
and it is not so bad as to be completely intolerable to the articulate
classes of the population. Conditions will have to become considerably
worse before the whole regime is threatened; and it is perhaps for this
reason that the literature of the period, full though it is of satire, and
reforming or humanitarian propaganda, remains on the whole con-
formist, and rarely sounds the note of individual protest of a really
radical kind. This curious and paradoxical situation may be summed up
by saying that it is the *fashion* to criticize, and that criticism is the new

form of intellectual conformity. So, although there are moments of genuine disgust and outrage, the best-known figures of the philosophical movement do not impress by any burning desire to tear up society by the roots. Montesquieu, for example, liberal and even republican in sentiment, is held back by a mixture of realism, empiricism and prejudice, from advocating anything more than a cautious reform of the monarchy. This would be on constitutional lines inspired by a somewhat defective understanding of the English system, and it would certainly not destroy the social hierarchy. Similarly Voltaire, though a devastating opponent of revealed or institutionalized religion, and the barbarities or absurdities of the legal system, is certainly no revolutionary, but a man who appears to have enjoyed to the full the civilization of his age. Even Diderot, a combination of sensibility and 'advanced' intellectual tendencies, shrinking from nothing, and making of the *Encyclopédie* a rallying-point for something like a political opposition, seems in the end to be in love with ideas for their own sake. He may take up extreme theoretical positions, of atheism, materialism or 'immoralism', but in practice, like the others, he does the commonsense thing and compromises to some extent with the existing order, even though it has imprisoned him for a time in the château of Vincennes.

Rousseau's own philosophy, or at least parts of it, could also be shown to be concerned fundamentally with the problem of *how* to compromise, and the quest for principles which will make of compromise a valid or morally worthy act distinguishable from mere complacency. For it is his sense of the underlying complacency of contemporary society, and even of its critics, which transforms Rousseau's assault upon it into something much more radical, and at times, puritanical. Whereas most of the *philosophes* pursue a line of intellectual criticism directed against the stupidities of the social system, many of which could be rectified or moderated by administrative tinkering and the application of 'reason', Rousseau is much more concerned to deliver a *moral* criticism of it, on the grounds that its basic principles are opposed to the liberty of the individual, and therefore inimical both to happiness and to moral dignity.

It is by no means certain, however, that he always felt this way about the society of his time; on the contrary, there are strong indications that he would have been glad to be able to feel at home in it; and this is why his detractors can always argue that in castigating and standing aside from a society in which he had failed to integrate himself, he was making a virtue of necessity. The truth of the matter seems to be that, from a social standpoint, Rousseau was his own worst enemy; but this is because he demanded more in the way of psychological reassurance than any society could possibly give him. We can hardly explain in absolute terms why this should be, although there is a considerable literature on the subject of his psychological peculiarities; but some idea of his position as an 'outsider' can be obtained from a brief survey of certain salient features in the record of his life.

Rousseau was born in Geneva on 28 June 1712, the second son of one Isaac Rousseau, a man of French descent whose social standing was, it appears, somewhat inferior to that of his wife, Suzanne Bernard. Nearly everything that is known about his personal background suggests that it was unsatisfactory, and not very conducive to a normal degree of conformity. His early years were spent, in fact, in a curious atmosphere combining freedom and insecurity, and there is little doubt that his philosophy as a whole bears the marks of this in so far as it seeks to establish security without the sacrifice of liberty.

His mother died a few days after giving birth to him; his elder brother simply disappeared from his employment as an apprentice watchmaker while Jean-Jacques was still a boy; the father, who was himself a watchmaker by trade and something of an adventurer by temperament, had also wandered off during the period between the birth of his two sons, and practised his craft for five years in the improbable setting of Constantinople. Moreover, it is on record that he was in trouble with the authorities of Geneva on at least two occasions, both of which involve a suggestion of violence. The second of these, which occurred when Jean-Jacques was ten, led in fact to Isaac Rousseau's hasty and final departure from the territory of Geneva, and the removal of any actual parental control over the boy. Rousseau's principal debt to his father seems to have been a precocious taste for novel-reading; and his nearest approach to any sort of formal education as a child came when his uncle, to whose care he had been entrusted, lodged him with a cousin in the household of M. Lambercier, pastor of the neighbouring village of Bossey. His stay in the country was short, however, and ended two years later when thoughts on the problem of earning a living led to his being placed in the office of a notary. When this experiment proved unsuccessful, he was articled for five years as apprentice to an engraver, one Du Commun. Rousseau was then thirteen, and according to his own account, the experiences of his apprenticeship did nothing but transform him into a lazy and furtive oaf. He was undoubtedly in need of discipline, but he seems to have received the wrong kind of treatment from a somewhat insensitive master. And so, one day in March 1728, returning from an expedition with some companions outside the walls of Geneva, and finding (not for the first time) that the city gates were shut against him, he decided to avoid the punishment which his master was certain to inflict upon him, by running away. It is possible that the idea of doing so had been in his mind for some time, but in the account which he gives in his *Confessions*, Rousseau uses all the resources of his art to invest the episode of the closing of the gates with a sinister symbolism, and mark it as one of the great 'moments' or turning-points in his emotional life, when he became conscious for the first time of being outside the social pale, for better or for worse.

A new direction was given to the existence of the young vagrant when, having called on the Catholic priest of a small village, he was sent on to the town of Annecy, with an introduction to the baronne de Warens, a recent convert to Catholicism and a pensioner of the House of Savoy, whose business it would be to gain Jean-Jacques for the Church. The impact of this twenty-nine year old blonde adventuress upon his adolescent sensibilities is faithfully recorded by Rousseau, but the relationship with the woman whom he came to call 'Maman' was not to develop immediately. Instead, she in her turn dispatched him to the Hospice of the Holy Ghost in Turin, where he abjured his Protestant faith and spent the spring of 1728. During this stay, his mind was scarred by certain revelations of sexual vice, but the rest of the time spent in Turin was not unhappy. In the course of it, he earned a living as a lackey, and later, in a secretarial post; but on being dismissed, returned in 1729 to Annecy and to Mme de Warens.

Over the next decade, an ambiguous relationship grew up between them in which this most remarkable woman, who, with her taste for speculation and business, seems to have been born out of her time, figures as something between mother and mistress. Rousseau himself appears in a rather unfavourable light as part of triangular arrangements involving successively Mme de Warens' amanuensis Claude Anet, whom he displaced, and a coarse-fibred young man known as Winzenried de Courtilles, by whom Rousseau himself was finally supplanted. So far as lasting emotional impressions are concerned, the outstanding feature in this decade is the establishment of the Warens household in the valley of Les Charmettes, on the outskirts of the town of Chambéry, and the periods spent there by Rousseau, notably between 1735 and 1737. In later life, he tended to look back on this time as a relatively settled one, and to surround it with illusions of security and 'belonging'; and there can be no doubt that the Winzenried episode came as a severe shock, particularly to his self esteem. On the whole, however, it was still a time of adventures and wandering, of great personal efforts of study, and of career-seeking in various ways, including a period of work in a survey-office, the teaching of music, and, from 1740 to 1741, an unsuccessful spell as tutor to the children of M. de Mably at Lyons.

One of the striking aspects of these early years of Rousseau is the actual range of his experience, and the continuing inability or unwillingness really to come to terms with the humdrum conditions of a provincial life. He appears inevitably as a drifter, but his drifting is caused partly by the restlessness of unsatisfied ambition, and it is possible to see in it the expression of both the *naturel indolent* and the *naturel ardent* of which he speaks in his autobiographical writings. There are in any case many facts in the history of this period which do not tally very well with the idea of simple or innocent rusticity, but which suggest, on the contrary, that Rousseau was actively seeking the paths of glory. Mme de Warens probably encouraged him in this, although the fact is not given much emphasis in his presentation of their life together; and it is certain, in any case, that when the relationship finally collapsed and he left for Paris in 1742, it was with the clear intention of becoming a success in this European centre of social sophistication, and of making a real reputation for himself.

His hopes of doing so rested on a new system of musical notation which he had devised, but in the event this earned him no more than compliments from the French Academy of Sciences; and the years from 1742 to 1750 show him struggling in various ways, mostly quite orthodox, to find his way in the social labyrinth and make a career. These include an extremely important interlude as secretary to the French ambassador in Venice, but are chiefly concerned with musical enterprises such as the opera *Les Muses galantes*, or the cultivation of literary men like Marivaux, the aged Fontenelle, and, of course, Diderot. It is interesting to note, however, that it was during the same period that he drifted into his notorious liaison with the unlettered Thérèse Levasseur, who was to remain with him for the rest of his life, and whom he finally 'married' in an unorthodox ceremony in 1768. This union, disastrous though it was in many ways, seems to have compensated Rousseau for his failures in more refined social relationships. It produced (according to his own account) five children, who were abandoned at the Foundling Hospital or *Enfants-Trouvés*; and both the liaison and the abandonment of the offspring are the subject of some extremely curious efforts of

R B

defensive rationalization by Rousseau, ranging from Platonic theories of state education to the description of his relations with Thérèse as a form of primitive behaviour having none of the moral and social refinements of 'love'.

In the years following his return from Venice in 1744, he was moderately successful in some of his social contacts, which included the Duc de Richelieu, the financier La Pouplinière and the d'Epinay family; and was able to provide for Thérèse and her rapacious relatives by accepting a secretarial post with M. de Francueil, a member of another family of financiers. Nevertheless, the period must really be reckoned one of failure. His musical talents in particular had not brought him the fame he had sought from them, and by 1750 the sense of frustration and discouragement weighed heavily upon him. Part of his response to this situation can be seen in his philosophical writings, as a tendency to lay the blame for his failure upon society, and upon its whole system of competition; but he had by no means abandoned his ambitions. What he does seem to have done, is to turn more particularly to literature, and to the exploitation of his friendship with Diderot, now engaged on the first volumes of the great *Encyclopédie*; and it was literature which in 1750 finally brought him glory of a sort, with the success of his celebrated *Discours sur les sciences et les arts*.

There is nevertheless a great irony in this initial success, in that Rousseau's ambition to shine in an urbane and cultured society was only achieved by denouncing the principles of that society. This is why his critics can question the sincerity of his views, and argue that the subsequent building up of a system of thought on the basis supplied by the *Discours*, and his attempts to live in conformity with the system, are really aspects of a great lie forced upon Rousseau by his inability to extricate himself from a trap of his own making.

It is certainly true that he retained a deep desire for complete social integration, and that at times he was acutely conscious of having placed himself in a difficult position by his attack upon the culture of his time. It is also true that in his later years he expressed bitter regret over his whole career as a man of letters; but it does not follow that his constant protests against the prevailing values of society were insincere; or that the philosophy which he developed from them is lacking in general significance; or that he ever repudiated it, even while regretting its publication. On the contrary, the moral element in his criticism springs from a genuine conviction that in trying to live according to the established rules, he had become a less estimable as well as a less happy man.

It is customary, following a lead given by Rousseau himself, to regard his real literary career (i.e. the production of 'literature' as opposed to autobiographical writing) as beginning with the first *Discours* in 1750, and including, as its best-known products, the second famous discourse: the *Discours sur l'origine de l'inégalité*; the *Lettre à d'Alembert sur les spectacles*; and *La Nouvelle Héloïse*; ending in 1762 with the *Contrat Social* and *Emile*. These are the major works of doctrine, showing a consistency of inspiration and development, and having a general import for society as a whole. They contain what may be called the public philosophy of Rousseau, and they have an intrinsic interest and an independent existence as a system, irrespective of biographical considerations. The period of twelve years which produced them falls into two halves, during the first of which Rousseau remained mostly in Paris, except for a visit to Geneva in 1754. He was now trying to adjust himself to success rather than to failure; but the following six years were spent in the country, chiefly at Montmorency, and in the course of them we find him detaching himself gradually from his Parisian friends and acquaintances such as Diderot and Grimm. The years 1757 and 1758 stand out, however, as the time of the great passion which Rousseau conceived for Sophie d'Houdetot, the sister-in-law of Mme d'Epinay. This episode, which could not end in any kind of fulfilment because of the established liaison between Mme d'Houdetot and the poet Saint-Lambert, is a very important part of the background to Rousseau's novel *La Nouvelle Héloïse*, but it was destined, ironically, to contribute to the final breach between him and the circle which included Mme d'Epinay and the leading Encyclopedists. Thus, it came about that after the publication and condemnation of *Emile* in 1762, Rousseau found himself at the same time bereft of old friends, and exposed to persecution both in France and in Switzerland, where he was obliged to seek refuge. In the course of these misadventures, he was prevailed upon to visit England, under the protection of the philosopher David Hume; but having by now convinced himself that he was the victim of a conspiracy in which Hume was playing a leading part, he returned to France, and ultimately to Paris, where he was allowed to spend his last years more or less undisturbed, except in mind.

In the general perspective of his life, the whole period from 1762 onwards appeared to Rousseau himself as an expiation of his previous activities. It produced, nevertheless, three more major works: the *Confessions*, the *Dialogues* and the *Rêveries du promeneur solitaire*, which are all highly subjective and may appear, superficially, to have little in common with earlier writings. One point of resemblance, however, is that they are written from the standpoint of a man who is outside society, whether he accepts the position or not. Apart from their obvious interest as an intimate account of a most remarkable personality, they all carry on, explicitly or implicitly, the work of criticism by one who has failed to find his place in society; and all of them convey their author's profound and tragic conviction of being a man of good intentions completely misunderstood and frustrated by his generation. Just what these intentions were, is a question which can still provoke controversy; but one thing at least is clear: namely, that Rousseau is not just a misfit or a malcontent, working off his frustration on society. He is also a constructive thinker dealing seriously with specific problems which he feels to have a real public urgency; and to see what they are, we must now turn to the philosophical, as distinct from the historical background.

The subject can be approached in two ways: first, through his actual knowledge of the great thinkers of earlier ages; and secondly, through the question of the immediate inspiration of his own philosophical enterprise. The first of these aspects is not particularly relevant to the present study, except in relation to the general question of his originality. One point which must be made, however, is that compared with many contemporary thinkers, Rousseau had little, if anything, in the way of formal philosophical training. In this respect as, indeed, in most things, he was very much a self-taught man; and although this leaves him cruelly exposed to technical criticism, particularly on matters of terminology, it is also one of the reasons why his books are still alive. He read the works of earlier thinkers not because he was forced to, or for abstract intellectual satisfaction, but because he felt the need to examine anything which could help him to make sense of his own troubled existence. For Rousseau, all philosophical problems are personal problems, or associated with personal difficulties in the first place; and the consequences of this are rather paradoxical. On the one hand, he can be seen to have acquired, with the characteristic perseverance of the autodidact, a fairly wide knowledge of philosophical and religious literature; on the other, he tends to select from it what is most relevant to his own problems, and to go on from there, laboriously working it out for himself. As a result, it is always possible to argue, after a study of the sources, that much, or even most of his thought is derivative in some sense; and yet, at the same time, everything is worked over and developed in a genuinely creative spirit, to produce a system which is inseparable from the personality of its originator, but which can hardly be expected to produce universal solutions. It is possible, incidentally, that Rousseau's final feelings of frustration and bitter disappointment derive from his failure to grasp this simple fact.

One source to which he can hardly help going back sooner or later is, of course, the philosophy of the Greeks. He never mastered their language, but he knew and reacted against Aristotle; and it has been said that his political thought owes more to Plato than to any other single philosopher. Apart from this, however, much of his knowledge of ancient Greece is second-hand and distorted, being derived from his reading of Plutarch and Montaigne. It appears to have left him with a number of prejudices, notably in favour of the Spartan ideal; and this, combining with a similar view of the virtue of republican Rome, accounts for a tendency to interpret ancient civilizations in terms of heroic personalities and vaguely Stoic values. His notions about the ancient world are predominantly literary, and the use which he makes of them in his own system shows almost invariably a moral bias and a moral idealism, which can be a serious handicap from a historical or philosophical point of view. All that can be said in mitigation of this criticism is that it is a common failing of his age.

On the whole, Rousseau is more at home with the moralists and thinkers of more recent times; and, to take one example, the account he gives of his stay at Les Charmettes includes references to a serious study of Montaigne, Descartes, Malebranche, Leibniz and Locke. Later, he acquired an extensive knowledge of the great jurists such as Grotius; and his reading also included numerous theologians, among them Pascal and the Jansenists, and Fénelon, with whom he has most affinities.

Following the course of his reading, Rousseau's reflections gradually extended to a wide range of problems, and show, inevitably, great indebtedness to his predecessors. It is the concern of specialized studies to point out the precise connection with the political thought of Plato, or Hobbes, or Grotius, and the way in which his educational theories are influenced by Montaigne or Locke; but in a general survey, it is more important to realize that while his moral, political and educational doctrines stand independently as contributions to particular currents of thought, they are in the first place no more than aspects of a central theme, which provides the immediate background and the real starting-point of all Rousseau's work.

This theme is the problem of evil, which is, of course, the concern of religion as much as of philosophy, and is perhaps the oldest of all fields of human speculation. It is a special and dominating problem for the eighteenth century simply because the thought of the Enlightenment, carrying on from earlier manifestations of humanism, represents a vast reaction against a religious tradition deriving much of its strength from the sense of the precariousness of existence, the awareness of imperfection and the aspiration to perfection. By the beginning of the century, the special status of the problem is quite evident, and can be seen not only in the works of the theologians, but in the writings of Bayle, Leibniz and many other philosophers. The effects of scepticism with regard to the providential ordering of the world appear, for example, in Bayle's half-serious flirtations with the old Manichaean doctrine of the co-existence of good and evil principles or powers. The reaction against these effects is visible, on the other hand, in the *Theodicy* of Leibniz, and the doctrine of 'the best of all possible worlds', with its literary posterity in Pope, or in the optimistic writings of Voltaire, before his change to a rather more pessimistic frame of mind after 1750.

This is also the time of Rousseau's emergence into prominence, and the situation confronting him reveals quite clearly the division of thinking and articulate men into two camps, as far as the aspiration to perfection is concerned. On the one hand, there is the Christian view of man as a fallen being with possibilities of 'salvation'; on the other, there is the rationalist spirit of the Voltairian type, which dismisses the idea of a Fall, and thinks in terms of 'progress'. One reason why Rousseau is more interesting than many, if not most contemporary thinkers, is that because of his own experiences, he is from the beginning attuned in some degree to both these ways of thinking; so that his own philosophy will involve, inevitably, some formidable effort of bridge-building between them.

He falls, in fact, between two dogmatic extremes, both of which are forced upon his consciousness by particular circumstances and personal associations. From his earliest years in Calvinist Geneva, he is aware, even if only vaguely, of the most rigorous application of the dogma of Original Sin, and of doctrines of predestination emphasizing not so much salvation, as the permanent possibility of *inevitable damnation*; and after his conversion to Catholicism at the time of his association with Mme de Warens, he records the oppression of his mind by similar lines of thought encountered among Jansenist authors. The fear of hell-fire and the consequent emotional disturbances are depicted in a moving passage of the sixth book of the *Confessions*, and there is no doubt that the whole of his thought is conditioned in part by the need to escape from the contemplation of this horror, even though it may be argued that he never quite succeeds in exorcizing the sense of sin. It is this, in all probability, which prevents him from accepting entirely the optimism of the liberal intellectuals whom he encounters later, and a system of thought which can lead, through the application of reason, to the other extreme dogmatism of *inevitable progress*.

The first consequence of all this is that Rousseau offers us the curious psychological spectacle of a man who contrives to be both a hedonist, sharing his century's belief in the right to temporal happiness, and a kind of puritan, convinced that happiness is ultimately inseparable from moral rectitude. The second is that his philosophy, in its general or universal aspects, is a compromise, cast into a pattern analogous to the religious scheme of Fall and Redemption, but modified by the rationalist sense of history, according to which the evil in human affairs can no longer be thought of as the necessary consequence of Original Sin, but must be seen as a series of contingent ills with specific historical causes, and therefore curable through historical processes, the direction of which will lay upon all men a burden of social responsibility.

The first step towards the appreciation of Rousseau's thought is, therefore, a recognition that while it expresses a personal search for consolation, it is eminently 'reasonable' in its origins. As a variant of Deism, it assumes that the Creation is a rational order, and that man occupies an appropriate and intermediate position in the scheme of things. It opposes an extreme religious view which would reduce man to a puppet, and God to a capricious will; but it also opposes a humanism which, tending increasingly towards atheism, would make man the measure of all things, a law unto himself, and the source of all values. This may not be novel or profound, but there is nothing extravagant about it; and it is worth keeping in mind as a corrective to the kind of view which seeks to condemn Rousseau as a dangerous extremist, or to dismiss him as an untutored psychopath, embarrassing to true philosophy.

He certainly puts himself into some curious and unhappy situations, both physically and mentally, but he never relinquishes the belief that he is treading the path of common sense between opposing forms of intolerant dogmatism, each of which is a threat to happiness simply because it chooses to ignore certain aspects of human experience. Rousseau, writing in the particular historical context of an age in which Christianity and current philosophies appear to be irreconcilable, sees no valid reason for this incompatibility, inasmuch as both work, or ought to work, towards the happiness of man. What matters is that they should promote the happiness of all men, and not merely that of clever men or ascetic men; and the thing that is really offensive to him is exclusiveness, which, deriving from pride and selfishness, is equally indefensible on religious or philosophical grounds. Accepting evil or imperfection as a fact, the worst that can be done about it is to destroy hope; and much of Rousseau's thought is directed against the particular forms of rationalism and religion which seem to him to do this in one way or another.

If Rousseau's philosophy is, in general, the outcome of considerations arising from the question of evil, the actual form and content of his works is determined by the ways in which he is brought to envisage this problem. Here, again, there is nothing extravagant, vague or abstract in his approach to it; and he is less inclined than some of his contemporaries—Diderot, for example, or even Voltaire,—to divide it into its metaphysical, moral or physical aspects for the pleasure of speculation. Sooner or later, of course, he will have to make the effort to systematize completely his ideas on the subject, as his *Profession de foi du vicaire savoyard* shows; but his first reaction to evil is, simply, to note that it hurts, and to tackle it where it most hurts *him*—namely, in the field of social relationships. It may be partly his own fault that he cannot come to terms with society, but society is, nevertheless, palpably defective; and so, although his thought will move ultimately to the metaphysical plane, his immediate concern is with evil in its social aspects, where something can be done about it.

This, too, must be kept in mind, because it implies that the aim of his philosophy is a practical one. He has been scoffed at as a dealer in visions, hypotheses and ill-founded schemes of logic, and the criticism is justified to some extent; yet we must recognize that these things are, after all, inducements to action. The crucial elements in Rousseau's system are, in fact, acts of will, and this is why his philosophy is dynamic, and why, although the ultimate aim seems to be one of reconciliation, the actual mechanism is 'revolutionary'.

The third and most precise way in which the problem of evil constitutes an essential and immediate background to his thought is in posing the question of responsibility both for its existence and its cure. This concerns chiefly the moral evil which he sees underlying the social ills of his time; and while it is closely bound up with his views on the complacency of contemporary French philosophers, it brings in also his own religious experience. He believes that God exists, and is near enough to orthodox tradition to accept His essential goodness, without worrying too much about the problem of divine responsibility for the *possibility* of evil; but on the other hand he is, as we have seen, sufficiently imbued with humanistic ideas to reject the essential corruption of man, and the whole notion of damnation, as being totally incompatible with the divine goodness. And so the principal preoccupation in his early writings is to find a way of meeting the accusation levelled against human nature by theological tradition, without involving the Deity in any kind of direct responsibility for moral evil. To do this, and to assert the Original Innocence of man, it is clear that he will have to seek a middle course. Man, in fact, will have to be shown as being responsible in some way, yet not in the way which would entail the consequences of damnation, so offensive to human sensibility and so incompatible with divine justice. Rousseau's solution to this problem is, as it turns out, devastating in its very simplicity. In plain terms, it consists in socializing sin, and transferring the responsibility and the burden of guilt from men as individuals to men collectively in society; in short, in making society the scapegoat, as though it were something distinct from the individuals composing it.

Now it is quite possible that when he began his philosophical career, Rousseau was not fully aware of what he was doing; and virtually certain that he did not foresee all the complications and the ultimate consequences of his idea. Nevertheless, viewed in retrospect, this is the process which constitutes the first or critical phase of a remarkably consistent philosophy. This phase includes, of necessity, a fundamental attack upon existing society, quite different from the relatively superficial criticisms of contemporary reformers; and it will also involve some sort of historical survey in order to justify the attack. These elements provide the main themes of the two early discourses which made him a celebrity, and which can now be examined, as the first step in the exposition of his system.

The Indictment of Civilization:
Discours sur les Sciences et les Arts

*

THE PUBLICATION in 1750 of the *Discours sur les sciences et les arts* is a notable event, not only because it marks the real beginning of Rousseau's philosophy, but because in later life he tended to look back on it as the source of much personal misery, and as a kind of accident which condemned him to a literary career for which he often felt himself to be unfitted by temperament. This interpretation is not, of course, entirely true, inasmuch as he had previously displayed a normal amount of personal ambition, which entered also, no doubt, into his motives for writing the work; but it is true in the sense that the discourse was not completely spontaneous.

It exists because in October 1749 Rousseau read that the Academy of Dijon was to give a prize for an essay on the question: *Si le rétablissement des sciences et des arts a contribué à épurer les mœurs?*; and its first claim to notice is, simply, that it was awarded the prize in the face of the efforts of a dozen competitors, the best of whom also, as it happens, took the same negative line as Rousseau. More important than its spontaneity or its success, however, is the question of its originality; and for two centuries this has aroused much controversy involving the figure of Diderot, with whom Rousseau was then on terms of friendship, but who was imprisoned at Vincennes because of official disapproval of certain of his writings.

The circumstances relating to the inspiration of Rousseau's essay and the decision to direct it to the condemnation of the arts and sciences as instruments of moral and social corruption, are the subject of two famous accounts by himself, one in his *Lettres à Malesherbes*, the other at the beginning of the eighth book of the *Confessions*, where he describes something like a mystical revelation, which came to him as he was walking out from Paris to visit the incarcerated Diderot.

Ce que je me rappelle bien distinctement dans cette occasion c'est qu'arrivant à Vincennes, j'étais dans une agitation qui tenait du délire.

Diderot l'aperçut; je lui en dis la cause, et je lui lus la prosopopée de Fabricius écrite en crayon sous un chêne. Il m'exhorta de donner l'essor à mes idées et de concourir au prix. Je le fis, et dès cet instant je fus perdu. Tout le reste de ma vie et de mes malheurs fut l'effet inévitable de cet instant d'égarement.

Mes sentiments se montèrent avec la plus inconcevable rapidité au ton de mes idées. Toutes mes petites passions furent étouffées par l'enthousiasme de la vérité, de la liberté, de la vertu, et ce qu'il y a de plus étonnant est que cette effervescence se soutint dans mon cœur durant plus de quatre ou cinq ans à un aussi haut degré peut-être qu'elle ait jamais été dans le cœur d'aucun autre homme.[1]

The description in the *Lettres à Malesherbes* is much more graphic in relation to the physical and emotional disturbances associated with this celebrated occasion, and, together, the two accounts leave an impression of truth, which is not greatly weakened by hints from Marmontel and others that Diderot was really responsible for Rousseau's attack upon intellectual and artistic culture. There is no doubt that Diderot was capable of suggesting this line, simply for the sake of provoking an enjoyable argument. He himself never claims to have done so, however; and this episode on the road to Vincennes, though it may have been dramatized in Rousseau's recollections, accords perfectly with what we know of his mental processes, which tend to move, like his philosophy, through a mechanism of crisis, revelation and revolution. Moreover, the line of thought is thoroughly comprehensible as an explosion of feelings of frustration resulting from the failure of his earlier projects.

In short, this first discourse, while it probably owes something to Diderot, and certainly owes a great deal to the literary influence of Plutarch, Montaigne, Seneca and Fénelon, can be considered, nevertheless, as the expression of an authentic and highly individual revolt against an intellectual tradition and a social atmosphere. It is also the testimony to a sudden and genuine expansion of awareness, in which Rousseau glimpsed a system of ideas which might make sense of his own existence, with all its dissatisfactions. Although he may not have retained this sudden glimpse of a whole, certain parts remained in his consciousness, to be developed gradually in later works; and in the essay which he produced in the following weeks we can see in fact the seeds of almost every important element in his later philosophy. It is, however, doubtful whether they would ever have come to fruition, had it not been for the encouragement given to Rousseau by the award of the prize.

The first thing to be said of the actual text of the first discourse, is that it does not deal precisely with the subject proposed by the Dijon Academy, because at the outset, Rousseau modifies the title by re-phrasing the question thus: *Le rétablissement des sciences et des arts a-t-il contribué à épurer ou à corrompre les mœurs?* As a result, what was originally a historical question on the effects of the Renaissance, is deepened and transformed in such a way as to bring in the idea of a positive corruption and lead to a polemical discussion calling into question the values which tend to be taken for granted as marks of any civilization. This man-oeuvre also makes possible a great deal of emotional protest, a fair measure of highly impressionistic 'history', and the use of the declama-tory style which, in some of the later works, is sometimes quite mis-leading, but is in this case merely tiresome. Because of these characteris-tics, the discourse is not very impressive, but it requires serious examina-tion not only for the actual stock of ideas, but for what it can tell us about the working of Rousseau's mind, and certain attitudes which will be encountered again later.

It is a short work preceded by a diplomatic preamble apologizing for making knowledge the object of attack in an academic discourse, and running to about sixty paragraphs, in which Rousseau treats his subject from two angles, and using two methods. The first part is an attempt at *induction*, seeking to establish from historical facts a general law to the effect that states and civilizations tend to decay as they allow the develop-ment of arts and sciences. In order to enforce the acceptance of the resulting paradox, Rousseau then goes on in the second section to examine the nature of these activities, and tries to apply a method of *deduction*, demonstrating *a priori* that the encouragement of artistic and intellectual culture entails necessarily the historical consequences which he has already indicated empirically. The essay is, therefore, boldly con-ceived, with a firm and definite structure; but unfortunately, this is of such a kind as to encourage repetition and leave the impression of being a mere collection of emotional outbursts, unless it is analysed with care. The execution, in fact, is not equal to the conception, though the work retains some interest as an early example of the mingling of empirical and logical methods, which is characteristic of most of Rousseau's writings.

Considered now in greater detail, the first part opens with an evoca-tion of the renewal of civilization at the Renaissance. This is a concession to the official title, and it provides exactly two paragraphs, after which Rousseau feels free to generalize about the civilization of his own day.

In directing the reader's mind to the present, he displays at once the tendentiousness of his thought, by associating the culture of the mind with the development of a defective political society, lacking both liberty and equality, and working to a spurious morality which is in fact nothing more than a façade of urbanity. This is the beginning of a rhythm of ironic presentations which are used to build up gradually a sense of the inauthenticity of civilization, although he is careful to temper the wind of his doctrine at first by flattering comparison with the refinements of Greek and Roman taste.

The main effort of argument at this stage is to set up the antithesis of nature and artifice in relation to manners; to suggest that manners have become a substitute for morals; and to point out that a collection of men going through the motions of social behaviour is not necessarily a society, but is more likely to be a herd. Rousseau is, in fact, developing the paradox that in existing conditions, the *more* men are together, the *less* they are together, because the real social tie involves what he calls a 'reciprocal penetration', which is rendered impossible by the uniform smoothness of men's artificially-created social façade. This passage has little direct reference to the arts and sciences as such, but it is worth quoting as one of his earliest and most succinct protests against existing society; and as an explanation of the main tendencies of his subsequent moral and political thought.

Avant que l'art eût façonné nos manières et appris à nos passions à parler un langage apprêté, nos mœurs étaient rustiques, mais naturelles; et la différence des procédés annonçait, au premier coup d'œil, celle des caractères. La nature humaine, au fond, n'était pas meilleure; mais les hommes trouvaient leur sécurité dans la facilité de se pénétrer réciproquement; et cet avantage, dont nous ne sentons plus le prix, leur épargnait bien des vices.

Aujourd'hui que des recherches plus subtiles et un goût plus fin ont réduit l'art de plaire en principes, il règne dans nos mœurs une vile et trompeuse uniformité, et tous les esprits semblent avoir été jetés dans un même moule: sans cesse la politesse exige, la bienséance ordonne; sans cesse on suit des usages, jamais son propre génie. On n'ose plus paraître ce qu'on est, et, dans cette contrainte perpétuelle, les hommes qui forment ce troupeau qu'on appelle société, placés dans les mêmes circonstances, feront tous les mêmes choses si des motifs plus puissants ne les en détournent. On ne saura donc jamais bien à qui l'on a affaire. . . .[2]

The very smoothness of social polish, which in Rousseau's view derives mainly from intellectual refinement, is, therefore, an obstacle to true social cohesion and integration; and although this mistrust is doubtless born of his own psychological insecurity in the face of an alien culture, it is something which he never abandons, but tends rather to ascribe to all men. Such an attitude is understandable in an 'outsider', but what is more questionable, is the insistence that this misleading and disconcerting urbanity is largely the product of letters, art and science. Refusing to consider the opposite point of view, Rousseau now puts this idea forward as his major thesis. Not only have the arts and sciences *not* been morally beneficial; they have caused a positive corruption in creating the social screen or façade; and to defend this thesis, he proceeds to make his historical 'inductions'.

The combination of cultural refinement and moral degeneration is not, he maintains, peculiar to this age alone, but can be seen throughout history as a regular movement, which he compares, using a characteristic image, to the tides of the ocean. First Egypt, then Greece, Rome and Byzantium are depicted as rising to prominence, only to sink again through the enervating effects of luxury and the arts which develop with it; and the process is brought up to date with the example of China. Conversely, Rousseau goes on to depict a selection of energetic nations such as the Scythians, which, being preserved from the contagion of vain knowledge, maintained their vigour, virtue and happiness; and this series of historical contrasts is summed up by the classic antithesis of Athens and Sparta. It is, needless to say, the legendary and dangerous spirit of Sparta which is approved by Rousseau in this early work and elsewhere—a fact which is sometimes overemphasized by his critics.

Having thus established his scheme of historical references, he now turns aside for a moment to introduce another historical current which, as we shall see, is of immense importance to him, and from which he derives a great personal inspiration. This is the tradition of *protest*, exemplified for Rousseau in the rather oddly-assorted figures of Socrates, Cato, and the Roman general Fabricius, whom his imagination evokes, in a famous tirade, denouncing the decadence of the later Romans, enervated by the arts, and fallen from their former austerity and courage. This is the great 'set piece' of Rousseau's discourse, written down, according to his own account, immediately after the revelation on the road to Vincennes. Whether this is true or not, the tone of passionate denunciation is impressive enough; and it is important as part of a device of association by which he contrives to project himself indirectly into his work. In fact, in this penultimate section of the first half of his discourse, Rousseau manipulates this tradition of protest in such a way as to appear, by suggestion rather than affirmation, as a latter-day Sage or Socrates, preaching a happy ignorance which is considered as the Providential dispensation for mankind. It is, therefore, under the protection of this borrowed prestige that he finally sets up his formal paradox and last induction, to the effect that probity is the daughter of ignorance, and that knowledge and virtue are incompatible.

The second or 'deductive' part of the discourse opens with Rousseau's observations on the origins and objects of the sciences and the arts, as a prelude to a further exposition of their effects as visible in history. His first argument is that they are tainted in their origins, being born of human vices; and thus, with magnificent disregard for the complexities of human activity, he derives astronomy from superstition; eloquence from ambition, hatred, flattery and deceit; mathematics from avarice; physics from vain curiosity; and all of them, including moral philosophy itself, from pride. Similarly, their immediate objectives are all connected in one way or another with some aspect of moral, political or social failing; thus, the arts in general are inseparable from luxury; jurisprudence is born of injustice; and history is concerned (exclusively, it would seem) with tyranny, war and conspiracy. Even if it is conceded that the aim of science is the discovery of the truth, Rousseau maintains (and it is a point of fundamental importance in relation to the subsequent tendencies of his philosophy) that truth is but one, whereas error is capable of an infinite number of variations. The chances are, therefore, bearing in mind the probable insincerity of the seeker and the absence of valid criteria, that the truth will never be recognized, or if it were recognized, that it would be abused.

Having delivered himself of his radical criticisms, Rousseau now turns to the effects of these tainted activities, which he denounces, in general, on utilitarian grounds. Born of idleness, the arts and sciences themselves perpetuate the waste of time which should be spent in doing good. He does not state what he means by doing good, but rushes ahead to argue that not even the most distinguished thinkers (his examples are Newton, Malebranche and Descartes) have brought any practical benefit to their fellow-men; and that consequently the lesser men—and particularly the men of letters—must be thought of as mere parasites. Moreover, having nothing positive to offer, they cannot but work to the detriment of society, by undermining virtue and destroying patriotism and religious faith. And worst of all, they do not even do it for the 'right' reason, that is, because they sincerely hate what they destroy, but merely to be different. It is, says Rousseau, a mania of ostentation which motivates them; and in this way he sums up the philosophical movement of his day as a manifestation of vanity. This is his first major 'deduction', and he must now direct his attention elsewhere if he is to continue his onslaught.

The next phase of the discourse turns, in fact, on the problem of luxury, which has been a source of perennial controversy, and was one of the hotly debated questions of Rousseau's time. It serves here for an attack upon the arts rather than the sciences, and produces one of the most developed passages of the work. His argument is that luxury is incompatible with morality; that arts and sciences are inseparable from luxury; and that they must therefore, in this respect also, contribute to the dissolution of societies. A particular objection to luxury is that by encouraging the pursuit of wealth, it leads to a form of social esteem based on economic rather than moral values. To the argument that the man of luxury is a public benefactor because the satisfaction of his desires creates employment, he replies that this is no true criterion for the worth and dignity of a man, but would be more appropriate to a herd of cattle; and it must be admitted that although his answer is not well developed, it is consistent with his earlier thought concerning a *society* and a *herd*. He does not, however, pause to explore the relations between economics and ethics, but presses on to make his second deduction, namely, that since luxury is fatal to moral stamina, rich nations must logically succumb to the assaults of poor nations. This proposition is then supported by further evocations of the 'rustic' Spartans, Scythians, Franks, Saxons and so on.

The third of Rousseau's deductions involves a change of ground, because it concerns the effects of luxury upon art itself, particularly through the increasing social influence of women. The time must come when refinement and effeminacy cannot but pervert genuine artistic gifts, and replace a manly vigour and nobility by a false delicacy and pettiness of inspiration. And so, having already denounced the mediocre *philosophes* of his age, he now, in one of his most piquant passages, 'deduces' the literary art of his contemporary Voltaire as the outcome of this movement of degeneration, and an example of the corruption of taste!

The fourth lesson in this short course of *a priori* history is on the decay of true military courage, and is illustrated with the usual collection of simplified examples from the annals of Greece, Rome and Italy. Like most things in the essay, this is in reality a wild generalization; it is important, nevertheless, as revealing a consistent tendency of Rousseau's thought to distinguish between 'long-term' and 'short-term' forms of the same human qualities. In this case, it emphasizes the difference between simple bravery on the field of battle, and sheer hardiness and staying-power, which for Rousseau is the true and authentic *vertu*; and the same tendency can be seen in the next section of the discourse, where he extends his comments to the whole field of moral qualities. This is a prelude to a sweeping condemnation of existing systems of education, which, in turn, brings him back to his original paradox of the apparent incompatibility of knowledge and virtue.

This time, however, instead of merely recording the facts and letting it be understood that they are the effects of vanity, Rousseau proffers his explanation of what makes possible this play of vanity. It is, he says, the different degree of esteem accorded to moral worth and talent which emphasizes the inequality of men, and makes of life a competition in which the prizes are awarded not to what is good or socially useful, but to what is clever. From a moral standpoint, men are more or less equal; in terms of intellect or special aptitudes, they are clearly *not* equal; and such is the perversion of the sense of values through the cultivation of the arts and sciences, that the man of special ability, whether he be poet or mathematician, is in danger of losing sight of his basic humanity, while the mass of the people, toiling to satisfy the real and universal needs of mankind, are denied not only material reward, but also any sort of moral dignity or recognition. What Rousseau is now arguing, in effect, although he does not make his point very clearly, is that the arts and sciences may be agreeable in themselves, but that they are nevertheless a form of specialized behaviour which, by destroying the common denominator of moral equality, constitutes a threat to the integrity both of the individual and of society.

In view of the radical nature of this criticism, it is not surprising that he should now press on swiftly and soothe the susceptibilities of the Academy of Dijon with a word of praise for institutions of this kind. Yet this too, on closer inspection, turns out to be part of a scheme of irony, revealing even at this early stage something of Rousseau's dialectical skill; for his next 'deduction' is that of the necessity of academic institutions, to impose a salutary restraint upon the dangerous propensities of artists and intellectuals in general. This gives a neat twist to the discussion, and opens the way to the last section of criticism, the main weight of which falls upon philosophy. The targets here are the

R C

dangerous systems of Hobbes and Spinoza, and what Rousseau sees as the half-baked elucubrations of contemporary scribblers, who follow a fashion of unbelief, and seek distinction in an activity for which they have no natural aptitude. The inference is that the mediocre figures whom Rousseau claims to see around him in artistic and intellectual circles would be better employed in producing textiles, or some similar occupation. This is, of course, a variant of an ancient tradition of literary satire, but it leaves open the vital question of whether humanity is in need of guidance and enlightenment, and if so, who is to provide it. Rousseau's answer to this is the last product of his line of logic, and it runs thus: that because the arts and the pursuit of knowledge as we see them are corrupt in their origin and corrupting in their effects, no true enlightenment can be derived from them. Such enlightenment may be needed, but it must come from *outside* the existing order; it must come, in fact, direct from nature, through a small élite of men of genius.

Rousseau believes that nature does provide such men at the right time; and he cites as examples, and as a kind of balance to Socrates, Cato and Fabricius in the first part of the discourse, the figures of Bacon, Descartes and Newton. Forgetting that he has previously hinted at the inutility of both Descartes and Newton (and this is one serious inconsistency in the work), he now extols them as men independent of the culture of their time, and possessing a special insight which enables them to be the true guides and teachers of the human race. Such men as these should be the counsellors of kings and political leaders, in order that power and reason may no longer be on opposite sides, but that they may be brought together for the happiness of all men. And for the rest, for the multitude (with whom Rousseau politely identifies himself), let them renounce their pretensions to literary or intellectual glory, and console themselves with the genuine happiness to be found in independence of the opinion of others, and in the enjoyment of a quiet conscience—for virtue is a form of knowledge which is given to all, and especially to simple souls.

Such are the outlines of the diatribe which determined much of Rousseau's subsequent career, brought him a certain notoriety, and called forth nearly seventy refutations, which are sufficient testimony to the extreme vulnerability of his position. Leaving aside the emphasis and emotionalism of the style, it cannot be denied that the work is in many respects puerile, especially from the standpoint of the serious historian, although it accords well enough with poetic traditions; and the refutations must have left Rousseau in no doubt as to its weaknesses. Nothing can alter the fact that civilizations do not perish necessarily or exclusively for the reasons which he alleges; but on the other hand, it can hardly be maintained that moral factors, or economic factors associated with luxury, for example, *never* play a part in their downfall. Since there is no absolute law in these matters, his views have no universal validity; but this does not mean that the discourse must be written off as a total failure. It means simply that Rousseau started off on the wrong foot, because the subject of the essay, even in its modified form, is not really appropriate for the expression of a system of ideas which, after all, was only just beginning to take shape in his mind.

Considered in the context of his philosophy as a whole, the first discourse has really two weaknesses. The first is that, as the refutations show, it attempts to lay upon the arts and sciences an unreasonable burden of responsibility for the ills of civilization. It is not necessarily absurd to argue that a price may have to be paid for the advantages of civilization, or that culture can go sour; but in writing upon a set subject Rousseau allows his thought to be diverted to the symptoms rather than the root causes of social evil. The second weakness is that the essay is too short to allow the proper development of any of the suggestive insights which it contains. Consequently, superficial denunciation takes the place of detailed argument in too many instances. In spite of this, however, a number of elements in the discourse can be, and are, powerfully developed in Rousseau's greater works, and so stand out as the important parts of a defective whole.

The first of them is the paradoxical nature of the essay, which explains the reluctance of many contemporaries to take it seriously. Superficially, the whole work could be regarded as a paradox, in that it sets up a challenge to received opinion in respect of the benefits of civilization. Yet strictly speaking, it is Rousseau who expresses the traditional moral view on such subjects as luxury, so that this sense of 'paradox' can only be sustained in relation to the rational optimism of a certain section of contemporary opinion. What is much more important is Rousseau's method of exposition, which is based largely upon a principle of contradiction: as, for example, when he considers intellectual culture as both gain and loss; or when he suggests that men in society are together yet apart. The understanding of this technique is indispensable, not only because it becomes one of his standard dialectical devices, but because it is a genuine expression of his view of life as a whole, reflecting, among other things, certain Christian influences upon his thought. The discourse shows, in fact, the beginnings of a famous and fundamental formula, to the effect that men are unhappy because they are 'in contradiction with themselves'.

This sense of the contradictions of life appears in other memorable aspects of the essay, notably in the antitheses which are set up between knowledge and morality, or talent and virtue, or society and the herd; and especially in an idea which runs through the whole work, although it is only given one direct expression. This is the notion of the discrepancy between reality and appearance, between *être* and *paraître*, which Rousseau sees as a source of conflict and unhappiness, and the special threat which civilization offers to the integrity of man. What is already taking shape here is the doctrine that, in turning from nature, the so-called civilized man has burdened himself with the necessity of living a lie, or a series of lies; and that life has become a competition in pursuit of spurious values. Most of the constructive thought in his later works will be concerned in one way or another with the resolution of this conflict between *être* and *paraître*, and the search for the authentic values which alone can restore to man his happiness and peace of mind.

These ideas have far-reaching implications with regard to both government and education; and although the subject of the essay does not require Rousseau to pursue these topics, he leaves the reader in no doubt as to their interdependence. Luxury (including the arts and sciences conceived as cultural superfluities) is already being considered as the accompaniment of an inauthentic and tyrannical political system; and the brief criticism of the prestige-factor and the tendency to specialization in intellectual life is an obvious starting-point for radical re-examination of the nature, aims and methods of education.

One of the most significant uses of paradox in this discourse relates particularly to philosophy, and is to be found in Rousseau's observation of the sterility of the movement which has occurred in the course of history, from ignorance to scepticism—i.e. to a different kind of ignorance. There is nothing new in the idea of the ignorance of the learned, but in the whole context of Rousseau's thought, it has a special importance because of its association with the problem of happiness. In moving thus from ignorance to scepticism, man is seen as exchanging a situation of unselfconscious limitation for one of selfconscious frustration, and being thereby rendered positively unhappy. Although it is not expounded very systematically, this is his most effective criticism of the idea of progress; and it is vitally important for the understanding of his whole philosophy, because it reveals already the modification of an original conception of the history of civilization in terms of the ebb and flow of a tide, and the first emergence of a dominant thought-pattern involving a vicious circle, and the possibility of breaking it through the intervention of *Genius*. Rousseau's subsequent political thought, for example, is in part a development from the vicious circle idea; and the brief observations on genius in this first discourse can be seen as leading to a 'Lawgiver' or legislator-figure, who will appear later in various contexts and in various forms.

What makes this element in the work doubly important, is that it also involves Rousseau's view of his own position as one standing out-side the vicious circle. Although he does not at this stage associate him-self with Genius, he undoubtedly does so later in his career, and the understanding of his autobiographical works, in particular, depends very largely upon this. The first discourse, therefore, already throws light upon his situation as an outsider—and what is more to the point, it suggests that there is more than one way of being an outsider. In the first part, he evokes in the figure of Socrates, the wise man or *Sage*, who has stood aside from the circle of corruption, and has in a sense lingered behind the general movement of humanity. On the other hand, the conception of genius in the second part is undoubtedly that of a leader or initiator, who is *ahead* of the general movement, and represents a new kind of enlightenment in the form of positive discovery. Although these notions can hardly be said to have taken formal shape in the dis-course, they represent in a nebulous way the beginning of a curious polarity, which can be traced right through to the last of Rousseau's works, and which has been a sore trial to his commentators, because of the possibilities of contradictory ideals and apparently conflicting lines of thought which it obviously contains.

The discourse offers us, then, some interesting keys to a way of think-ing which is, indeed, paradoxical, but which, as we shall see, is based on the possibility of an ultimate meeting of opposite extremes, and the resolution of paradox in nature, or the author of nature. If this is accepted from the beginning as a permanent feature of Rousseau's mental processes, it becomes possible to understand why some of his works are written from the standpoint of the active Genius, while others emphasize rather the passivity and resignation of the Sage, who, in Rousseau's mind, seems to have become increasingly associated with the idea of the primitive. The line of demarcation is not always very clear, and the position which he will adopt at a given moment will vary according to circumstances; what will remain constant is the radical opposition to the ambiguity of existing civilization and its values, as expressed in this early work.

For this reason, the *Discours sur les sciences et les arts*, although it is full of suggestive glimpses, and poses enough problems to give it a great power of expansion in the mind, retains its interest mainly as a simple act of protest, the force of which can still be felt in spite of its obvious absurdities. It proclaims, with a kind of evangelical fervour, a state of evil; and indicates its presence in places and activities where the fashionable intellectuals of Rousseau's time prefer, on the whole, not to see it. But if the tone of the essay is evocative of the tradition of religious protest, its content already hints at the great and significant difference from the position of the Christian preacher: namely, the belief that however illusory the idea of progress may seem, there has at least been no essential change for the worse in human nature. Although most of Rousseau's efforts are directed to a denunciation of civilization, he does state explicitly that even in the natural state preceding the reign of artifice, human nature was not *better* in itself. In the face of eighteenth-century optimism, he denies that man's life is what it should be, and insists at the outset that there has been some sort of degeneration. What he does not admit, here or anywhere else, is that there has been a fall in the strict theological sense. But it is evident that the attempt to lay the blame for the contingent evils in human affairs upon the arts and sciences is not an adequate way of making these evils compatible with the goodness of human nature, which he believes to be fundamentally intact.

In conclusion therefore, the first discourse can be said to keep its place in the literature of protest; but it is not plausible enough to be taken very seriously as a contribution to philosophy. Rousseau's whole position requires rethinking, in fact; and it is the consciousness of this and the seriousness of his efforts to do it, which make of his next major work— the *Discours sur l'origine de l'inégalité*—something far more impressive. This does not mean that he will abandon the position taken up in the *Discours sur les sciences et les arts*. The protest will stand, and also the method, particularly the deductive method of the second part, which consists in establishing some primary hypothesis and tracing the history of man on a more or less *a priori* basis, without too much regard for the 'facts' as such. The main difference will be that the subject will allow Rousseau more scope to probe into the problem of human nature, without being held on the surface by the necessity of dealing with a specific, but limited, range of activities.

CHAPTER III

The Historical Hypothesis:
Discours sur l'origine de l'inégalité

★

THE CONTROVERSY stirred up by the first discourse had a number of immediate consequences, one of which is particularly interesting from a biographical point of view. Rousseau seems to have decided that one way to meet his critics would be to make an exemplary gesture, and attempt to live in accordance with his theories; and to implement this decision he resigned his position with M. de Francueil, abandoned most of his social pretensions, adopted a simple mode of dress, sold his watch, and took to music-copying, as an honest craft and an uncomplicated way of earning a living. Since the effect of all this was to make him even more of a celebrity, it has been found easy enough to question his sincerity. The simplest way of dealing with this problem is to admit that he was a complicated man, and that his motives may have been mixed. What matters, so far as this discussion is concerned, is that this *réforme* was not entirely insincere, that it was at least consistent with his ideas on *être* and *paraître*, and that it shows already a preoccupation with what is destined to become the most pressing of all Rousseau's problems: namely, that of bridging the gap between a system of thought and the order of reality.

These gestures were not, however, a complete substitute for argument. Rousseau did reply to certain of his critics, and although he did not succeed in overcoming the inherent weaknesses of the position adopted in the discourse, the necessity of self-defence sharpened his wits considerably, and the general level of the exchanges gave him much more confidence. We need not follow these controversies in detail, but two of his declarations are worth mentioning for what they tell us of the man and the doctrine at this particular stage. Both are to be found in the preface which he added in 1752 to his play *Narcisse*, and which he uses as a convenient pretext for summarizing and answering the main criticisms of the discourse. The first occurs where, having reiterated his belief that knowledge—meaning, apparently, philosophical reflection—

is not meant for mankind in general, Rousseau raises again the question
of the man of genius, working for the good of all.

> J'avoue qu'il y a quelques génies sublimes qui savent pénétrer à travers
> les voiles dont la vérité s'enveloppe, quelques âmes privilégiées, capables
> de resister à la bêtise de la vanité, à la basse jalousie, et aux autres
> passions qu'engendre le goût des lettres. Le petit nombre de ceux qui
> ont le bonheur de réunir ces qualités est la lumière et l'honneur du
> genre humain: c'est à eux seuls qu'il convient, pour le bien de tous,
> de s'exercer à l'étude, et cette exception même confirme la règle.[3]

He again avoids any idea that he himself belongs to this category, but
there can be no doubt that he is becoming increasingly convinced of his
own special position as a man with a mission, a repository of wisdom,
and the recipient of a 'revelation', all of which accord with his external
reform.

The second declaration shows a considerable clarification of his ideas
on the contingent nature of existing evils, and expresses again the conviction that paradox and contradiction are the characteristic forms of
evil in society.

> Etrange et funeste constitution, où les richesses accumulées facilitent
> toujours les moyens d'en accumuler de plus grandes, et où il est im-
> possible à celui qui n'a rien d'acquérir quelque chose, où l'homme de
> bien n'a nul moyen de sortir de la misère, où les plus fripons sont les
> plus honorés, et où il faut nécessairement renoncer à la vertu pour
> devenir un honnête homme! Je sais que les déclamateurs ont dit cent
> fois tout cela: mais ils le disaient en déclamant, et moi, je le dis sur des
> raisons: ils ont aperçu le mal, et moi j'en découvre les causes; et je
> fais voir surtout une chose très consolante et très utile, en montrant
> que tous ces vices n'appartiennent pas tant à l'homme qu'à l'homme
> mal gouverné.[4]

This is one of the most important passages in any minor work of
Rousseau, and it stands out in the present context for two reasons: first,
because it shows him changing his position to the more solid ground of
politics; and secondly, because for the first time he succeeds in reducing
his thoughts on moral evil and injustice to a formula. The conclusion
concerning 'ill-governed man' can be taken, in fact, as the effective
beginning of his great 'alibi', and his defence of human nature against
the doctrine of Original Sin. The preface to *Narcisse* shows, therefore,
both in its content and its harshly ironic tone, that Rousseau was ready,
given a suitable opportunity, to deliver a much more cogent attack
upon the established order of his time.

The opportunity came in 1753, when the same Academy of Dijon proposed for a new essay competition, the question: *Quelle est l'origine de l'inégalité parmi les hommes, et si elle est autorisée par la loi naturelle?* The subject was so appropriate to the needs of Rousseau at this particular moment that he was inclined to regard it, retrospectively, as another indication of the hand of fate; and although on this occasion the boldness of his ideas seems to have been too much for the sensibilities of the judges, and he received no prize, his essay, published in 1755, is one of the most forceful responses ever made to an academic initiative. One curious thing about it, however, is that in spite of its appearance and ultimate consequences, it is possible to see it as a 'reasonable' rather than a revolutionary work. Like other writings of Rousseau, it tends to change its appearance according to the context in which it is considered; and the best way of getting it into perspective is to leave aside for the time being the question of its consequences, and to think of it in relation to the previous discourse.

The essay on the arts and sciences is essentially, as we have seen, an attack upon the dogmatic extreme of the belief in inevitable progress, inspired partly by private frustrations, but also by the conviction that this belief is simply a source of complacency. In the *Discours sur l'origine de l'inégalité*, Rousseau turns his attention to the opposite extreme of a religious dogma which is repugnant to him on personal grounds, and which he also thinks of as being conducive to complacency. Both positions, in short, seem to him to lead to moral laziness, the one because of the feeling that nothing very drastic *needs* to be done, the other because it suggests that nothing much *can* be done, to alter the human condition. Underlying this second discourse there is, clearly, an increasing desire to clear the ground for action; and in order to do this Rousseau has no choice but to take up some central position between two very different forms of complacency.

The particular issues confronting him at this stage can be put quite briefly. Having already simplified the problem of evil, and reduced it to social terms, expressed in various kinds of conflict and paradox, he must now come out into the open and decide unequivocally whether social ills are symptoms of a tainted nature, as Christian moralists would suggest, or whether they are simply examples of bad behaviour whose causes are contained in society itself. His observations on ill-governed men, in the preface to *Narcisse*, leave no doubt as to which way he will decide; and it is worth stressing that he acts entirely as an eighteenth-century rationalist in choosing the most accessible explanation. On this

point, at least, there would be no great disagreement with the attitude of
Voltaire, and his emphasis on the historical causes of existing evils. But
the elaboration of a historical hypothesis containing Platonic elements,
within a framework of degeneration inspired by the theological notion
of a Fall, is the first outstanding example of Rousseau's eclecticism. It
produces a theory which, while imputing injustice and moral evil to
human agency, depersonalizes responsibility in such a way as to cancel
the individual sense of sin, and the depressing prospect of damnation.
By implication, it also, of course, rules out the idea of Redemption, at
least in the orthodox sense, thus rendering inevitable a conflict with all
shades of Christian opinion.

There are various ways of studying this second discourse, the most
usual being to read it as the starting-point of a political philosophy.
This is perfectly appropriate, but the simplest way of grasping its importance in the whole system of Rousseau's writings, is to consider it
first as an alternative to the early chapters of the Book of Genesis. There
are, of course, many special sources for the work, including, besides
Plato, the Golden Age philosophies of the past; the favourite eighteenth-
century myth of the Noble Savage; travel accounts; and later thinkers
such as Grotius, Condillac and Buffon. For most practical purposes,
however, the essay can be accepted simply as Rousseau's rationalization
of the idea of Paradise Lost, appearing, like other aspects of his work,
almost as a parody of the Judaeo-Christian tradition.

Seen against the religious background, such an undertaking suggests
rebellion and dangerous extremism; if, on the other hand, it is set in the
total historical context, it is simply a work of compromise and reconciliation. In rejecting belief in the literal truth of the Genesis account of
human origins, Rousseau is following a long-standing practice of the
freethinkers; unlike some of them, however, he retains a respect for the
spirit of the biblical tradition; and there is no reason to think, in spite
of his subsequent conflicts with religious authority, that he ever departs
from this position. In short, the second of Rousseau's influential works
suggests a reasonable belief that it is the letter which kills; and that even
if the Genesis account can no longer be thought of as more than a myth
or allegory, of human invention, it is at least rooted in human experience,
and contains enough of what, in later life, he will call 'general truth'
about human nature, to warrant re-statement in terms acceptable to the
eighteenth century. Needless to say, Rousseau's re-handling of the
theme of Paradise Lost takes him very far from the simplicity of the
biblical account, and it is doubtless right to stress the differences rather

than the similarities; but it is easy enough to pick out analogies, especially
in such fundamental things as the stirring of the moral sense; the
necessity of labour (which recalls the curse of Adam); the division of
labour and specialization (which seems to echo the story of Cain and
Abel); the invention of metallurgy and agriculture (comparable to the
activities of the race of Cain), and so on. These aspects of biblical
inspiration must on no account be overemphasized, because they are
almost inseparably interwoven with elements deriving from Plato (e.g.
the thought on the division of labour); nevertheless, they are worth
remembering for their bearing upon the ambiguity of Rousseau's whole
religious position.

For the rest, his *Discours sur l'origine de l'inégalité* is a hypothesis, semi-
introspective and semi-historical in character, showing the origins and
downfall of man as a moral, social and political being. It consists of an
important preface, a brief preamble, and a main text in two parts, which
present, respectively, Rousseau's conception of primitive man, and his
'fall' into the existing and unhappy social state. The whole work, which
is about twice as long as the previous essay, is extremely dense; and some
idea of its complexity can be gained from the preamble, where Rousseau
expresses rather deviously his principal aims in writing it. There are
five of them, the first of which is to 'defend humanity', presumably
(though this is not stated explicitly) against a moral accusation and an
iniquitous political system linked to it. The second is to define and explain the kind of inequality which involves human acquiescence (and is
therefore theoretically curable); the third, to examine when and how
this acquiescence or consent came about; the fourth, to put forward
the thesis that the essential qualities of human nature have been debased
but not destroyed; and the fifth, to stimulate a desire for change, and,
indeed, for a retrogression to the condition which has been lost.

Rousseau's sense of the difficulties facing him is expressed by a
characteristic two-edged criticism, directed on the one hand against the
failure of the philosophers to give an adequate idea of the original nature
of man; and on the other, against the Scriptures, as being another source
of confusion. The method by which he himself seeks to avoid the pit-
falls is to lay aside both historical 'facts' and dogma, and to arrive, by
stripping off accretions acquired in the social state, at a hypothetical
'natural man' who can serve as a starting-point for historical deductions,
of the type to be found in the earlier discourse. Logically, of course,
Rousseau's position is flawed, because his introspective method assumes
the 'intact' nature which is one of the things he is trying to demonstrate

and, like all such schemes, can be criticized as a projection upon human history of a prejudiced view of the writer's own personality. His idea retains, however, considerable psychological interest, and stands as a sincere attempt at radical re-thinking, confused and laboured, but fruitful nevertheless.

The description of man in the hypothetical state of nature begins, after a significant hint at the possibility of a long evolutionary background, at the purely physical level. When stripped of both supernatural gifts, and artificial or acquired characteristics, man appears as an animal, existing at a level of pure sensation, and able to satisfy the simple needs of food and rest in the immediate environment. He survives if he is robust; and in this crude doctrine of the survival of the fittest, Rousseau makes an important comparison between the laws of nature and the laws of Sparta, the effects of which will be seen later in his political thought. Given this initial physical robustness, however, the primitive is in other respects self-sufficient; and since he is conceived as living in solitude, among the animals, is not naturally predetermined either to timidity, or to that aggressiveness which is the foundation of the political thought of Rousseau's predecessor Hobbes. In competition with the animals, he can at least hold his own, or find a refuge, when force is not counterbalanced by skill or ingenuity; and as a result, he quickly conquers any disposition to fear. His only aim is self-preservation; and in the simplest conceivable state this is ensured by an appropriate development of the senses, particularly those of hearing, sight and smell.

In this situation, evil simply does not present itself as a problem, because of the limited range of consciousness. The primitive man is, no doubt, vulnerable in infancy and in old age; but as an infant, he does not *know* this, and as an old man, does not *care* about it, but, when his time comes, undergoes not death so much as 'extinction', in a way which is free from anguish. Between these two states, the only internal enemy is illness; and it is Rousseau's contention that susceptibility to disease is mainly of social origin, so that the primitive would have nothing to fear on that score. Since this particular suggestion is often held up as an example of the absurdity of Rousseauism, as though he were saying that savages are never ill, it must be pointed out, in justice to him, that he is after all putting a hypothetical case, according to which it is in fact highly probable that the primitive who is robust enough to survive the perils of infancy will not be much troubled thereafter in physical health.

Rousseau also maintains, however, that his hypothetical primitive will not be subject to mental illness either; and in doing so, makes one of his most 'shocking' statements, to the effect that 'the state of reflection is against nature, and the man who meditates is a depraved animal'. Since this too has been thought to indicate that Rousseau is pushing paradox to the point of madness, it should be emphasized that it is merely a logical development from his premises, and that in any case the word 'depraved' is probably used in a non-moral sense to avoid the moral connotations attaching to a word such as 'corrupt'. All that Rousseau is saying, in fact, is that in the state of nature the range of mental activity is so limited that it is impossible for the hypothetical primitive to worry himself into ill-health; and the point arises not as a matter of history, but as part of a philosophical view which insists that man is responsible for evil, either by the physical abuse of nature, or by creating a false mental picture of the world, in which things seem evil, although they are really neutral. He does not, however, develop all the consequences of this idea (which include the implication that philosophy itself is merely an elaborate form of worry), but presses on to discuss the primitive from a moral and metaphysical standpoint.

Here, the main aim is to indicate the characteristics by which even primitive man is distinguishable from the animals; and he begins by insisting that the possession of freewill is the fundamental difference. This is vital to the whole of his system, as a philosophy of action and initiation; and it is the source not only of danger, but also of the essential dignity of man, because of the ability it gives him to refuse the impulsions of the senses or of instinct.

The second distinguishing feature ascribed to man is a spiritual soul, revealed in the consciousness of freewill, and vital, also, for the subsequent development of Rousseau's religious thought. The third is perfectibility, which, ironically, carries with it the risk of imbecility, error and consequent unhappiness. In the primitive state which, at the mental level, is almost entirely passive, these attributes remain as potentialities; and apart from divine intervention, with which Rousseau is not here concerned, cannot be conceived as developing, except over a very long period of time. Intellectual evolution is linked to the passions, which are themselves born of needs; and although Rousseau thinks that needs as well as wants multiply with knowledge, those of his primitive are limited to the immediate physical requirements of food, rest and sexual satisfaction (which has, of course, none of the social and moral implications of 'love').

The point he is making here is that the primitive cannot be unhappy, because where needs are so restricted and immediately fulfillable, no sense of deprivation can be felt. Conscious only of his existence, through the senses, he has no capacity for abstract thought, no awareness of time, and no imagination. Again, a long, slow process is necessary before the primitive can move from pure sensation to simple knowledge (*connaissances*); and this consideration brings Rousseau to the problem of language, both in its origins and its relation to thought. At the primitive stage, the only communication conceivable is some instinctive 'cry of nature', involving gesture, imitation, or crude vocal articulation, but no abstract or analytical thinking. Rousseau is, indeed, baffled by the question of the origins of language; but what matters is that he is asking the question, in common with contemporary philosophers like Condillac; that he is opposed to the idea of monogenesis; and that his reflections on the subject show once more his desire to penetrate beyond what he sees as the convenient myths of the Bible.

The main conclusion emerging from these observations is that in spite of his potentialities, Rousseau's hypothetical primitive remains amoral in his actual behaviour; and that where there is no social relationship or obligation, there can be no question of vice or virtue. The man created by a good God must himself be good, so far as Rousseau is concerned, but his goodness can only be interpreted in terms of passive innocence. Apart from private religious considerations, the reason why he is anxious to stress this conclusion, is that it will enable him, later, to strike at the root of the abhorrent absolutist political doctrine, based partly on the idea of the inherent wickedness and aggressiveness of men, and of which he considers Hobbes to be the most dangerous exponent.

He is still left, however, with the problem of the moral and social potentialities of man, even in the state of nature; and this he attempts to deal with by proposing two pre-rational instincts or 'feelings', to serve as a kind of foundation for right conduct and rational morality in the social state. The first is the instinct of self-preservation (which is obviously 'right' because God himself must logically wish His creatures to maintain themselves). The second, which Rousseau introduces as an immediate reaction against the Hobbesian line of thought, is a balancing instinct of pity, which expresses a natural repugnance at seeing a similar creature suffer, and which constitutes a sentimental basis for all human sociability. It must be admitted that Rousseau's handling of this idea is not very convincing, and that it complicates his system very considerably; but it is essential to his ultimate aim of a philosophy of action addressed to all men. It implies an awareness that some men act on reason, but that most men act on feeling; a belief that an appeal must be made to both; and a conviction that all things are possible if sentiment and reason are brought into line.

The life of Rousseau's primitive, taken all in all, is relatively peaceful. It is a state of limitation, but not one of unhappiness, because there is a balance between needs and the possibilities of fulfilment; and the natural inequalities between individuals are scarcely noticeable. The sources of the kind of irksome inequality which he has set out to discuss must, therefore, be sought in the social rather than the natural state; and accordingly, Rousseau is now poised for the consideration of the subsequent history of his hypothetical man.

The question which faces him at the end of the first part of his discourse, is how man ever left the primitive state at all, in view of the limitation of his awareness and the lack of incentives within himself. The answer to it is that man was set on a course leading to unhappiness by a combination of external circumstances, for which he cannot be held responsible in the way suggested by theologians. What is proposed, in fact, is a doctrine of *chance*, operating on natural man in such a way as to produce certain inevitable results; but while this disposes of sin in a personal sense, it still leaves open the question of the weak point in human nature which exposes men to such historical hazards. This problem is extremely important, because Rousseau's handling of it lays the foundation for the whole of his subsequent constructive thought. We must therefore pause to consider it, before passing on to the second part of the discourse.

In discussing the pre-rational equipment of his primitive, he postulates, as we have seen, the two instincts of self-preservation and compassion the first of which is the driving-force in all life, while the second, involving rudimentary relations with other men, has a restraining or humanizing effect. As he sees it, the passage from the peaceful and balanced primitive state to an aggressive and unbalanced social state implies some upsetting of the relation between these two principles, one of which must, therefore, be susceptible to change of some kind. In Rousseau's opinion, it is the active principle of self-preservation which is subject to change and debasement; and this gives rise to a distinction without which none of his philosophy is really comprehensible, but by virtue of which all his works can be seen to hang together, even though they may sometimes be difficult to appreciate in detail.

The distinction (which is systematized rather than invented by him) is between what he calls *amour de soi* or *amour de soi-même*, and *amour-*

propre. These terms are difficult to translate, but may be rendered roughly as Self-Interest and Selfish Interest (although 'enlightened self-interest' is a term which the English reader will tend to associate with the first of them).

According to Rousseau's treatment of the subject, the two terms can be applied over the whole range of human activities and experience. The point is that the first of them—*amour de soi*—is legitimate, and the second is not; that the first can be traced back to the state of nature, and thence to the will of God, whereas the second only arises in the social state, because it is *comparative*, and depends upon a level of awareness which, on Rousseau's premises, is simply not present in the state of nature. Selfish Interest or *amour-propre* may, indeed, be regarded as a degenerate or debased form of Self-Interest, operating from a point in man's mental evolution when he becomes capable of reasoning, and above all, of making judgments of value, and applying these judgments to himself and others by a process which Rousseau calls 'reflection'. This form of self-seeking *relative to others* is, for Rousseau, the beginning of conflict and competition between men; it is also the source of another conflict within the individual, between the desire for long-term and short-term well-being or satisfaction.

At the 'primitive' level of Rousseau's thought, Self-Interest means simply the urge to survive; at the most evolved level of his philosophy, it will appear as a maximum individual response to the Creation, and to the eternal values of truth, beauty and goodness; involving every kind of satisfaction—sensuous, intellectual, moral and spiritual—provided that such satisfaction does not encroach upon the similar satisfaction of other individuals. In the long run, it points inevitably in the direction of Utilitarianism, and in this respect is an important element in Rousseau's political thought; but in the *Discours sur l'origine de l'inégalité* the distinction between Self-Interest and Selfish Interest is made as the most rational way of interpreting the tradition and meaning of the Fall.

Having noted this possibility of the debasement of the principle of self-love, Rousseau is now in possession of a formula which will enable him to press on with the second part of his discourse, in which he 'deduces' the course of human history in terms of chance discoveries exploited in a selfish spirit, which may be thought of as weak or blind, but is at least not 'sinful'. This undertaking is a formidable one, including both moral and political analysis of a succession of changing situations; and the skill with which Rousseau follows this double line in a short and dense discussion is a testimony to his development as a writer since the first discourse. It involves him in a selective account of changes in man's relation to the physical environment, and then of the interaction of moral and political factors which are conceived as resulting from them; and the strands are so tightly intertwined that it is difficult to condense his argument. We can, however, pick out certain major phases in this hypothetical history of man, separated by 'revolutions'; by which Rousseau appears to mean not, necessarily, violent changes, but rather the acceleration and consummation of very long historical processes.

The first phase and theoretical point of departure is, of necessity, the pre-social State of Nature, in which human behaviour is neither moral nor political. Although at this stage, men are deemed to be living mainly in isolation, Rousseau does allow for two kinds of ephemeral association, the first of which is sexual, and the second a temporary herding together to meet some passing need or immediate threat. In these 'free associations' there is no calculation for the future, and no reflection of the kind that will produce, later, a competitive attitude between individuals; since the only kind of pride or vanity conceivable at this point is a vague collective sense of the superiority of men over the other animals. On the other hand, Rousseau does not claim that even this phase is static, since the need to cope with the physical environment is enough to lead to activities such as tool- or weapon-making; and the discovery of fire can be invoked as a fortuitous event causing the first refinement of physical existence, i.e. the cooking of food. The most important development in this primitive state is, however, a mental one, involving the perception of physical characteristics and relationships, and a rudimentary process of comparison to produce such notions as big and small, or strong and weak. This is the kind of awareness which precedes judgments of value properly speaking; and is, in fact, the beginning of a theory of knowledge which Rousseau will apply in the educational system of his *Emile*.

The first historical Revolution postulated in this discourse results from the acceleration of these developments to produce a permanent family life, which is the first and natural society. Physically, it is bound up with the use of tools to construct primitive artificial dwellings. The potential political importance of this lies in the emergence of a rudimentary, but real sense of *property*, deriving from the labour which is involved; and there is an accompanying moral development connected with the permanent emotional relationships of the family, described by Rousseau as a 'reciprocal attachment'. Ironically, however (and this is a typical manifestation of his sense of paradox), this growth of permanent

RD

human relations is accompanied by the first signs of *specialization*, in the lives led by the two sexes; and this is paralleled on the 'public' scale, by the division of the race into natural social groups as a result of further chance events, such as earthquakes, floods, the detachment of islands and so on. This marks the emergence, in Rousseau's theory, of *nations*, although the division is, as yet, purely natural, and has no formal moral or political sanction.

What Rousseau is now presenting, in fact, is a second and modified state of nature, which can be considered as his Golden Age, although he does not actually use the term in this discourse. For him, this is the most pleasant and most durable phase of human history; the real youth of the world, as opposed to its infancy; and a period which is happy precisely because it is least exposed to revolutions. It is, indeed, a phase of equilibrium, when man is equidistant from brutishness and from the refinements of civilization, and protected from evil by a happy combination of instinct and reason.

Once more, however, he is careful to point out the changes operating beneath the surface, and offering a threat to this happiness. The most important mental development associated with this Golden Age is the use of human comparisons arising in primitive assemblies, to produce judgments of value, and ideas of merit and beauty. This is the beginning of moral awareness, and of aesthetic pleasure associated with amusements such as singing and dancing; but again, ironically, it implies also the growth of vanity and the search for public esteem. It is, in fact, the crucial point in this historical hypothesis: the point where Selfish Interest begins to appear as something distinct from Self-Interest or the fulfilment of legitimate needs; and it now requires no more than some other chance event to set men on the road to disaster.

This, therefore, is where Rousseau, drawing inspiration both from Plato and the fourth chapter of Genesis, postulates a Second Revolution, which is brought about by agriculture and the fortuitous discovery of the usefulness of metals, and which demonstrates the consequences of Selfish Interest. Its different aspects include the necessity of labour to provide more than the minimum requirements for subsistence; a further development of the idea of property; the division of labour; and the multiplication of special skills, leading to a competitive existence. In this new way of life, the element of selfish calculation renders active the sense of time, and completes the development of the natural faculties. Any further change must, therefore, have a social and artificial origin; and Rousseau hastens to repeat his condemnation of social behaviour, based on the distinction between *être* and *paraître*, and mutual deception as to individual worth.

This is the stage which marks the end of man's original independence and self-sufficiency; and in a few famous phrases Rousseau indicates their replacement by dependence and social slavery.

> . . . de libre et indépendant qu'était auparavant l'homme, le voilà, par une multitude de nouveaux besoins, assujetti pour ainsi dire à toute la nature, et surtout à ses semblables, dont il devient l'esclave en un sens, même en devenant leur maître: riche, il a besoin de leurs services: pauvre, il a besoin de leurs secours; et la médiocrité ne le met point en état de se passer d'eux.[5]

From now on, it becomes almost impossible for men merely to maintain their position passively; on the contrary, in a competitive social environment, they must seek to acquire more than they need, in order to make sure of having enough, so that acquisitiveness and ambition become the typical forms of social behaviour. The outcome is inevitable; and the ultimate effect of Rousseau's Second Revolution is now seen to be a State of War, in which every man's hand is turned against his neighbour, and the honourable qualities of human nature are transformed by abuse into a source of shame.

And so the Fall of man, as rationalized by Rousseau, gathers momentum, and is presented from now on almost exclusively in political terms, as, indeed, it must be, since religious explanations are ruled out, and he has already dealt with moral and mental development. His political theory proper begins with the problem of moderating and controlling the State of War, and leads to the first of his applications of the idea of Contract. For it is to escape the inconvenience and insecurity of the State of War, that the powerful, i.e. the rich, and those who have acquired the most property, are held by Rousseau to have conceived the most selfish (or, as he puts it, the most 'reflected') plan ever concocted by the human mind: namely, to protect their own interests by reducing the universal conflict of individual men (or state of anarchy) to a conflict of groups or associations brought together under their own leadership, and held together by the fear of an artificially invented 'common enemy' in the form of similar associations. In the whole perspective of Rousseau's hypothesis, this constitutes virtually a Third Revolution, engineered by the corrupt and the clever, ostensibly as the means of a general escape from the worst vicissitudes of fortune. To the natural divisions of the human race produced by geographical factors, it adds arbitrary distinctions based on the appearance of national unity, but having no proper

moral basis whatever. It creates, indeed, new shackles for humanity in
general; and from this additional constraint upon the instinct of compassion for all men, only a privileged few have remained free. These are
the true citizens of the world—

> grandes âmes cosmopolites qui franchissent les barrières imaginaires
> qui séparent les peuples, et qui, à l'exemple de l'Etre souverain qui les
> a créés, embrassent tout le genre humain dans leur bienveillance.[6]

It is by evoking these unspecified philosophic souls, that Rousseau finds
an expression for the conscience of the Outsider, and the permanent
possibility of rejecting the false society, just as he does, in the first discourse, through the symbolic figure of Socrates.

This Third Revolution marks, therefore, the passage of mankind from
a State of War to what looks like a social state (and is so called by
Rousseau himself), but is in fact a bogus political order which would be
much better described as a state of government. The acquiescence of the
mass of humanity in this adroit manœuvre, in the mistaken belief that
they are safeguarding their liberty, is treated by Rousseau as a kind of
contract. It is not, however, a genuine Social Contract; as an *ad hoc*
arrangement between the rulers and the ruled, it might be made to pass
for a contract of government, at the most; but the government which it
sanctions is a tyranny. It marks, in fact, the point in human history
where moral and political development get out of step with each other,
because of the selfish exploitation not only of material wealth, but of
inequalities of intelligence; and if it is viewed in the light of the whole
system of Rousseau's thought, it might be conveniently described as the
inauthentic or anti-social contract, to which the subsequent political
treatise *Du Contrat Social* is conceived as a corrective.

This false contract does not create true political society, or the rule of
law; it merely perpetuates, through a façade of legitimacy, an order of
power and expediency based in the first instance upon property. Men
have accepted it as being for the best, but in so doing, have jumped out
of the frying-pan of anarchy into the fire of Tyranny. What Rousseau is
really saying, although the point seems to get lost in the details of his
exposition, is that existing political orders are the logical and inevitable
outcome of the play of *amour-propre* or Selfish Interest, in which, whatever the original form of government may be, all power tends sooner or
later to be concentrated in the hands of an individual. All that remains
for him to do now is to show the kind of processes by which this can,
and indeed has, come about; and so the last section of his discourse com-

pletes the exposition of the socialized and 'innocent' Fall of man, with an account of the degeneration of the state of government into the kind of absolutism which Rousseau finds so repugnant, especially in France.

The hypothetical history of *government* (for Rousseau is still, of course, avoiding particular facts) begins with the establishment of authority on an opportunist basis. The precise form of the original political institutions varies from one nation to another according to chance and circumstance; but the one thing of which he is quite convinced, is that no existing government was accepted from the start on the arbitrary basis of Divine Right. He believes that the magistrates existed before the law, but it is unthinkable that men should have willingly surrendered the whole of their liberty. To do so would be an offence against both reason and nature; a rejection of freewill and, by implication, a denial of the Creator's intention for humanity, tantamount, indeed, to 'sin'. It is for this reason, i.e. as a philosophical necessity rather than a historical 'fact', that Rousseau accepts the idea of an original agreement in which there has been simply a psychological error, a miscalculation of interest concerning liberty. Theoretically, the rulers are obliged to act for the good of the community; in practice, there is no moral or legal authority to prevent abuses on the part of the rulers, and, by the same token, nothing to prevent the rebellion of the ruled. And, according to Rousseau, it is to remove the latter possibility that the rulers have pushed Selfish Interest to its logical conclusion, and thought up the doctrine of Divine Right to sanctify their usurped authority.

An important aspect of this argument, and one with far-reaching implications, is that it does not deny the possibility of a religious sanction for *any* form of political order; it merely denies a religious sanction to existing forms of absolutism; maintains that the Divine Right of Kings is an afterthought rather than a principle; and leaves Rousseau free to explore the possibility of a political society whose principles would be *genuinely* in accordance with the divine will. There is, in short, no formal or final rupture between politics and religion, although many critics have believed that this is implied by Rousseau's theories.

Having dismissed the absolutist version of the doctrine of Divine Right, he can now argue that all governments, whether monarchical, aristocratic or democratic, were originally elective, maintaining only, as an indication of personal preference, that democracy is nearest to the state of nature. His problem now becomes that of explaining the degeneration of the elective principle; and this he does once more on a basis of chance and opportunism operating in the absence of clear moral principles. Thus, the choice of experienced men to guide public affairs means in practice the choice of old men. This, in the nature of things, leads to frequent elections, encouraging the spirit of faction and intrigue, and resulting in civil wars. For the sake of peace and quiet, the people acquiesce once more, and end by accepting the hereditary principle, which transforms the state into the *property* of the ruler. And so, the history of political power and political inequality can be summed up on an economic basis, producing a distinction between rich and poor, then between the strong and the weak, and finally between master and slave. This is the existing order, and one which must continue, unless government is dissolved entirely, or reconstituted on a legitimate foundation.

Although the discourse as a whole is an attempt at compromise, when viewed in the broadest context of eighteenth-century thought, the revolutionary implications of this political sketch are clear enough; and Rousseau now strengthens his critical position by prolonging the rhythm of his presentation, to include a moral analysis of society in an absolutist state. Here, his aims are to extend the review of the operation of Selfish Interest, and show how it leads to a stratification of society, and a system of illusory liberty whereby individuals accept the dictates of those above them, in order to have the gratification of forcing their own petty authority upon their inferiors. In this situation, however, they are not exercising any genuine will of their own, but are merely transmitting a superior will, gaining thereby an entirely false esteem. The only self-esteem which is relatively genuine is that of the man at the top; and the logic of the system requires some individual in whose hands all power and authority are finally concentrated.

The last stage, therefore, of Rousseau's new account of the Fall, brought right up to date in political terms, is the emergence of naked Despotism, as a devouring monster established on the ruins of the republic, and subsisting because it flatters to some degree the sense of spurious values derived from Selfish Interest. The theme of paradox and inauthenticity visible in the first discourse is here taken up and extended, as Rousseau postulates a form of honour without virtue, reason without wisdom, and pleasure without happiness; and suggests to the sensitive mind that the whole of civilized life is composed, at best, of short-term satisfactions gained at the expense of true contentment and self-esteem. And once more, his sense of irony breaks through as he presents Despotism as the final closing of a vicious circle. At the end of this passage through three states and three major revolutions, mankind finds itself back where it started, in a new state of nature worse than the original one, in the sense that it is a state of positive unhappiness. Inequality, when pushed to the limit, means that all men are now reduced to the equality of moral nullity, and that the only law discernible is the law of the jungle. The Despot himself, having no moral status or authority, lives in the same fear as his subjects, and must confront perpetually the threat of revolution which is the inevitable accompaniment of the despotic system.

Thus ends the main argument of the *Discours sur l'origine de l'inégalité*, enabling us to summarize Rousseau's view of man in the inauthentic social state resulting from his 'innocent Fall'—a state in which the driving-force is not Self-Interest, but Selfish Interest.

On the material plane, property has been sanctified as the concrete symbol of prestige and selfishness, and a store of superfluous value; and the logical outcome of this is the reduction of the men forming an association to the status of chattels. The state is, in fact, the property of the Despot.

On the intellectual plane, learning and the arts are a façade. They are corrupted by a competitive urge for esteem; and themselves corrupt by encouraging a false system of education.

Morally, man is a nonentity. He has lost his natural freedom—i.e. his independence of the will of fellow-men—without gaining political freedom. He is no longer self-sufficient, but has become a slave to *wants* born of his passions. He has lost his dignity; and above all, has exchanged happiness (a negative happiness, it is true) for a state involving a sense of deprivation and frustration.

Finally, from a political standpoint, man is indeed a 'political animal'; and for Rousseau, this is neither true animal nor true man, but a monstrous collection of contradictions resulting from the processes outlined in this 'common-sense' alternative to the dogma of Original Sin.

At the end of this discourse or master-hypothesis, Rousseau can be said to have expressed the principal elements of his critical thought. The expression is not necessarily complete, even taking the two discourses together, and some of his points will be taken up and expanded in later writings; but he has obviously created a basis for the working out of a constructive philosophy. After this diagnosis of the ills of mankind, there arises the problem of the cure; and with it a complication which has caused frequent misunderstanding of Rousseau, and whose source is the gulf between logic and history.

It does not require great insight to realize that after giving his eighteenth-century version of the Fall of man, he is likely to seek some variant of the idea of Redemption, and so complete his rationalization of the central theme of Christianity in some way compatible with current philosophies, and especially with ideas about political progress. This is, indisputably, what he sets out to do in the works written for the edification of the public in the late 1750's; but although the intention is clear enough, the actual performance does not follow the simplest line.

In the *Discours sur l'origine de l'inégalité*, he has avoided the word and concept of sin, but has argued nevertheless that man has lost his happiness through deviating from his original state. The logical solution would be to invite man to retrace his steps; and 'back to nature' is, indeed, what many contemporaries, including both admirers and scoffers, thought that he was preaching. But it must be understood that although the idea of a return to nature obviously does run through Rousseau's philosophy, it is not to be taken simply in the literal or 'primitive' sense, except in a private sector of his work, with which we are not yet concerned; and that even here, it is not a complete expression of his aspirations. So far as the working out of an active philosophy for the future of mankind as a whole is concerned, it is clear that the principle of a return to nature must be applied in a way compatible with history, if it is to have any value at all. The society of 1750 may not be to Rousseau's liking, but it is the product of irreversible historical processes; a brute reality, the liquidation of which is just not a practical proposition. Therefore, if man is unhappy in his existing state, but unable to return to his original simplicity, the only alternative is to press forward and *complete* the historical process by a further revolution which will in some way allow him to be true to his *own* nature. The essential point, here, is that while Rousseau believes man to have been happy in a negative way, in his original animal-like existence, he does not really believe that the race was intended by the Creator to remain in that condition. Human nature is seen from the start as perfectible and capable of evolution; and the fact that men have taken a wrong turning socially does not rule out a return to a happiness involving rational, moral, political and spiritual factors. This putative happiness in the historic future will not, of course, be the same as that of the primitive state; but it can be *like* it, in so far as it may consist of the absence of a sense of deprivation, to be brought about through moral and political equality.

The necessity facing man is, in short, that of creating, by the use of the faculties of reason and will provided by nature itself, an artificial moral and political environment reproducing, as far as possible, the conditions described or implied in Rousseau's original state of nature. Having, as it were, 'contracted out' of that state by negative but universal processes of acquiescence, men must, again by universal consent, contract positively into the true social state, as the only way of escaping from an ambiguous state of government, which is neither natural nor social, and in which they are neither amoral nor moral, but immoral.

When his public philosophy is considered in this way, in relation to historical processes, it is clear that Rousseau is not saying 'back to nature', or back to anything; but rather: *forward* to the fulfilment of human nature, which is something very different from primitivism in a literal sense. This is why, from now on, the movement of his thought tends to complete itself as the downward swing of a pendulum is completed, by an upward movement involving a change of direction, but also a continuity. His problem is now that of showing how to change the direction of human history; and a review of his version of the Fall suggests that there is only one course for him to follow. He has claimed, in the *Discours sur l'origine de l'inégalité*, that man's departure from his first state has involved four principal factors: namely, freewill, perfectibility, an element of chance in the relationship with the physical environment, and the principle of self-interest. Of these, the only one shown by Rousseau to be modifiable through human initiative is self-interest, which has, in fact, degenerated into *amour-propre* or Selfish Interest. Thus, the only change for the better which can be envisaged is the extension of the range of understanding of self-interest; and the only rational motive which may induce men to contract into the true social state must be an 'enlightened' self-interest, or evolved *amour de soi*, in which the safeguarding of the moral integrity of the individual must take the place of the original and non-aggressive instinct of self-preservation at the physical level.

With these problems and implications, therefore, the conclusion of the second discourse brings us to a turning-point in Rousseau's scheme of thought. The constructive works which follow are all concerned with the maintenance or extension of true self-interest in a social context; and although they differ in scope or tone, all of them develop in some way the idea of contract, as a social act of reason and faith inseparable from this principle. This is the key to the moral regeneration in which he sees the hope of true progress; and which is at the same time the counterpart to the idea of Redemption in the religious tradition.

CHAPTER IV

The Politics of Regeneration:
Du Contrat Social

*

THE MOST impressive phase of Rousseau's career is the period from 1756
to 1762, most of which was spent at Montmorency, and which produced
apart from relatively minor writings such as his attack on the theatre in
the *Lettre à D'Alembert sur les spectacles*, three major works. The novel
La Nouvelle Héloïse was published in 1761, and was followed in 1762 by
the political philosophy of *Du Contrat Social* and the educational theory
of *Emile*, which appeared within a few weeks of each other, though not
in the order intended by their author.

The actual chronology of composition and publication is still a subject
of some argument, but this is less important to the present discussion
than the simple fact that the three books are the outcome of the same
surge of creative energy, or 'effervescence', as Rousseau calls it in his
Confessions; and that they may reasonably be expected to show the
same trend of thought. But such is the range of feeling and style, from
pure passion in parts of the *Nouvelle Héloïse* to pure logic in the *Contrat
Social*, that his commentators have sometimes hesitated to affirm, or
have frankly denied, any fundamental unity, even of intention. With
the *Nouvelle Héloïse*, conflicts of opinion arise over what Rousseau is
trying to say, not only because of apparent ambiguities in the text, but
also because the whole history of the book is complicated by the dis-
turbance of Rousseau's emotional life through the presence of Mme
d'Houdetot. In the case of *Emile* and the *Contrat Social*, critics usually
have firm views about what Rousseau is saying in each book; but some
of them have felt that the doctrine of one contradicts the other, and
that human beings brought up on the 'individualist' principles of
Emile would not be able to breathe in a 'collectivist' political society
which is often thought to be the only possible outcome of the *Contrat
Social*.

The three books do present real difficulties, and the only way to hold
Rousseau's ideas in perspective is to keep firmly in mind the nature of the

problem confronting him after the publication of his two discourses. It is, of course, a total problem, involving nothing less than the whole destiny of mankind, as well as his own destiny as an individual; and since it concerns all aspects of human nature and behaviour, it would not be very realistic to expect the whole of the solution (if there is one) to be set out in a single work, or demand that the constituent parts should be capable of standing entirely alone. What we may reasonably expect, is that Rousseau should produce at least one book calculated to communicate as much of his doctrine as possible to as many people as possible; and devote himself otherwise to exploring those aspects which have the most immediate bearing on man's future. This is precisely what he appears to have done in these major works; and instead of criticizing him for not harmonizing every detail of his thought, it is more fitting and useful to emphasize what really is consistent in his speculations. This, as it happens, can be done more effectively by disregarding strict chronology, and discussing the *Nouvelle Héloïse* after the *Contrat Social* and *Emile*, which carry on fairly directly from the critical positions of the discourses.

The line which Rousseau must take after the *Discours sur l'origine de l'inégalité* is that of working out the social and political future of humanity, without necessarily ruling out all possibility of a compromise with religion. Privately, he need not show any preference for the social state, but as a philosopher, he is committed to the consideration of principles by which it can be made, on the one hand, tolerable; and on the other, a source of positive value to individuals. Since society is composed of individuals, and must have been accepted, even in its inauthentic form, as being for the good of those individuals, it follows for Rousseau that any attempt to think out the advance of man into the true social state must include a discussion of these principles in relation to society as a whole, and to the individual. As he puts it in *Emile*:

> Il faut étudier la société par les hommes, et les hommes par la société: ceux qui voudront traiter séparément la politique et la morale n'entendront jamais rien à aucune des deux.[7]

He obviously does not intend to compartmentalize his doctrine, but the impossibility of saying everything at once explains why his thought now bifurcates temporarily to produce the *Contrat Social* and *Emile*, and why some confusion has arisen. There is, however, no confusion in the intention, which is, in the first instance, to explore the social problem in its political and moral aspects; and it must be pointed out that *Emile*, though technically a work on education, is perhaps more significant as a moral treatise in the broadest sense. And if Rousseau goes further than the establishment of abstract principles, it is certainly not to advocate, in either work, anything like a return to the primitive life, or an abandonment of the social state. The *Contrat Social*, in particular, is explicitly concerned with the completion of a social evolution, and the arrival of man at a point of political enlightenment which, while it is intended to provide a similar situation in terms of happiness, is in other respects as far removed as possible from the animal-like primitive state. And although *Emile*, being concerned largely with the child, is bound to concentrate more upon human nature in its 'raw' state. Rousseau says unequivocally that the product of his educational theory is to be, not a savage, but a social being, with all that this implies in the way of reason, morality, political consciousness and spiritual awareness; for such is, in fact, man's destiny.

If these points are kept in mind, it is clear that there is no fundamental discrepancy; that these works are simply complementary, as attempts at logical exposition of different aspects of a total evolutionary process; and that neither can be fully understood without the other. The kind of society in which Emile will find fulfilment and integration could only be a society based on the principles of the *Contrat Social*; and conversely, this society can only be fully realized if its members have undergone the process of moral awakening indicated in *Emile*. The fact that, from a practical point of view, there are the makings here of a very fine vicious circle, need not affect our appreciation of the theoretical relationship between the two books.

Beginning, therefore, with the *Contrat Social* and the political aspect of regeneration (or rationalized Redemption), it must be observed first of all that it is, manifestly, an imperfect work. This need disturb no-one, since Rousseau himself said as much, and would conceivably have rewritten it if he had felt equal to the task. One reason for its shortcomings is that it represents only a part of the political reflections upon which he had embarked at least as early as 1743, at the time of his stay in Venice. His original intention was to produce a comprehensive study of political institutions, but circumstances prevented him from doing much serious work on it, until the publication of the discourses gave him a new impetus; and even after that, his progress was so desultory that in 1759 he decided to confine himself mainly to theory, and sacrifice the rest. As it stands, therefore, the book is a second version of a much-modified undertaking, re-cast again, and including, as a late addition, a chapter on State Religion which has caused much controversy.

One result of this salvage operation is that although the *Contrat Social* preserves the essentials of Rousseau's political theory, it also includes a certain amount of rather confused historical discussion of institutions, of little importance today, but containing a few vital points of theory detached from the central doctrine.

It would be unjust, however, to think of it as a bad book, because the second general observation to be made about it is, precisely, that its pattern is dictated very largely by the immediate political issues arising from the *Discours sur l'origine de l'inégalité*, and that it does try above all to answer these specific problems.

Outwardly, it consists of four books, of which the first discusses, principally, the legitimate political society and its conventional basis; the second, Sovereignty and the Law; the third, Government and its forms; and the fourth, relations between the Sovereign and the Government. The divisions relate to subject-matter rather than to themes, but the order in which these topics arise is determined mainly by the following statement of intentions in Rousseau's preamble.

> Je veux chercher si dans l'ordre civil il peut y avoir quelque règle d'administration légitime et sûre, en prenant les hommes tels qu'ils sont, et les lois telles qu'elles peuvent être. Je tâcherai d'allier toujours dans cette recherche ce que le droit permet avec ce que l'intérêt prescrit, afin que la justice et l'utilité ne se trouvent point divisées.[8]

The first striking thing in this statement is that Rousseau is concerned, here as elsewhere, to strike a balance or resolve a conflict. The second is that the search for a political organization which shall be both legitimate and effective carries on speculatively from the point at which the second discourse stops; for Rousseau's condemnation of Despotism is grounded, precisely, in the belief that it is not only illegitimate, but also ineffective and unstable, and so fails to meet the claims either of right or expediency. The third notable point in the preamble is Rousseau's intention to think in terms of a *potential* legality, and of human nature as it actually exists, which for him means, it must be remembered, something debased but not essentially corrupt. One important implication of this is that his thinking is not entirely Utopian (especially since the Genevan background is a factor in it); the other is that the Social Contract described in this book is not conceived as an actual event in man's historic past. A certain amount of critical labour has been wasted in the belief that Rousseau is explaining here the historical origins of society; and this view is supported to some extent by his order of exposition, and the fact that he does tend to think in terms of a contractual origin, for philosophical purposes. The point which must be grasped at the outset, however, is that the whole range of his political thought includes two 'contracts'; and that the only one which has any real importance for past history is the spurious 'contract of government' which appears in the *Discours sur l'origine de l'inégalité*.

The importance of this will be seen later; but the immediate value of Rousseau's preamble is in its bearing on the form of the *Contrat Social*. Although the subject-matter gives rise to four books, the theme indicates that this is not a true division, but that the first two books are both concerned with issue of legality (*administration légitime*), while the last two deal broadly with the issue of stability or effectiveness (*administration sûre*), which involves a more empirical approach. This latter half of the work raises different problems of appreciation, and provides important links with other aspects of his thought.

In outline, Rousseau's thoughts on legality develop as follows. He begins by observing that since men have accepted the shackles of political organization as an escape from destructive anarchy, there arises the fundamental problem of who is to decide upon and impose the constraint implied by the organization. Before giving his answer, he takes up some of the points made in the second discourse, and clears the ground of what he considers to be the false justifications of the State. These include anything having a natural origin in the physical sense; and first, the analogy of the family, which is indeed the only natural society, but one which also dissolves naturally when the children cease to be dependent. In making this point, Rousseau attacks, characteristically, both the philosophical traditions exemplified by Hobbes, Grotius or Aristotle, and the kind of religious fundamentalism which would have recourse to the figures of Adam or Noah.

In the second place, arguing that Might is not Right, he disposes of the law of the strongest; and re-establishes the distinction made in the *Discours sur l'origine de l'inégalité* between power and authority. Proclaiming thus that no man has natural authority over another, and prudently avoiding the question of the Divine Right of Kings (on which his views are, in any case, seen clearly enough in the discourse), Rousseau concludes that legitimate political authority must have a conventional basis, but qualifies this by saying that one form of alleged contract is invalid. This is the arrangement, sometimes justified by reference to slavery, and found in Hobbes and others, by which a people is supposed to alienate voluntarily its liberty and place its destinies entirely in the hands of a monarch, in return for the promise of order and tranquillity. Rousseau rejects this by going back to his belief that freewill is the distinguishing characteristic of man; and maintaining that to renounce liberty is to renounce any moral or, indeed, human status whatever. He must, of course, take this line, because as the discourse shows, this is what he thinks has actually happened, through a contagious process of tacit consent, to produce an order of Despotism composed of beings who are, strictly speaking, neither animals nor men.

His point is that this cannot be the authentic convention, but that some primary contract would have to be invoked before one could arrive at the origin of a true political society. It must be emphasized once more that although Rousseau is prepared to accept a past historical development which is summed up in this 'contract of government', he does not actually say in this book that there *was* a previous Social Contract. He merely claims that even if the contract of government were acceptable on other grounds, its validity would still be conditional upon the prior constitution, by some unanimous and positive act of will, of a genuine society which could then elect a king or ruler. In short, whether there ever was a Social Contract in the past or not, the contract of government cannot stand as the legal foundation of society, although, as the second discourse suggests, it is the foundation of existing political orders. Having made this point, which is fundamental to his hatred of Despotism, Rousseau now feels free to discuss the true Social Contract, not as a matter of history, but as a necessary postulate for the legitimacy of any form of political organization.

On the supposition that men have reached a position where they can no longer overcome individually the obstacles confronting them, they must unite and organize their forces by some engagement which will not be inimical to their self-interest as individuals, or to their freedom, which is the characteristic that must be preserved if human nature is to remain intact in its essence, during the transition to the social state. The problem is stated thus by Rousseau in his famous sixth chapter.

> Trouver une forme d'association qui défende et protège de toute la force commune la personne et les biens de chaque associé, et par laquelle chacun s'unissant à tous n'obéisse pourtant qu'à lui-même et reste aussi libre qu'auparavant.

The solution is the Social Contract, which consists of

> l'aliénation totale de chaque associé avec tous ses droits à toute la communauté.

This conventional surrender of All to All, being total and equal, is the guarantee of justice, removing all cause for complaint and (by implication) maintaining the 'happiness' of the state of nature, which consists, as we have seen, in the absence of a sense of evil. It also preserves liberty, inasmuch as a surrender to All is a surrender to no-one.

The instantaneous product of this reciprocal act of surrender is a true society or Public Person (as opposed, presumably, to a Public Thing or *res publica*: i.e. the potential chattel of a Despot). This is an entity having a moral personality, a life and, above all, a will of its own, to which Rousseau gives the famous name of General Will, and to which all are equally required to submit, as members of the society. It is in this Will that all political authority resides, and the whole community possessing it is, therefore, the Sovereign.

After laying the foundation of his hypothetical *administration légitime* with the principle of the Sovereignty of the People, Rousseau concludes the first book of the *Contrat Social* with two chapters which review the Contract from a moral and material standpoint respectively, and indicate the consequences with regard to the property and the social status of individuals. Property, which is condemned in the second discourse as the symbol of unrestricted selfishness, is now given a legal recognition, subject to the General Will and the restrictions which it may authorize; and the moral implications of the Contract are presented as so important as virtually to transform an animal into a man: that is, an intelligent being, who exchanges natural independence for moral liberty, and the restrictions of nature for the rule of reason. As Rousseau puts it:

> On pourrait . . . ajouter à l'acquis de l'état civil la liberté morale, qui seule rend l'homme vraiment maître de lui; car l'impulsion du seul appétit est esclavage, et l'obéissance à la loi qu'on s'est prescrite est liberté.[9]

Here, in fact, is the beginning of that *virtue* which, in Rousseau's doctrine of regeneration, will emerge as the social and 'artificial' counterpart of the passive *innocence* of the state of nature.

Having stated clearly where Sovereignty must reside, Rousseau opens the second book of the *Contrat Social* with an analysis of it through the concept of the General Will, as a prelude to the discussion of the Law. His first point is that Sovereignty, being the exercise of the General Will, is *inalienable*, and that the collective being which is the Sovereign cannot be represented. Power may be transmitted (e.g. to a government), but the Will itself, in which lies legitimate authority, cannot; and in advancing this belief, Rousseau not only disposes of the claims of absolute monarchy, but also opens up a line of thought which is likely to prove hostile to representative government of a relatively liberal kind.

The second characteristic of Sovereignty is that it is *indivisible*, a point which enables Rousseau to make a distinction between the decree of an executive body and a genuine law, which must emanate from the people as a whole; but also predisposes him to suspicion of doctrines of the separation of powers, or checks and balances, in more empirical thinkers like Montesquieu.

The third, and much more complicated assertion concerning Sovereignty as operating in the General Will, is that this Will is *always right*, and tends always to the public good. Apart from the difficulty of defining a will in this context, this appears to imply that the people as a whole are always right. Since such a doctrine of popular infallibility is bound to be unacceptable at the level of practical politics, it must be pointed out that what Rousseau is doing here is to reiterate in a rather roundabout way his belief in the essential goodness of human nature, and his objection to the idea of an inherent and disabling corruption. It is, in fact, to distinguish between corruption and error that he now first points to a difference between the General Will of the community, and the Will of All, which is the sum of particular wills of the members. This remarkable manœuvre will have to be considered later, since so much of Rousseau's doctrine hangs upon it; for the present, however, it is more convenient to add to the points already noted, a fourth assertion by Rousseau which occurs, not in Book II, but at the beginning of Book IV, and is to the effect that the General Will is *indestructible*.

In summary, therefore, the central core of theory in the *Contrat Social* runs thus: that by a single contract involving the voluntary surrender of All to All, there is created a true society or Public Person, possessing a General Will which is different from the Will of All. This Public Person is the Sovereign; and its Will is inalienable, indivisible, incorruptible and indestructible. The expression of this Will is the Law, which is thereby dissociated from the arbitrary and despotic caprice of any individual; and since the Law is put above all individuals, there is created a situation of moral equality and moral liberty, providing the basis of the artificial environment which is necessary if man is to regain his lost happiness.

R E

As a theory, this is neat and simple; it is also, unfortunately, extremely difficult to translate into anything like practical terms, and the rest of the work shows Rousseau's desperate struggles to do this; to put real meaning into his concepts, and to bridge the gulf between their absoluteness and the relativity of politics in crude reality.

In the remainder of Book II, for example, his sense of these difficulties comes out first in an attempt to pose certain limits to the sovereign power, and to make the absolute surrender of the individual to the community tolerable, by maintaining (II, 4) that the risks to the individual in the true social state are less than in the state of nature, where he must in fact be constantly fighting for himself. There is here a hardening of his conception of the state of nature; and a corresponding harshness in his conception of its political equivalent can be seen in the fifth chapter, where he discusses the criminal, and the right of the State to inflict the death penalty. According to this passage, the criminal is to be dealt with simply as a public enemy; and the chapter presents a distressing revelation of the inhumanity to which a most humane thinker can be drawn by the pursuit of a logical argument.

The most noteworthy of all examples of the difficulties arising in the movement from theory to practice occurs in the seventh chapter, where Rousseau faces the problem of the practical formulation of a body of law to express the Will of the Sovereign People. The people may, as he says, be 'incorruptible', but this does not prevent them from being mistaken as to their own ultimate interest as a community. So great, in fact, is the probability of the blind multitude not seeing the good that it wills, that Rousseau can see no other solution but the introduction of a figure who, to many critics, has seemed altogether alien to the context. This is the Lawgiver, whose appearance has always been offensive to those seeking to interpret Rousseau in a purely 'democratic' way, but who, as a special kind of Genius, will not be at all surprising to anyone who has carefully studied the *Discours sur les sciences et les arts*. The Lawgiver is an 'extraordinary man in the State'; neither sovereign nor magistrate, and completely apart from the exercise of actual power or executive functions. He is, in short, a kind of prophet, enabled by superior intelligence and intuition to grasp the conditions likely to develop in the future from the play of the various factors in the given or present situation; and to draw up positive laws or suggest institutions to meet these conditions, and ensure the smooth functioning and survival of the State.

The Lawgiver is thus a theoretical necessity, invoked by Rousseau to make the transition from abstract principles to the concrete realities of the lawful society; and his appearance brings to a somewhat unsatisfactory end the main theory of legitimacy. What can now follow is a discussion of the conditions required for an *administration sûre*.

Book III of the *Contrat Social* leads on fairly smoothly from the point where Rousseau, having conceived his ideal state and brought it to birth with the help of the Lawgiver, comes to the problem of who is to run it. This produces the discussion of Government, bearing first upon its principle and its forms; and then upon its relation to the Sovereign, and the dangers arising from its presence.

Rousseau's first preoccupation is to distinguish clearly between the Sovereign People and the Government, which appears as an intermediate body established between the Sovereign and the subjects (i.e. the citizens in their private capacity), and charged with the legitimate exercise of executive power. The Government can, in certain circumstances, be thought of in terms of kingship, so long as this is not made synonymous with sovereignty. The point is, simply, that Government, whether monarchical or not, has no permanent contractual basis, but exists, when properly conceived, merely by virtue of a commission from the Sovereign, which may be revoked if the Government is seen to be acting against the interest of the Public Person. Nevertheless, in order that the Government may act efficiently, it must be admitted to have a personality and executive will of its own, distinct from that of the whole body politic from which it derives its legal authority. This, clearly, is a source of a possible conflict, which, if it becomes intolerable, can only be resolved, on Rousseau's principles, by sacrificing the government to the people, and not the people to the government. And it is the calculation of the probabilities of such conflicts that leads him now to consider the principles and the different forms of government: i.e. democratic, aristocratic, monarchical, and 'mixed'.

It is at this stage that the *Contrat Social* ceases to be a theoretical work and moves on to a more empirical plane, with some interesting consequences. Rousseau now appears, indeed, as much more of a realist than he is sometimes thought to be; and a sign of this is that although he might be credited with a theoretical preference for a democratic state, he seems prepared to settle for an elective aristocracy as the best government in practice. He is, in fact, sufficiently imbued with the ideas of his age, and the influence of Montesquieu, for example, to be able to approach the practical problems of government in a thoroughly relativistic spirit; and it is not inconsistent with the views on the origins of government expressed in the second discourse, that he should now admit that no one form of government is best for every country, and that democracy is only appropriate to a small state. What he is really concerned about, as a result of his reflections in the discourse, is the inherent tendency of any government, even if lawfully established, to degenerate and abuse its power at the expense of the Sovereign. Thus democracy may degenerate into ochlocracy, aristocracy into oligarchy, and monarchy into tyranny. It is typical of Rousseau that he provides for each legitimate form of government a spurious or inauthentic variant, and then uses these variants as different ways to the same Despotism, which is the usurpation not of powers of government, but of Sovereignty itself.

The safeguarding of the Sovereign against the risks deriving from the necessary presence of the government is the leading theme of the last nine chapters of Book III. Rousseau's first point here (and it is a very important one as an argument against those who have held that his political society is a complete God-substitute) is that all states must perish sooner or later. The most that can be done is to preserve them as long as possible by an appropriate ritual designed to maintain the sense of the authority of the Sovereign People. This means in effect regular popular assemblies; and it leads him into a position which is incompatible with the more compromising spirit of liberal democracy: namely, an opposition on principle to any system of *representative* government. On this point, he differs from a number of contemporaries in such things as the attitude to the English system; and his influence is often quoted as one of the obstacles to the establishment of workable democratic institutions in post-revolutionary France. Yet it must be said that Rousseau's ideas on the subject are quite consistent with his main theory, and the desire to preserve the principle of popular sovereignty above all else. It is, moreover, in the same spirit, that he concludes this third book with further insistence on the subordinate position of the government, and reminders that it is revocable; although he concedes that revolution too, particularly in a violent form, is a risk to the Sovereign and must be avoided if possible. This point is to be stressed, because it means that he is no advocate of violence, even though he is often accused of exercising a destructive influence.

To the modern reader, the fourth and last book of the *Contrat Social* is the least interesting, because much of it is devoted to a discussion of Roman institutions, natural enough in the eighteenth century, when

Rome was still the great source for political commentary, but less relevant today. Nevertheless, the first, second and last chapters are among the most important in the work; and the book as a whole carries forward Rousseau's intention to preserve the strength and purity of the General Will against usurpation or dilution. In this, success depends upon the right institutions and the maintenance of a psychological climate favourable to civic ardour; and the real driving-force behind all this section is his deep conviction that the political health of a society is inseparable from the moral health of its members. The essential factor in its preservation must be their sense of responsibility, and willingness to participate actively in political affairs, by voting, and also, ideally, by a readiness to assume the burden of public office, which Rousseau would prefer to see distributed by lot. It is this preoccupation with active participation and the associated question of voting, which, in the first two chapters, directs his thought back to the indestructible General Will, and the fundamental difficulty which the concept raises as to its expression. At the inception of his State, Rousseau evades this issue by the heroic measure of invoking a Lawgiver, but even if it is assumed that such a genius is available, and that his foresight is such as to reduce subsequent law-making to a minimum, there must still be some occasions when the General Will has to be determined. In practice, it seems that the only way of doing this is to accept a majority vote, even though in principle the General Will implies unanimity. Looking at the realities of politics, Rousseau is driven to concede that apart from the original contract, his society must be directed by the voice of the majority, in the interests of expediency or, as he might say, of an *administration sûre*. But because the acceptance of any and every majority vote is clearly incompatible with his original distinction between the General Will and the Will of All, he is compelled to add that the validity of the majority vote is conditional upon a true love of the public good in the majority.

But how is this to be ensured? Rousseau has, as yet, no real answer to this question, because it can only be dealt with empirically, by the encouragement of a healthy public opinion and the inculcation of the habit of virtue. The ground of his discussion is now changing, in fact, from politics to morals; and it continues to do so throughout his review of Roman institutions, until, in the final chapter, he raises belatedly the question of religion and the State.

There are three main reasons for the addition of this chapter to the *Contrat Social*. The first is the obvious importance of religious influences in the formation of a moral climate; the second is that in the *Discours sur l'origine de l'inégalité* he has already condemned the religious sanction accorded to an illegitimate political order by the doctrine of the Divine Right of Kings, and must find some alternative; the third is that the degree of secularization implied by his political theory points to a perpetuation of a conflict of loyalties as between Church and State. For Rousseau, it is axiomatic that where there is conflict or 'contradiction', there is unhappiness; and to solve this difficulty he proposes, with relentless logic, that the State should capture the religious loyalties of the citizens, as far as possible, through the device of a civic religion. This involves a profession of faith, the articles of which must be fixed by the Sovereign, not as dogmas, but as 'sentiments of sociability', with a view to the maintenance of a true public spirit. These articles are few and simple, consisting of a belief in God (whose attributes are given as power, intelligence and beneficence, plus foresight and the ability to provide for the future); a belief in a life to come; in the happiness of the just and the punishment of the wicked; and in the sanctity of the Social Contract and the Laws. The one thing which is specifically excluded is intolerance; and this must be taken to apply to atheists as well as to the kind of religious attitude which holds that there is no salvation outside the Church. Aggressive expression of intolerance on either side must entail expulsion from the state; and once an individual has made a public profession of the new creed, any subsequent conduct in contravention of it to be punishable by death, as constituting a kind of social blasphemy.

With this well-meaning but singularly dangerous chapter, Rousseau concludes the discussion of topics arising from the relations between Sovereign and Government, and brings to a close one of the most controversial works of political philosophy. In a broad survey, it is, of course, impossible to probe into all the problems which it raises, but a number of questions must be considered because of their bearing on Rousseau's status as a philosopher. One of these concerns the degree of historical importance to be accorded to particular elements in the book, and the first case to be examined is clearly that of the Contract itself.

It is often said that the title of the book overemphasizes the significance of the Social Contract for Rousseau's standing as a political thinker; and this is certainly true inasmuch as many philosophers from Plato onwards have used the idea of contract, or something like it. In this respect, his thought is unoriginal, and his claim to particular notice can only rest on the fact that in contrast to thinkers like Hobbes, who manipulate the idea in such a way as to include a primary and secondary compact, in order to justify absolute monarchy, Rousseau clings to a firmly democratic interpretation, using a single legitimate contract and reducing the government to a mere executive body authorized by a revocable commission. For the historian of Western political thought, therefore, the importance of Rousseau's contract is very limited; but this does not mean that it is unimportant within his whole system. On the contrary, if it is remembered that he is concerned to create above all a practical philosophy, the Contract itself is seen to be of crucial significance; for it represents the formal gesture of commitment without which no man can be said to have completed his development as a political or a moral being. Indeed, the implications go so far beyond the common range of politics that it is better thought of as the threshold of a 'state of grace', than as a mere political event, real or hypothetical. It is not for nothing that Rousseau, borrowing the language of the theologians, attaches the word 'sanctity' to it; for beyond the Contract is the Citizen, or the New Man.

Other elements of the book have had considerable influence in history, independently of the idea of contract with which they are nominally bound up, and through force of expression as much as originality. One of them is the setting up of a Public Person instead of the *res publica*, which has the effect of bringing the state itself under moral law; and another is Rousseau's definition of Sovereignty, and the proclamation, in face of the doctrine of the Divine Right of Kings, of an idea which is tantamount to the Divine Right of the People. This is not very helpful at the level of practical politics, but, so far as the history of France is concerned, there is no denying the importance of the theory of Sovereign People and Revocable Government, during and after the Revolution of 1789. Because of it, Rousseau figures inevitably as the true revolutionary and 'proletarian' among the eighteenth-century *philosophes* although this conception of him is an oversimplification, encouraged by failure to realize that his favourite word 'citizen' can mean, in the mind of an eighteenth-century Genevan, a species of aristocrat.

The second kind of question arising from this brief exposition concerns the philosophical worth rather than the historical importance of certain ideas; and here again, a few of them, at least, must be examined because of their bearing on other aspects of his thought.

With regard to the Contract itself, it must be observed that it is inadequate, from the empirical standpoint, as an explanation of the origins of society, and also logically invalid; and that Rousseau's handling of it is no more convincing than that of any other thinker. A simple way of exposing the flaw, as it appears in the sixth chapter of Book I, is to point out, first, that the contract is void because it is unenforcable; and that in any case, the unanimous act of will which it necessitates assumes the very condition of enlightenment and reason which the Contract is supposed to create. Putting it another way, it could be said that at the moment of the Contract there is a complete coincidence of the Will of All and the General Will; but if this is possible, there seems no need to postulate a General Will at all, so that the concept is simply superfluous.

Most of the controversy let loose by Rousseau's book does, in fact, concern the General Will, which many critics have considered to be dangerous, useless or meaningless. One thing which can be said of it with absolute certainty is that its effect on his thought extends far beyond the *Contrat Social* itself, so that some effort of understanding is essential, whether the concept is ultimately accorded any real value or not.

Examination of the sixth chapter, where it makes its first appearance, shows that the Public Person created by the Contract is a generalization of the moral characteristics ascribed by Rousseau to individual men; and since the distinguishing feature of men even in the state of nature described in the second discourse, is freewill, it follows that the distinguishing characteristic of any community of men must be its 'free' will. The initial aim of the doctrine of the General Will is nothing more mysterious than the preservation in a political context of the fundamental source of human dignity. The challenging element in it, however, is the further distinction between the General Will and the Will of All; and the scepticism and dislike which this engenders comes from what appears to be a qualitative difference, setting up the will of a society as a metaphysical entity which is in some way more than the sum of the individual wills composing it. This, it is said, offers an opening to perversion, emotionalism, and the kinds of political mystique which various totalitarian regimes have inflicted on the world since Rousseau's day.

He himself would have detested such systems as forms of Despotism, and it is not fair to detach his politics from the context and accuse him of acting in the spirit of these regimes. He does not arrive at the concept of the General Will by an intuitive leap into some vague metaphysical darkness; he reaches it logically from original premises, and one simple way of appreciating the movement of his thought is to recall the inauthentic social state described in the *Discours sur l'origine de l'inégalité*. Even that equivocal position has been reached, according to Rousseau, by a common willing to leave the state of nature, or at least through a general acquiescence from which only a few Socratic souls have been able to stand aside. The outcome is a common agreement to accept despotic government as being for the best as compared with the state of war, and a historical 'Fall' which, seen from the standpoint of the outsider, already involves a unanimous willing on the basis of individual interests, but which has turned out for the worst. To the outsider, in short, it must appear that unanimity is not in itself a criterion for the rightness of an act of political willing; and this is why Rousseau cannot be content with a Will of All in a quest which is, after all, for something comparable to Redemption. What he requires, in fact, is a form of political willing which, while it must *ideally* become unanimous, must first of all be *right*, if it is to reverse the previous trend of human history as he has interpreted it.

The distinction between the General Will and the Will of All to which this leads is, indeed, a qualitative one, but it is to be sought not in the will itself, but in the degree of enlightenment in the motivation, which in both cases is a form of self-interest. These forms of self-interest are, of course, those already postulated in Rousseau's theory of *amour de soi* and *amour-propre* applied to individuals; and because of this it appears, in the final analysis, that the General Will is just as much a sum of individual wills as is the Will of All. The theoretical difference is that the Will of All is the sum of wills motivated by Selfish Interest or 're-flected interest', whereas the General Will is the sum of wills motivated by Self-Interest (or, if the term is preferred in the social context, en-lightened or long-term self-interest, which is rational enough to see that the good of all is its own good). At the historical level of Rousseau's thinking, the difference between them is that the Will of All has already expressed itself fully and characteristically in the despotic governments which symbolize the historical Fall, whereas the General Will is a permanent potentiality, not yet realized, but towards which political society is tending, although it has got its priorities wrong. What Rousseau is suggesting is that if this is corrected, man will be on the road to 'redeeming' himself through the fulfilment of the highest possibilities of his nature.

If this connection between the two Wills and the concepts of Self-Interest and Selfish Interest is kept firmly in mind, it now becomes possible to express the sense of Rousseau's doctrine in terms of historical processes in man's future, developing in the following way to produce ultimately the ideal rule of Self-Interest through the General Will.

As the final product of Selfish Interest, the *Discours sur l'origine de l'inégalité* has already set up the Despot; and the first requirement is clearly a 'right' substitute for this figure, representing the principle of Self Interest. This substitute does, of course, exist in the person of the Lawgiver, with whom the regeneration of society must begin, and who is superior to the ordinary citizens in wisdom, as the Despot is superior to the subjects in power. Rousseau says firmly that the Lawgiver is necessary, and this necessity seems to be a matter of internal logic. The *possibility* of the Lawgiver, however, is a historical or empirical matter, and could only be justified by the examples of Moses, Lycurgus or Calvin, by whom Rousseau is evidently inspired. He obviously believes, on empirical grounds, in the appearance of 'men of destiny' who do *in fact* shape human affairs. They are supplied through Nature herself, but whether this is the result of Chance or Providence is open to argument. The Despot-figure is apparently the product of Chance, but it seems that the emergence of the Lawgiver must be regarded as the work of Providence. Rousseau does not, however, actually say so in the *Contrat Social*, and can hardly be shown to believe it, on the basis of his political thought alone. But assuming, in any case, that a Lawgiver *can* appear, the reason why he *must* appear, in Rousseau's system, is the inability even of well-intentioned citizens to see the good which they will in theory. If, because of limited intelligence or moral insight, they cannot find viable forms of expression for their goodwill, the Lawgiver must do it for them.

All this raises, however, the question of unanimity, which is one of the most troublesome elements in the *Contrat Social* because ideally, as we have seen, the General Will is not only right but unanimous. On the other hand, as the 'anti-social' contract or contract of government shows, it is possible for a unanimous will to be in error as to its true interest; and it is to extricate himself from this difficulty which may still arise after the disappearance of the Lawgiver, that Rousseau also accepts, pending the final establishment of unanimity *and* the enlightenment of Self-Interest to which his system aspires, a provisional solution in the form of the acceptance of majority votes as expressions of the General Will.

The consequence of this is that in the new society the minority vote is the expression of a lack of enlightenment, and cannot represent the authentic will even of the minority, who are deemed not to have understood their own ultimate interest. Naturally, the apparent implication that minorities are necessarily wrong, or that people do not know what is good for them, is extremely offensive to liberal thinkers; but it should be observed that this is one of the stages in his doctrine where it is better to concentrate on the spirit rather than the letter. In fact, at least three things can and should be said in defence of Rousseau's position. The first is that he is, after all, trying to set up an effective as well as a legitimate political order, and that it is, on the whole, more liberal and more expedient to prefer majority opinion. The second is that in discussing the problem (in Book IV, Ch. 2), he considers the voting not in terms of absolute rightness or wrongness, but in a perfectly reasonable and commonsense way, as the giving of *estimates* of the long-term interest of the community. This enables the community to exploit in its actions such probability-value as is vested in majority opinion; but it also offers the great political advantage of holding open a door to reconciliation. In associating the minority opinion with honest error rather than malevolence or corruption, Rousseau continues to lay claim to the loyalty of the defeated, and also, of course, remains faithful to his optimistic view of human nature.

The third point in his favour is that he is well aware of the dangers of his position, and is prepared to make the validity even of the majority vote conditional upon a public spirit or enlightenment which cannot be guaranteed by logic, but only by the right institutions and atmosphere. He also indicates that there can be a majority vote which runs counter to the General Will, and is merely the result of the careful organization of sectional interests. Rather ironically, however, this leads to another element of his doctrine which tends to shock liberal opinion: namely, an abhorrence of political parties, which is inimical to the right of association. Rousseau's critics often attack him because his theory offers no scope for parties, independent churches or trade-unions; and all that can be done is to admit this, but to insist that his thought is really orientated to a state which may evolve, but has not yet evolved. In the best of all possible states or New Jerusalem, dissent is demonstrably superfluous; and with the advent of universal enlightenment, transcending what Rousseau calls elsewhere 'the yoke of opinion', political parties and religious sects (to say nothing of the government itself, which also tends to encroach upon the prerogatives of the Sovereign) must presumably wither away. Once more, it must be emphasized that he is making a logical point in a special context, and not actively preaching indiscriminate persecution of any and every minority opinion in the present or the immediate future. If he dislikes political parties, it is because he sees them as capable of becoming ends instead of means and his view is not entirely unreasonable.

The fact is, of course, that Rousseau's political theory cannot be reduced to liberalism or totalitarianism, as these terms have come to be used. Parts of it can be invoked to justify some very unpleasant kinds of political behaviour; but if this is done, it means almost invariably that some contrary truth is being ignored. The classic example would be, precisely, the potential tyrannizing of minority opinion which is alleged against him. It is easy to see that his doctrine can, if suitably perverted and divorced from its total context, be made to authorize the crushing of minorities; but it is equally true that the realization of his own scheme of political redemption is impossible without a respect for minority opinion. It begins, in fact, with a minority of one, i.e. the Lawgiver. In this case, the 'minority' is right by definition, but his influence must be a moral and rational influence, to be justified by the test of history, and certainly not imposed by violence or restraint. If it could be so imposed, the Lawgiver would be a Despot.

In the *Contrat Social* as a whole, there is just one passage which could be thought to condone persecution: namely, the final chapter on State Religion, where intolerance is met with intolerance, and where backsliding after a profession of faith is punished by death. This is supposed by some commentators to show Rousseau's cloven hoof, and reveal the fanatic, the inquisitor, and the potential mass-murderer; and there are, no doubt, dangers in it. Rousseau himself, however, would have been appalled by the sinister interpretations which have been made; and it is important, when passing judgment on this chapter, to keep a sense of proportion, and realize that he is trying desperately to deal with a unique problem, the special status of which can only be seen through a brief review of the sense of his whole doctrine.

It starts, as we have seen, from the position where Chance has impelled men down the slope of Selfish Interest in such a way as to produce the Despot, in whom the particular wills of the people are vested through the contract of government postulated in the second discourse. Meanwhile, the General Will, which is an expression of the principle of Self-Interest in a social and rational form, is always present as a potentiality waiting to be realized in the consciousness of men; but before this can happen, a breach has to be made in the unanimous acquiescence which Despotism implies. This breach comes with the providential emergence of the 'minority of one', whose wisdom, conscience and reason are the pledge for the ultimate triumph of Law over Chance, and over the manifold expressions of Selfish Interest. From now on, a generalization of awareness of the public good, and its coincidence with the good of the individual, can begin to take place through the wise institutions of the Lawgiver. This will move inevitably through a phase of conflict (of which Rousseau's views on minor associations give some idea), until a point is reached when the General Will may be assumed to be expressed in the will of the majority. Thereafter, sectional interests (including those of the Government itself) must surrender to the common good, until the General Will is fully realized in a unanimous surrender of Selfish Interest to a Self-Interest which is indistinguishable from the good of the State. When this happens, the Social Contract or surrender of All to All will be complete, and man will have created his substitute paradise.

But will this ever happen? The chapter on State Religion shows Rousseau's awareness of an ultimate obstacle in the form of an intransigent religious attitude, which, by claiming exclusive rights in Heaven, pushes the term of fulfilment of Selfish Interest beyond the political term of Self-Interest itself, and so cannot associate its good with the good of the State. Theoretically, the existence within the State of an individual claiming that outside the Church there is no salvation is incompatible with the existence of the State itself, which has been devised by Rousseau in the first place precisely to take over the business of salvation. This is clearly the crisis for his whole theory; and instead of condemning him in sweeping terms as a potential inquisitor, it is only just to point out that even here, when faced with a choice between destroying or exiling this particular opposition, he chooses the latter and 'liberal' alternative.

There still remains, of course, the death sentence on the hypocrite who, in his conduct, goes back on his profession of faith. This is certainly offensive; but while we may not like it, we can at least understand it, and realize that it proves, not that Rousseau is illiberal, but that his liberalism has a back which can be broken by a last straw. And this particular case is a last straw for a very good reason: namely, that the offender who 'lies in the face of the Law' can no longer be conceived as being in a state of error, as could the previous type of dissonant individual, but would have to be thought of, even by Rousseau, as being in a state of sin. This is because the failure to abide by the Contract and the profession of faith that goes with it is a refusal of enlightenment tantamount to a rejection of Divine Grace. In other words, it is a deliberate flouting of a divine order which has been formally acknowledged; a blasphemy, in fact, which must be utterly extirpated because it destroys the belief in Original Innocence, i.e. the fundamental premise of a system which its author would certainly claim to be a liberal compromise.

It is always possible, therefore, to defend the allegedly illiberal elements of the *Contrat Social* as measures of expediency essential for the preservation of a liberal conception; but even if the most favourable interpretation is accepted, this can hardly save Rousseau's political theory from the logical defects which it shares with other versions of the contract, or from the practical difficulties which arise to hinder its full implementation. The fact that he has to envisage the exiling of a religious dissident against his will suggests that he has not yet offered a complete solution to the problem of social solidarity, and that there are forms of resistance to 'enlightenment' which cannot be dealt with satisfactorily at the purely political level.

In this sense, then, the *Contrat Social* breaks down; but the limitation of its central doctrine does not oblige us to write it off as a complete failure. Rousseau has simply exhausted one line of exploration of the total problem of human destiny, but his doctrine is at least novel and challenging, and there remains always the more empirical side of his book. This is more derivative, on the whole, but important in showing how his thought can move out of the fall-and-redemption perspective, and assume forms much more compatible with an evolutionary doctrine, or a desire to let Nature take its course.

The most significant example is the eighth chapter of Book II, entitled '*Du Peuple*', where Rousseau asserts that nations, like individuals, have stages of growth and should not be forced beyond the natural pace. He cites the experience of Russia, whose people, he maintains, will never form a true polity because Peter the Great, a mere imitative genius, tried to make them into Englishmen or Germans before they were even Russian. This doctrine of national character and natural development is important for three reasons. First, it tallies exactly with the educational theory of *Emile*; secondly, it projects on a national scale that 'individualism' which stems from the outsider's personal sense of uniqueness, and leads towards a cult of patriotic feeling which in some respects separates Rousseau from the vaguer forms of contemporary cosmopolitanism; and thirdly, it throws light on his failure to complete his political theories by discussing a federation in which the general wills of sovereign states might surrender to a greater general will involving all men. Certain remarks in Book V of *Emile* make it clear that he did contemplate this logical extension of the *Contrat Social*, but he may have been held back by his sense of realities, and the fear of forcing human nature too quickly.

Considerations of this kind are interesting precisely because they raise the question of the empirical value of Rousseau's book as a whole. This is often disputed on the grounds, for example, that those sections which attempt to come to terms with reality are out of date; that ideas which might just pass in a community the size of eighteenth-century Geneva are irrelevant in the modern world; or that they are in no sense 'true', however comprehensible they may be in the closed circuit of Rousseau's logic. One example often seized upon is the Lawgiver, a theoretical necessity whose presence cannot be guaranteed, except in so far as he is a projection of Rousseau himself; and who is therefore dismissed by 'realists' as the mask for a total failure to translate theory into workable institutions. It may be admitted that the criticism is valid from the practical standpoint of those who make it; but it should be added that if he had worked out a complete system of institutions, these almost certainly would have been outdated. As it is, his theories are still sufficiently alive to present a challenge to political ingenuity; and it may be that his reluctance to institutionalize them stems from an awareness of realities rather than blindness to them.

The real test-case, however, is provided by that most notorious of Rousseau's contributions to political thought, the 'indestructible' General Will, which may be thought of as an interesting piece of idealism, but as having no more relation to reality than, say, the lingering grin of Lewis Carroll's Cheshire Cat. The trouble is that in spite of the criticisms which can be brought against it (e.g. that nobody except a prophet could ever interpret it, so that it is simply useless) a feeling may well persist that some sort of meaning does lurk behind the concept. It may be said, for example, that if the General Will is not a 'fact', it is at least a necessary assumption or working hypothesis of politics; and that politicians are constantly striving either to express it or to create it. It is because of this that attempts are still made to rescue Rousseau from the charge of complete absurdity. One way of doing so is to work backwards from the observation of actual political behaviour, and to suggest that in the doctrine of the General Will he is trying to describe the emergence, through democratic processes, of the kind of agreed policy which, on a small scale, is recognized vaguely as 'the sense of the meeting', following reasonable discussion in good faith. This view is supported to some extent by the third chapter of Book II, where Rousseau attempts to identify the General Will as a kind of average of particular wills, obtained by the cancelling of extremes; and it may well be that 'the sense of the meeting' is the nearest practical approximation to the General Will. The drawback, from the liberal point of view, is that this too is susceptible to totalitarian perversion.

In the long run, therefore, the empirical justification of this idealist concept requires a broader psychological foundation. It might even be argued, for example, that in postulating a Will which exists without being expressed or realized, Rousseau is groping towards a theory of the subconscious, for which his Lawgiver is a substitute; and that his meaning could be clarified with the help of psychological concepts which simply did not exist in his day. Support for such an argument could be drawn from his undoubted flair for psychological analysis, and the attempts, especially in his last writings, to go beyond the normal range of consciousness. On the other hand, it is an anachronistic interpretation, and superfluous in so far as the theory of the General Will is intelligible to some extent at the level of consciousness. It is, after all, a fact of experience that people are constantly faced with conscious choices between long-term and short-term interest, and that having one bird in the hand does not destroy the hankering after the two birds in the bush. Rousseau's appeal to individuals to take a chance on the latter is not likely to meet with much response, but at least it can be maintained that the doctrine of the General Will is based on real psychological conflicts.

Its other main claim to empirical value is that it shows Rousseau's genuine insight into the psychology of the group, deriving partly from his peculiar position as an outsider, and partly from reflection on the nature and methods of organized religion. The political regeneration of man has to begin with the Genius-Lawgiver, but thereafter, it is a collective enterprise in which the generalization of enlightenment and commitment is obviously based on the analogy of religious enthusiasm and conversion. And it is a fact of experience, once more, that integration in a community does change individuals, if not in their nature, at least in their behaviour, which is Rousseau's primary concern. Such modifications of behaviour in the group are not, of course, necessarily for the better, since the energy activating them is emotional, and may lead to a lynching as easily as to the quasi-religious exaltation which his General Will appears to require for its realization. It is this emotional supercharge which explains why the General Will can be interpreted as more than a sum of parts, and why, in spite of liberal intentions, Rousseau's political theory is so dangerous, unless it is combined with a moral scheme designed to preserve the goodness of human nature.

This, however, is irrelevant to the immediate point, namely, that the General Will, introduced into the *Contrat Social* as a logical extension of the earlier distinction between Self-Interest and Selfish Interest, can be related to reality in a number of ways. Some of them point downwards, as it were, to the facts of human behaviour; but it is clear that this is not the only kind of 'reality' which Rousseau has in mind, since human behaviour is variable, and a characteristic of the General Will is constancy. On two occasions, indeed, he calls it the *volonté constante* of the political community; and no empirical approach can exhaust the meaning of this formula. This, in fact, is where political discussion must finally give way to a moral discussion involving Rousseau's other constructive works; but before we move on to these, it may be useful to clarify one last point arising from the *Contrat Social*.

Many readers of this book, believing justifiably that the likeliest outcome of it in practice is the regimentation of the individual in some kind of police-state, have felt quite unable to equate this with the idea of 'getting back to Nature'. The theoretical answer to this difficulty is that Rousseau is seeking to establish, not a police-state, but a rule of Law as impartial as the forces of Nature, and so impassive as to dominate the human scene like the peaks of his favourite Alpine landscapes. In the face of this, a relative equality is created, which is the key to 'freedom', by which he means, above all, freedom from the enslaving power of passion, selfishness and opinion; and the social evil of *resentment*, which is the real obstacle to happiness. This condition is supposed, moreover, to represent an advance from the original state, in that to the first and negative happiness is added a bonus of satisfaction deriving from the creative exercise of the will, and the choice of morality. In this sense, the virtue of the citizen or New Man is its own reward.

Rousseau's conclusions are certainly consistent with his premises concerning the potentialities of human nature; and to the inevitable protests that this may be all very well in theory, but that his regenerated society still looks like a police-state, the only possible answer is that Nature itself is like a police-state in some respects: for example, in that everybody is condemned to death without right of appeal; that all must accept restrictions or perish; that no reasons are given; and that Nature's operations are completely ruthless, from the standpoint of ordinary human sensibility. No confusion need have arisen on this point if Rousseau had expressed as clearly in the *Contrat Social* as he does elsewhere, his belief

R F

that men's independence in the state of nature relates only to other human wills, and that in all other respects they are in a state of total but *tolerable* dependence; or if too many of his readers, misled by certain passages of lyrical enthusiasm in his writings, had not assumed that his conception of Nature was 'soft'. In fact, the conception which prevails in his public philosophy is 'hard'; and an appreciation of this is not only essential for the understanding of the *Contrat Social*, but must be carried forward also to the study of *Emile*.

CHAPTER V

Education and Natural Morality:
Emile

*

ROUSSEAU'S interest in education developed even earlier than his first reflections on politics, having been stimulated in 1740 by his rather unsuccessful experience as tutor in the household of M. de Mably, at Lyons, and strengthened by subsequent discussion with other acquaintances, especially Mme de Chenonceaux. It is also suggested that *Emile* is his atonement for having abandoned his own offspring, but the evidence for this is not very convincing. A likelier source of general inspiration is the sheer fascination of the subject for one who, in this as in other respects, was in the position of an outsider, with a strong sense of the unorthodoxy of his own upbringing.

Although he has been credited with the initiation of a revolution in the attitude of educators, and a so-called 'declaration of the rights of the child', there are distinguished precedents in French literature, particularly in the educational criticism of Montaigne and Fénelon. Moreover, the eighteenth century as a whole is unusually rich in educational discussions, to say nothing of Locke, whose influence is considerable. Consequently, part of Rousseau's impact in this field as in others must be accounted for less by absolute originality than by his unfailing knack of reducing complicated and much-discussed questions to formulas which impress, but which may turn out in the end to cloud his real meaning. Nevertheless, *Emile* remains an outstanding landmark in the literature of education, and may still be considered his best book, although it is less fashionable nowadays than his autobiographical writings.

Like the *Contrat Social*, it has been imperfectly understood, and for various reasons, one of which is, simply, that it is a long book and very dense. One consequence of this is that if the reader loses the thread of argument, he may well feel that there is a discrepancy between the individualistic tone of the opening, and the social orientation of the conclusion. Another is that attempts to put Rousseau's principles into practice are apt to lead to emphasis on the first sections, which relate to the young child, somewhat at the expense of the last parts, which bring him through adolescence to manhood, and were undoubtedly of vital importance to Rousseau himself. There are, in addition, special difficulties arising from his tendency to become emotionally involved during his discussions of general or philosophical problems. In this case, the result is the expansion of a pedagogical treatise into a moral survey of the human condition, followed by its gradual transformation into a kind of novel, in which the main figures of Tutor and pupil both show a strong autobiographical inspiration. Ostensibly, Rousseau justifies his educational principles by the device of the happy marriage of the pupil Emile to a suitable young lady, Sophie, whose name has obvious associations with the author's own emotional life. And as if this fictional element were not enough of a complication in itself, it is not even complete. As his imagination took hold of him, Rousseau found himself planning a sequel entitled *Les Solitaires*; and this is an embarrassment because the existing fragments upset completely the conventional happy ending, and reveal that Emile will have to face severe trials, including marital infidelity, before attaining the *sagesse* which is Rousseau's ultimate aim for him.

Fortunately, the moral issues raised by *Les Solitaires* recur to some extent in Rousseau's autobiographical writings, so that the present discusssion can be confined to the main text, with a preliminary clarification of certain problems which are fundamental to its interpretation, and are of two kinds. They concern, respectively, the relationship of *Emile* to the other philosophical works, and its internal plan or structure.

The starting-point must be the fact that when Rousseau finally produced *Emile*, it was not only because of a genuine interest in pedagogical matters as such, but to complete the pattern of his thought concerning the prospects of man's successful adaptation to the physical and moral environment. Because of this, *Emile* can be related very directly both to the two discourses and to the *Contrat Social*. It completes the *Discours sur les sciences et les arts* as a constructive work following upon a criticism of the false culture of a false society; and it also carries on from the *Discours sur l'origine de l'inégalité*, in starting from the morally neutral position of 'original innocence' and attempting to work out how the child ought to be allowed to develop, in accordance with the principle of perfectibility. To the *Contrat Social*, on the other hand, *Emile* stands in a lateral relationship, as Rousseau's effort to break immediately into the vicious circle set up by the political theory in isolation. His empirical observations on the natural development of political societies suggest that there must be a 'moment' for the realization of the General Will and the Contract giving it formal expression, when moral and political evolution, after keeping in step with each other, can, as it were, converge. The Contract, in short, may 'happen' when the individuals are ripe for it; but not if they are rotten, which is what Rousseau considers men to be, in the existing order. There must be a new beginning, therefore, in morals as in politics, if the theory of social redemption is to be worked out; and Rousseau turns to education as the only field of human activity offering any possibility of the *controlled* moral development which his system requires. There is little or nothing to be done with individuals who have grown up in and accepted the existing order; but there may be hope for future generations if sound principles can gain sufficient acceptance.

Although there are many practical elements in it, like the empirical aspects of the political thought, *Emile* can hardly be related to the order of history except as a programme of enlightenment for a hypothetical future; and the immediate problem is, of course, that of its initiation. It does not require much reflection to see that this is another occasion for a gesture of faith in Nature, and, through Nature, an appeal to Providence. Thus, *Emile* contains and depends upon a new personification of prophetic intelligence and wisdom, corresponding to the Lawgiver of the *Contrat Social*. This is the *Gouverneur* or Tutor, who may be thought of as a further manifestation of the kind of Genius postulated in the first discourse, and also as another projection of Rousseau the outsider. Almost the first thing he does is to instal this Super-Father in a position of moral responsibility and authority, so placing the whole work on the same philosophical plane as the *Contrat Social*. And it is on this assumption that his own insight is sufficient guarantee for faith in the future, that Rousseau can feel free to tackle the moral aspect of his total problem, and work out an educational programme for Emile, the abstract and hypothetical New Man.

So far, the links with the other works are reasonably clear, but now the difficulties appear; because the theoretical relationship does not seem to be borne out by the opening of the actual text. The reader who turns to *Emile* after the *Contrat Social* may well expect Rousseau to propose an educational theory or institutions aiming directly at the formation of a 'citizen'. In fact, after asserting that one cannot form at the same time a man and a citizen, and that a choice must be made, he proclaims his own intention to form, not an *homme civil*, but an *homme naturel*; and in

pursuance of this aim, removes the pupil from normal human relationships, and claims that his programme is simply to follow the course of
Nature. Yet, at the end, Emile is brought back into social relationships,
and, through marriage, into the responsibilities of citizenship; so that the
whole scheme starts in the direction of rampant individualism, and ends
with some sort of social integration. In the circumstances, it is not surprising that the work has been thought inconsistent, both internally and
in relation to the *Contrat Social*; and that there is a temptation to abandon
it as a hopeless paradox, and salvage those elements which can be applied
in educational practice.

Part of the explanation is that in spite of occasional resistance to the
idea, *Emile*, seen as a whole, is the work of a man who has come to
believe that there is not necessarily a permanent conflict between nature
and society, and become increasingly aware of the evolutionary character of natural processes. Because of this, it appears more and more clear
that the true citizen can only be he who has realized himself, or is in the
process of realizing himself as an individual and a man; who has preserved
his dignity in the free exercise of his will; and who, if kept from the
corruption of the inauthentic society, can be assumed to be capable of
accepting the burden of moral responsibility at an appropriate stage in
his development. This is why Rousseau insists, in the fifth book of
Emile, that liberty is not to be found in, or guaranteed by, this or that
form of government, but resides 'in the heart of the free man'; by which
he means, apparently, one who has been kept as close as possible to
Nature, and correspondingly independent of other human wills. The
difficulty of applying this principle is illustrated by the fact that Emile
seems to be totally dependent on the Tutor; but the principle itself explains why, instead of some scheme of positive instruction for citizenship, which a 'realist' might expect as a complement to the *Contrat Social*,
Rousseau offers a *negative* system organized primarily with a view to
letting Nature take its course—and requiring, as he admits, a great deal
of art.

The short answer to the assertion that *Emile* is not a logical complement to the *Contrat Social* is that it is perfectly acceptable as such when
all the premises are taken into account; and that it is the product of a
practical reason or Wisdom which, as Rousseau says, may sometimes
consist in doing nothing. The alternative which short-term logic might
propose would be, no doubt, to rush ahead of Nature and try to form
'citizens' by public instruction. Rousseau was tempted to do this, but
his final handling of the problem is entirely in accordance with his whole

system, in that the social unity at which he is ultimately aiming, and into which Emile must be fitted, is that of the General Will, and not that of the Will of All. As he would see it, instruction in a public institution, however well-intentioned, will mean, in effect, tyrannizing the young mind; and the result will be, not education, but indoctrination, or, at best, the handing on of mere erudition or a set of ready-made values. Although ostensibly these may be good values, they will not be authentically possessed; and so, apart from being unreliable, cannot provide any positive satisfaction, which is the reward for *choosing* the path of virtue. Putting it another way, indoctrination may well be the swiftest way to unanimity; but it will produce, instead of true morality, a spurious automatism which is more likely to be a Will of All and a source of unanimous error, than to form a General Will. In short, Rousseau's decision to express the major part of his educational thought as a theory for the private formation of a 'man', is conditioned as much by the precedence of Right over Unanimity in his theory of the State and the General Will, as by a resurgence of primitive individualism, to which at first sight it might be attributed. And it is because the morality to which Emile is brought is conceived as an authentic personal achievement, and not a meaningless mask of conformity, that it can be treated as the condition and basis of true Citizenship.

To the practical educationist, all this may seem excessively devious; but it must be said in justice to Rousseau that not only does he remain completely faithful to his principles, but that these principles are utterly opposed to anything like the indoctrination seen in modern totalitarian states—a point which has an obvious bearing on the spirit of his political thought.

The second kind of preliminary problem, concerning structure and planning, arises because *Emile* is partly a treatise and partly a narrative with a strongly subjective inspiration. Although it is not easy to reduce the work to simple outlines, one way of grasping the sense of the whole is to consider first what kind of movements it may be expected to display, in view of the co-existence in Rousseau's mind of the two perspectives of fall-and-redemption and natural evolution. These expectations can be reduced to four main points: first, a continuous development from the physical to the moral and even spiritual planes; secondly, a crisis or crises involving the appearance of Selfish Interest and the risk of a Fall on the lines of the *Discours sur l'origine de l'inégalité*; thirdly, a major effort to combat this danger by emphasizing the principle of Self-

Interest; and finally, the opening-up of a 'natural' way into the true social state, or just political society.

Broadly speaking, the book does conform to this pattern, although outwardly it is not immediately apparent. The reason for this is that Rousseau's speculations opened up such a wealth of ideas that he found difficulty in cramming them into the confines of any formal structure at all. Thus, at one stage, he seems to have thought in terms of a kind of dialectical process in three phases, involving 'man', 'social man', and 'citizen'; whereas later he uses the terms 'act' and 'dénouement', suggesting a dramatic approach to the life of Emile. Towards the end of the book, on the other hand, he refers to his thoughts on education simply as 'these essays', implying that considerations of structure have lost most of their importance for him. It must be pointed out, however, that the division of the text into five books is the outcome of a theory which is quite distinct from the conceptions mentioned above, and which, although it was much modified by Rousseau, still offers the best practical approach to the doctrine of *Emile*.

This theory divides human life from birth to maturity into a system of 'ages', and the key to it is a marginal note in one of Rousseau's manuscript drafts. According to this, the original idea was to work out an educational and moral scheme based on an 'age of nature' (extending to the twelfth year), an 'age of reason' (from twelve to fifteen), an 'age of force' (fifteen to twenty), and an 'age of wisdom' culminating at twenty-five, with the rest of life as an age of happiness. One interesting aspect of this plan is that it can be related to society as well as to the individual, and therefore to Rousseau's whole conception of history. The analogy must not be pushed too far, however, because he obviously found the original scheme unworkable, and had to change it. As a result, the final text of *Emile*, so far as it can be thought of as a pedagogical system, reflects a modified scheme of ages working out approximately, but not rigidly, as follows. Book I presents the Infant in his first three years, living through what might be termed an Age of Instinct, in which behaviour is almost wholly mechanical; Book II covers, roughly, the period from four to twelve, in which the Infant becomes the Boy. This is above all the Age of Sensations; and both of these phases are derived from the original concept of an age of nature. Book III deals with later childhood up to the age of puberty, treating it primarily as the Age of Ideas, with certain elements of 'force'; while Book IV presents adolescence proper, which is the period of crisis, and above all, the Age of Sentiment, although reason and imagination are also involved in it. Finally, in Book V, the educational and moral scheme is brought to its novel-like conclusion with the introduction of Sophie, and the love and marriage of the young couple. This phase cannot be described by any one term, but may be thought of as an age of morality, or social and civic responsibility, depending on the harmonious functioning of all the faculties previously brought into operation. It has an important political aspect, but ends in conventional domestic happiness, symbolized by the prospect of the birth of a child, and the generalization of enlightenment in the upbringing of the next generation. All that is lacking, so far as Emile himself is concerned, is the ultimate Wisdom or personal self-sufficiency outside the social context. The attainment of this lies beyond the scope of any pedagogical theory, but is envisaged, as we have seen, in the fragmentary sequel *Les Solitaires*.

This, then, is the general framework which serves Rousseau for the expression of almost everything of importance in his philosophy, including his theory of knowledge; a good deal of 'psychology'; parts of his aesthetic and political doctrines; most of his ethical system; and, in Book IV, his most comprehensive discussion of metaphysics and religion, in the famous *Profession de foi du vicaire savoyard*. These elements cannot be analysed here in detail, but the following outline will show how Rousseau brings them to bear upon the problem of education and natural morality.

Book I, presenting the Infant, opens with a preamble including the inevitable proclamation of the social Fall, and deviation from Nature.

Tout est bien sortant des mains de l'Auteur des choses, tout dégénère entre les mains de l'homme.[10]

And this deviation is associated with servitude, in resounding phrases which recall the opening of the *Contrat Social*.

L'homme civil naît, vit et meurt dans l'esclavage: à sa naissance on le coud dans un maillot; à sa mort on le cloue dans une bière; tant qu'il garde la figure humaine, il est enchaîné par nos institutions.[11]

From this, it is not difficult to deduce that the first positive principle of this scheme of regenerative education is *liberty*, although the precise significance of the word will only emerge gradually in the text.

The second positive principle is *equality*, and this implies that Rousseau is concerned, not with specialized pursuits in particular vocations, but with what is common and universal, i.e. the urge to live a full, happy and satisfying life, and the need to develop the resources required for successful adaptation to all the vicissitudes of an uncertain existence. The complement to the criticism of specialists in the *Discours sur les sciences et les arts* is the following paragraph, which sets the tone of the whole book.

> Dans l'ordre naturel, les hommes étant tous égaux, leur vocation commune est l'état d'homme; et quiconque est bien élevé pour celui-là ne peut mal remplir ceux qui s'y rapportent. Qu'on destine mon élève à l'épée, à l'église, au barreau, peu m'importe. Avant la vocation des parents, la nature l'appelle à la vie humaine. Vivre est le métier que je lui veux apprendre. En sortant de mes mains, il ne sera, j'en conviens, ni magistrat, ni soldat, ni prêtre; il sera premièrement homme: tout ce qu'un homme doit être, il saura l'être au besoin tout aussi bien que qui que ce soit; et la fortune aura beau le faire changer de place, il sera toujours à la sienne.[12]

Emile is, therefore, another contribution to the conquest of *Chance*; and also an 'art of living', in which Rousseau is concerned to maintain and develop the self-sufficiency of the individual, which is the *general* condition for successful living, irrespective of *particular* occupations or activities; and it is clear from the outset that sooner or later we may expect a convergence of the educational and moral theory, and the politics of the General Will.

What is immediately striking in this declaration, however, is the distinction between the vocation of Nature and the vocation of the parents, the paradoxical implication of which is that in the existing order of society the 'natural' guardians and educators of the child cannot be assumed to express the true intentions of Nature in their methods of training. They will the child's good, but may not see it; so that from the start, its upbringing is likely to be no more than a projection of the Selfish Interest of the parents. However offensive this may seem (and there may be more truth in it than most parents would care to admit), the inexorable logic of Rousseau's New Order clearly requires the substitution of a more enlightened authority before the presentation of his theory can proceed. It is at this point that a typical vicious circle is broken by the Tutor, whose active control cannot begin at once, but who is assumed to exercise a general supervision from the time of the child's birth; and who represents the conscience of all parents.

This remarkable figure assumes legitimate authority through a kind of contract which, while it is not particularly relevant to the actual theory of education, throws a great deal of light on the analogous intervention of the Lawgiver in the *Contrat Social*. Its terms are simple. From the parents, it calls for the transfer of all authority to the Tutor; from the Tutor, it requires complete dedication to his charge, the recompense for which will be the ultimate gratitude of the pupil, and the moral satisfaction accruing from a task well done. The authority of the Tutor is essentially a moral authority, and his motives and rewards represent an appropriate application of the principle of Self-Interest. Finally, from the infant himself, all that is and can be required, initially, is physical health, corresponding logically to the robustness of the primitive man of Rousseau's second discourse.

The exposition of the system can now begin; and the basic mechanism is shown at once in terms of the satisfaction, not of wants, but of genuine and natural *needs*, which during the age of instinct or infancy can only be physical needs. They are: sustenance (i.e. the mother's milk, as opposed to the system of the wet-nurse); pure air (i.e. that of the country rather than the town); rigorous hygiene based on clean cold water; and freedom of movement. These requirements are simple opposites of current practices in Rousseau's day; and the only one which calls for special comment is that of freedom of movement. This is because the more extreme 'individualistic' interpretations of Rousseau have assumed that because he demands that the baby shall be free to kick indiscriminately, he is demanding the same thing for the grown man. We shall see later, however, that this is not a fair indication of his meaning.

From a philosophical standpoint, more importance may be attached to the subsequent passages of Book I, which give the first stage of Rousseau's theory of knowledge, inspired to a great extent by Locke. The first point is that like the hypothetical primitive, the baby has no sense of time, because memory and imagination are not yet active. Its consciousness is restricted to immediate sensation; and its most important instrument for learning is the sense of touch, although the other senses naturally play their part as well. The point to be taken here, is that the basis of Rousseau's eloquent plea for the banishment of restrictive clothing is neither 'sentimental' nor 'Spartan'; freedom of movement is simply the key to the first stage of knowledge, i.e. the conquest of *space*; and also a means of *communication*, like grimaces and crying.

It is, in fact, with the discussion of the problems of infant communication that Book I draws to a conclusion which reveals the different planes of thought in Rousseau. At the mechanical level, his main argument is that Nature has provided the infant with adequate means of expressing its real needs; and that the development of movement or speech should not be forced in any way. Nature ensures that its faculties develop together at a suitable pace; and that at an appropriate time there will be a sudden acceleration, which is clearly analogous to the processes of 'revolution' postulated in the second discourse, with regard to society as a whole. The almost simultaneous mastery of the techniques of talking, eating and walking constitutes the consummation of the first phase in the child's life. It is a perfectly natural process; but it is characteristic of Rousseau that before concluding the book, he should point out also the risks of disaster which accompany even this limited development.

These risks exist because the efforts of the baby to communicate its requirements are also the first links in the chain of the social organization; and the whole future of the child and the man may be jeopardized by a defective response to them. The first tears of the infant are, as Rousseau says, 'prayers', and must be met promptly and justly by the satisfaction of the legitimate—i.e. physical—needs. Any other demand is unnatural and therefore illegitimate; and must be countered by the most uncompromising impassivity on the part of the responsible adult. Otherwise, the prayers of Self-Interest will become the commands of Selfish Interest, and the natural expression of dependence will become the unnatural expression of a tyrannical and capricious will.

This principle must be understood at the outset, because all the *social* implications of the theory of *Emile* depend upon it; and because it disposes once and for all of the notion that Rousseau's belief in Original Innocence implies any sort of flabby sentimentality in his approach to the child, or that the basis of his doctrine is indiscriminate free-expression. On the contrary, his fundamental belief is that the child must be rigorously conditioned from birth to expect a response only to what the enlightened adult can recognize as the legitimate claims of Self-Interest; because *every* child, according to Rousseau, is not only *not* a little angel, but must be assumed to be a potential public pest or Despot, and treated as such by being brought up against resistances in his environment, as soon as possible. Rousseau's cure for Despotism begins, in short, with indifference to infantile tantrums; but the corollary to this point (which is entirely in accordance with his theory of the State), is that this resistance must be strictly 'depersonalized' and not associated with another individual and frustrating will. It must, in fact, be carefully emptied of morality, and made to appear as the physical resistance of *things*, and not that of human wills. This is the first stage of what Rousseau calls 'the education of things'; and it leads directly to the main topics of Book II of *Emile*, which takes the child through the Age of Sensations, as he elaborates his theory of knowledge.

The second book starts from the point where the child can be deemed to have enough sense of its individuality, and control of its physical faculties, to be treated as a person or *être moral*. This transition is associated mainly, however, with the power of articulate speech which, etymologically, distinguishes the *puer* from the *infans*; and this leads Rousseau to a reconsideration of what the child wishes to communicate, which is still, for the most part, physical needs or the sense of physical discomfort. Philosophically, therefore, this section begins with a new discussion of the fundamental problem of evil, which stresses once more the harsh realism underlying the whole system.

The first thing which the child must learn is to *suffer*, for this is the beginning of that ultimate Wisdom which consists in the understanding of, and adaptation to, the risks and limitations of the human condition. At this early stage, the question of moral evil hardly arises, any more than it does for Rousseau's primitive; and the principle of Self-Interest requires simply that the young child be allowed sufficient physical liberty, within the bounds of common-sense, to follow nature and come to terms with risks of the physical environment. Just as the baby is to be freed of its swaddling-clothes and allowed to learn about the world by the simple process of stubbing its toe on it, so the mobile child must be allowed a reasonable number of cuts, bumps and bruises, in order to register the essential lesson of the relationship between its physical capacities and its surroundings; for the key to all the liberty and happiness of which man is capable lies precisely in the balancing of desire and the possibility of fulfilment, and this must be learnt first at the physical level.

It is at this stage that Rousseau, in one of the most significant paragraphs that he ever wrote, makes the first formal link between the scheme of *Emile* and the ideas on liberty and dependence which govern the whole of his political theory.

Il y a deux sortes de dépendances: celle des choses, qui est de la nature; celle des hommes, qui est de la société. La dépendance des choses, n'ayant aucune moralité, ne nuit point à la liberté, et n'engendre point de vices: la dépendance des hommes étant désordonnée les engendre tous, et c'est par elle que le maître et l'esclave se dépravent mutuellement. S'il y a quelque moyen de remédier à ce mal dans la société, c'est de substituer la loi à l'homme, et d'armer les volontés générales d'une force réelle, supérieure à l'action de toute volonté particulière. Si les lois des nations pouvaient avoir, comme celles de la nature, une inflexibilité que jamais aucune force humaine ne pût vaincre, la dépendance des hommes redeviendrait alors celle des choses; on réunirait dans la république tous les avantages de l'état naturel à ceux de l'état civil; on joindrait à la liberté qui maintient l'homme exempt de vices, la moralité qui l'élève à la vertu.

These lines not only explain the political thought, but provide the precept which dominates the first three books of *Emile*, and gives practical expression to the principles of liberty and equality.

Maintenez l'enfant dans la seule dépendance des choses, vous aurez suivi l'ordre de la nature dans le progrès de son éducation.[13]

Nothing could be simpler than this, or show more clearly the absolute consistency of Rousseau's thinking. Its logical outcome in the actual educational theory, is that in the ensuing years the child's consciousness must be restricted as far as possible to the material world, and that his permitted activities must be predominantly physical. This does not mean simply exercise, fresh air and plenty of sleep, although these things are, of course, of prime importance. It means anything which, at the child's level, can be directed to the education of the senses; and it is in pursuance of this idea that Rousseau devotes the last sections of Book II to a penetrating analysis of the role and relative importance of the five senses in the life of the child. This discussion, inspired largely by the works of Locke and Condillac, is technically out of date, but still makes stimulating reading. It treats the senses on a kind of hierarchical basis, beginning with the primordial importance of touch; and considering in turn the greater range and the unreliability of sight; the training of the ear; and the relative importance of taste, and unimportance of smell, as far as the child is concerned.

This section contributes greatly to the detailed theory of knowledge in *Emile*, and, as we shall see later, has a very direct bearing upon Rousseau's aesthetic doctrine. If read superficially, however, it could easily be taken as being far too negative, and as implying an absurdly limited view of the mental and moral potentialities of children below the age of twelve. In justice to Rousseau, therefore, it must be emphasized that he is concerned, not to impose limitations, but to make sure that within the limits imposed by Nature itself, the child's experience shall be as rich as possible. He contends that because of society's indecent haste to condition children by intellectual exercises, the sensory potential of most men remains permanently unfulfilled, and the relationship to 'things' impoverished and falsified from the start; and it must be admitted that his position is defensible.

As to the question of moral and mental development, Rousseau is certainly not so naïve as to think that they can be left out of account at this age, in any conditions conceivable in real life. On the contrary, he states explicitly, at the beginning of Book II, that as soon as the child is recognizable as a person, one must begin to consider him as a moral being. His main argument, once again, is that the pace of moral development must not be forced by a type of formal instruction which can have no real meaning for a creature who is 'neither animal nor man, but a child'.

He cannot, of course, evade the problem of controlling the child; and his logical solution of it is to reject reasoning and rely on 'force', by which he means the careful exploitation of impassive resistances. In circumstances which necessitate a veto for the child's own good, the 'no' must be absolute and final. This implies that the child must on no account be allowed to feel that he is at the mercy of an arbitrary and capricious human will, either through positive commands or through punishment. It does *not* mean (as opponents of this kind of education are apt to assume) that the child must not suffer the consequences of what his elders can see to be an anti-social act, such as lying; it merely means that he must experience punishment not *as* punishment, but as the natural and inevitable consequence of certain actions. In theory, the false statements of the child cannot be deemed to be 'lies', and so do not call for 'punishment'; but provided that the whole process is maintained strictly on an amoral cause-and-effect basis, Rousseau is perfectly happy to see the ill-effects of not telling the truth rain down on the head of the luckless boy.

It would require a very long discussion to exhaust Rousseau's handling of the moral aspect of what he conceives primarily as the Age of Sensations. What matters, for our just appreciation of his position, is that he is fully aware of the difficulties; that much of Book II is in fact devoted to them; that his theoretical handling of them is carried out unsentimentally and with impeccable logic; and that, at the practical level, he is enough of a realist to admit that every child is an individual, and that everything depends ultimately upon the patience, intelligence and good example of a dedicated adult. The comparative rarity of such a paragon does not of itself dispose of Rousseau's arguments.

There remains the question of mental development in this same age;

and this again needs special consideration, partly because it relates to the transition from Book II to Book III, and partly because it is precisely the kind of question which can lead the unwary critic to reject Rousseau as hopelessly unrealistic or positively eccentric.

Since he regards the period from four to twelve as an age of sensations, rejects book-learning, and maintains that it is pointless to reason with a child before the age of reason, it is easy to assume that he is obstinately flouting common experience and denying to the child any rational powers at all; and that his Emile will be a real savage, without any mental discipline. Rousseau does not, of course, teach anything so absurd. What he does claim is that the reason of the child is different from the reason of the adult, because his experience does not allow the same degree of abstraction, and because during the early years the mind registers, not ideas, but images of objects experienced passively through the senses. Ideas or *perceptions* come later, and are notions of objects involving relationships, and requiring for their development the participation of an active faculty of judgment which is not yet operative.

Far from denying that the child thinks, or ought to think, in this age of sensations, Rousseau argues simply that it is through the senses that he *begins* to think; and that the richer the stock of sense-experience, the sooner and the more efficiently the active power of judgment will come into operation. Thus, physical pursuits not only strengthen the body, but, in that they can involve rudimentary judgments about the material environment, lead to the only kind of 'reason' which Rousseau thinks possible at this early age. This he calls a *raison sensitive* or *raison puérile*, to distinguish it from a *raison intellectuelle* or *raison humaine*, which is the prerogative of the human adult, the development of which will be traced in the later books.

In short, the apparently arbitrary division between the Age of Sensations and the Age of Ideas is merely a device for the exposition of a theory of knowledge based really upon a *continuity* of development. It may be out of date, but it need not be dismissed as inherently unreasonable just because of the lateness of the turning-point, which is put roughly at the twelfth year. All that Rousseau means to suggest is that by then any normal child could be assumed to have had a rich, free and happy experience of the *pays des sensations*, and to have acquired, not a useless load of second-hand knowledge, but the ability to think for himself in a simple way, by using a 'sixth sense' to combine several sensations or images. The slowness of the tempo is explained by the insistence upon authenticity of experience, and by the great difference between a child really thinking for himself, and merely parroting the uncomprehended 'reasoning' of surrounding adults. The point of emergence of this *raison puérile* is the maturity of childhood; but it also represents, in the scheme of *Emile*, the completion of a second 'revolution'.

The period from twelve to fifteen covered by Book III is to all intents and purposes the Golden Age of youth: a fleeting phase distinguished from the others as the only time when Nature allows the forces of the child to outstrip the growth of its needs. In these years immediately preceding puberty, there is a surplus of energy which it is of vital importance to direct in the most profitable manner: namely, to accumulate a stock of resources and knowledge for the future. This, therefore, is the time for study, and more positive guidance by the Tutor; when mental curiosity naturally succeeds a merely physical restlessness, and can be exploited in the same way with the willing co-operation of the child.

It is time, in fact, for him to take the first step of manhood, the *premier pas d'homme*, which consists, precisely, in the transformation of sensations into ideas. But, true to his principles, Rousseau insists that this should be a gradual process, still based directly upon sensation; and that the knowledge acquired should be gained at first-hand, without the mediation of books. To this rule, however, there is one famous exception: *Robinson Crusoe*, which offers the only kind of vicarious experience compatible with Rousseau's views on self-sufficiency, and relevant to the actual situation of his hypothetical pupil. For the rest, the world is Emile's book, and can provide all his immediate needs in the way of positive knowledge—about geography, for example, or the physical sciences.

Viewed superficially from the standpoint of the practical educationist, whose thinking is geared to the methods and tempo of public instruction, this is the most vulnerable part of Rousseau's theory; and one which it is difficult to rescue from the aura of absurdity hanging over the highly artificial demonstrations and illustrative anecdotes with which it is decorated. The difficulties arise because on one hand Rousseau wants to accelerate the educational process, to make the most of this short-lived 'peaceful age of intelligence' preceding the awakening of the passions; while on the other he is committed, through the refusal of the second-hand symbolism of books and the denial to the child of powers of abstraction, to an empirical method of object-lessons, which is consistent with the whole scheme, but very slow in practice.

RG

His chief resource is to argue that the method is more important than the amount of knowledge acquired; and that the educator's main consideration at this stage should be to communicate not only the method, but an enthusiasm which will lead the pupil to find out for himself what he really needs to know. In fact, when faced by the possibility of sheer inertia and laziness, Rousseau falls back, with his usual consistency, upon the universal principle of Self-Interest, and asserts that the pupil will make rapid intellectual strides when convinced that knowledge is *useful*. It is to give immediate support to this utilitarian principle that he invokes the aid of *Robinson Crusoe*; and it may be conceded that the choice is a good one, although the desire to confine the reading of an intelligent boy of fifteen to a single book must seem ridiculous if it is taken too seriously. What is important about *Robinson Crusoe*, from Rousseau's point of view, is not so much its appeal to boyish imagination (since, technically, that of Emile is hardly stirring, as yet), as the fact that it provides an admirable demonstration of Self-Interest, and a suitable introduction to a discussion of the practical and social aspects of education, which forms a natural complement to his criticisms in the two discourses.

The best and most famous suggestion in this section of *Emile* is that the pupil should devote a part of this period to the mastery of a basic manual skill or 'useful art', such as carpentry, instead of flirting with intellectual activities and 'agreeable arts' which he is in no position to understand. There is, of course, nothing very original in this suggestion; it is already in Locke, for example, and it tallies with the interest in 'mechanical arts' shown by Diderot and the Encyclopedists. Nobody is likely to disagree, in any case, that it is a good thing for a boy to be able to use his hands; but Rousseau is not passionately interested in the skill as such. It is true that he took a pride in his own craft of music-copying, but his advocacy of manual training is based on a number of philosophical considerations, all of which have a logical place in his scheme of thought. To begin with, the acquisition of a basic trade or skill is relevant to his theory of knowledge, in that it offers the right combination of physical and mental activity for a particular stage of development; secondly, it relates to the principle of Self-Interest, in that the possession of a necessary skill is an insurance against the revolutions of fortune (though this is a point which has lost its force); thirdly—and this is the most important aspect—the cultivation of manual skill and the *Robinsonade* with which it is associated provide a natural way of encouraging in the young mind the beginnings of a sense of social values.

There is, of course, a temptation to regard this *Robinson Crusoe* element as a piece of faintly comic Romanticism, or to associate it with Rousseau's own psychological peculiarities; but as it stands, it is a sincere and sensible attempt to induce the child to make for himself the great step from *raison sensitive* to *raison intellectuelle*; to awaken the active judgment; and to start him working out for himself ideas on such things as the dignity of labour or the laws of economics. The main lessons, in fact, are a sense of the mutual dependence of men, and an awareness of the natural values, which will enable Emile to judge the perversity of the conventional values of Selfish Interest in the false society which he must encounter. Without being subjected to direct moral indoctrination, the Emile of the end of Book III will be conditioned to make his own 'right' moral judgments, when the range of experience is extended a little further; and will have ideas about social relationships without having been exposed to the risks of active participation in social life. As Rousseau sums it up:

> nous avons fait un être agissant et pensant; il ne nous reste plus, pour achever l'homme, que de faire un être aimant et sensible, c'est-à-dire de perfectionner la raison par le sentiment.[14]

At the end of childhood, Emile, who has been firmly conditioned to accept the dependence on things and the 'yoke of necessity', is ready to enter into relations with men, and to acquire thereby the social virtues. In theory, he has, moreover, remained as happy as Nature will permit; and free at least from the shackles invented by society, i.e. those of opinion and of the passions, which are the way to Selfish Interest. But can this position be maintained beyond childhood proper? With this question, *Emile* now moves towards its climax.

During each of the phases covered by the first three books, Rousseau recognizes certain risks to happiness, involving Selfish Interest; and deals with them by force or ruse. In Book IV, he leaves us in no doubt that adolescence is the period of the greatest risk; and his thoughts on this crisis of his educational drama find expression in a double set of images, which reflect both the evolutionary and the fall-and-redemption perspectives. In terms of the first, the hazards appear as a storm which cannot be weathered without all the skill of the Tutor (who is presented momentarily as a 'Ulysses', with a play on the etymology of *gouverneur*); in terms of the second, Emile is depicted as a sleepwalker on the edge of a precipice, whose awakening must be carried out with the greatest care, if he is not to fall to destruction. Without lingering on the imagery, the importance of which will be discussed in connection with the art of Rousseau, we can assume from it that the scope and subtlety of this book will be much greater than that of the preceding ones; and that the handling of the complex problems of the adolescent cannot be reduced to easy formulas. Nevertheless, the main intention is simply to enable the pupil to take the second step of manhood, and enter into the moral and social order; and it is carried out in three stages. A first section poses and analyses the new range of moral, intellectual and social problems and hazards; a second (which is in fact the *Profession de foi du vicaire savoyard*) shows how to direct the pupil's mind to philosophy and religion, and counters the risk of a Fall by the simple, logical and 'evolutionary' process of extending the range of operation of Self-Interest; and the third, under the protection of this safeguard, brings Emile into contact with the world at large, and begins his gradual awakening to a social future.

Rousseau's investigation of the problems begins with their causes in the passions, which, as might be expected, he defends in so far as they have a natural source. This defence involves a re-statement of the fundamental distinction between Self-Interest and Selfish Interest; and this in turn is essential to the next point: namely, that during adolescence Nature itself creates a new need, the satisfaction of which falls, or should fall, within the range of Self-Interest. This new factor is, of course, the sexual drive, which is so important as to constitute virtually a second birth; and is in any case an inevitable breach of the theoretical isolation in which the pupil has so far been kept. This new need marks, therefore, a reorientation of Rousseau's scheme, to provide for the first social relations and a new kind of emotional life. From now on, his working assumption must be that the pupil cannot be preserved from Selfish Interest merely by negative methods. The educator may defer sexual preoccupations up to a point (about the age of twenty, in theory), but sooner or later he must intervene in a much more positive way than hitherto, in order to combat two specific threats. These are offered, not by the passions themselves, but by 'opinion' and imagination; and Rousseau contends that the educator now has at his disposal the means of controlling them. The first resource is reason, which is already largely developed in the adolescent, and can be used to vanquish the rule of opinion; the second (and new) factor is *sentiment* or feeling, which, if used judiciously, can direct the imagination in healthy ways.

It is sentiment which Rousseau calls upon first; and although this might seem a risky way of dealing with the problem of sex, it is reasonable enough within the system. The procedure depends, in fact, upon two points made in the *Discours sur l'origine de l'inégalité*: namely, the distinction between sexual desire, which is physical and natural in a primitive sense, and love, which is social; and the existence of a pre-rational instinct of compassion. Assuming that the physical manifestations of sexuality can be controlled by a healthy and active life, Rousseau concentrates heavily upon the sentiment of compassion, in order to deflect the pupil's thoughts away from the particular relationship of love, and towards friendship and the general sense of human community, which in his view has a natural priority. This means, first, that the Tutor-Pupil relationship becomes more of an equal friendship than before; and secondly, that the attention of Emile is now directed to all that can develop fellow-feeling, and particularly to the spectacle of human suffering. The emotional response to the limitations and common misfortunes of humanity is regarded as a partial antidote to Selfish Interest; the rest depends upon Emile's estimate of his own position in relation to those around him. If he can be made to see that he has no reason to envy others or compete with them, Selfish Interest can be defeated.

This, therefore, is the point where Emile must undertake a vital part of his education, i.e. a study of the social organization, and the ills and inequalities which are of social origin. It is evidently one of the stages at which *Emile* begins to link up with the thought of the *Contrat Social*; and is the place for the introduction into the educational programme of history and didactic literature. Once more (as with *Robinson Crusoe*) Rousseau allows his pupil a measure of vicarious knowledge and experience; but he is far too cunning to allow Emile the dangerous satisfaction of thinking that he is immune from the stupidities and catastrophes to be found in fable or history. The remedy is to make sure that he undergoes an occasional personal humiliation, sufficient to deflate the youthful ego, but not serious enough to leave a lasting resentment.

Up to this point, the main emphasis is upon the control of imagination by sentiment; but towards the end of the first section of Book IV, Rousseau turns to the prospects for the rational control of the rule of opinion, which is the other great threat to adolescent Self-Interest. This is unquestionably a major step, not only on account of its ultimate moral implications, but in relation to the actual theory of knowledge; for it is here that Emile must be seriously exercised for the first time in the use of what Rousseau has called the *raison intellectuelle*. In other words, the Age of Sentiment is also the Age of Reason in the full sense of the term;

when the natural acquisition of ideas takes the pupil beyond the range of sensory experience and empirical control, and on to the plane of abstract thinking. It is also, says Rousseau, another time of 'acceleration', which, as we know, is tantamount, in his terminology, to another 'revolution'. In this case, the accelerated progress of the passions calls for a corresponding acceleration in the development of *lumières*, if the pupil is to maintain the equilibrium which is the rule of Nature and the key to happiness. And so the first part of Book IV ends by raising the problem of metaphysics and abstract speculation, and leading into the field where Rousseau believes the rule of opinion to be most powerful, and most dangerous to liberty and happiness. Emile, who has hitherto been carefully kept from such discussions by the rigorous application of a theory of knowledge, must now face the question of religion. And since, on Rousseau's principles, this 'natural man' must not be forced into any particular sect, all that can be done is to put him into a position where he can choose for himself, through the best use of his reason.

Because of its implications for Rousseau's philosophy as a whole, this is not the place to discuss the actual content of the *Profession de foi*, except to say that it expounds the only doctrine compatible with the principles of *Emile*, which is that of natural, as opposed to revealed, religion. Our immediate concern is with its relation to its context, in respect of the method and the practical consequences for the pupil; and here the first point to make is that although it can be treated as a separate entity, it continues the practice, observed elsewhere, of making cautious use of vicarious experience, in appropriate circumstances.

Disclaiming any dogmatic intention, Rousseau gives the *Profession de foi* ostensibly as a mere example of the kind of extended reasoning which the pupil can now be expected to follow. The degree of religious awareness resulting from it must remain a personal and individual matter. Apart from this, what Emile, as a representative figure, is expected to derive from such an exercise in metaphysics and comparative religion is an understanding of the value and, above all, the limits of human reason; an extension of the range of feeling, which must take over where reason breaks down (provided always that it follows the lines indicated by reason); and the basis for a personal morality, which consists in an expanded understanding of Self-Interest, taking into account a life to come. As the boy, or even the baby, develops its faculties and maintains its happiness by exploring and coming to terms with the physical environment, so the adolescent must use his growing reason and sensibility to explore the moral environment, and, likewise, to maintain his happiness through a just appreciation of his own relation to it, which makes for liberation from selfish desire. Rousseau sees this as a natural and painless transition from the study of Nature to the search for its author; and when the idea of God is acquired, as the most reasonable explanation of the cosmos, it follows that with the natural love of self, there will be associated a natural love of the Creator of the self and the universal order, of which the self feels itself to be an integral part.

To cut a long story short, Emile will emerge from the kind of experience suggested by the *Profession de foi* with an active conscience which, although it operates through feeling, does not supplant reason, but supplements it, particularly in the creation of a sense of personal relationship to the Deity. As a result, he will now see both his behaviour and his prospects of happiness in a new perspective—*sub specie aeternitatis*—and associate his true, i.e. longest-term—interest with being and doing good for love of a benevolent God, and irrespective of particular laws and social sanctions. When this happens, Emile is on the threshold of manhood, and ready for a new kind of submission; not this time, to necessity, but to the rule of reason, that other 'yoke' which man must learn to bear voluntarily in the course of his natural fulfilment.

It is by exploiting this new form of control that Rousseau seeks to guide the hypothetical pupil through the storm of adolescence, or—if the alternative symbolism is preferred—to save him from the Fall into the abyss of Selfish Interest, and the slavery to passion. And it is clear that at this point the convergence of the doctrines of *Emile* and the *Contrat Social* has been taken a stage further. Indeed, in the third section of Book IV they not only converge but begin to interlock, at a moment which stands out as a great turning-point in the scheme of *Emile*, and finally confirms what has become increasingly apparent, i.e. the analagous roles of Tutor and Lawgiver.

This third section begins at the 'true moment of nature', when the sexual development of the young man makes it imperative that he should be told the facts of life. In spite of the conditioning which has already taken place, nothing is left to chance; and the revelation is staged in a way which, it must be admitted, prompts some uneasy reflections on the kind of spellbinding to which Rousseauism can lead. In the face of the spectacle of nature, and with all the religious and emotional stops pulled out, Emile is informed of the 'inconceivable mysteries of generation', and of the status of marriage as the most sacred of contracts; and it might well be thought that this liberation from ignorance is also the moment for the abdication of the Tutor. But such is the effect of the conditioning he has received, that the young man cannot bear immediately the burden of liberty thus conferred on him, but prefers to prolong voluntarily the state of dependence on the wisdom and moral authority of his mentor. Unsure of himself, unable to exploit his sexual maturity with the amorality of the primitive, and frightened by the consequences of immorality or Selfish Interest, of which he is now aware, he has no alternative but to lean upon the enlightenment of the Tutor, just as, during the evolution of Rousseau's New State, the individuals must depend provisionally upon the enlightenment of the Lawgiver. This intensely interesting psychological situation is symbolized by Rousseau as a voluntary surrender to moral authority, in the following terms.

O mon ami, mon protecteur, mon maître, reprenez l'autorité que vous voulez déposer au moment qu'il m'importe le plus qu'elle vous reste; vous ne l'aviez jusqu'ici que par ma faiblesse, vous l'aurez maintenant par ma volonté, et elle m'en sera plus sacrée. Défendez-moi de tous les ennemis qui m'assiègent, et surtout de ceux que je porte avec moi, et qui me trahissent; veillez sur votre ouvrage, afin qu'il demeure digne de vous. Je veux obéir à vos lois, je le veux toujours, c'est ma *volonté constante*; si jamais je vous désobéis, ce sera malgré moi: rendez-moi libre en me protégeant contre mes passions qui me font violence; empêchez-moi d'être leur esclave, et forcez-moi d'être mon propre maître en n'obéissant point à mes sens, mais à ma raison.[15]

This act of submission is sometimes referred to by commentators as the Pedagogical Contract, but its implications go far beyond the educational theory as such. It is clearly the counterpart, expressed in individual and moral terms, of the situation depicted in public and political terms in the Social Contract. In the light of it, we can see more clearly how the realization of the General Will or Constant Will of the community is the agreement of individual constant wills directed, as in the case of Emile, by true Self-Interest, but requiring initiation and mediation by a more enlightened mind.

This is not, of course, the conclusion of *Emile*, but all that follows in the main text (and disregarding *Les Solitaires*) is worked out in relation to a social context, mainly domestic, but with a political aspect also. Book IV itself ends, naturally enough, with the introduction of Emile into the world, under the protection of the Tutor, who, it may be noted, makes a point of not using his new authority in any way which could appear 'despotic'. Instead, he proceeds purely on a basis of friendship and mutual trust—a point which again reminds us of the true spirit of Rousseau's politics.

Following as it does the *Profession de foi* and the great moment of 'contract', the end of Book IV must seem rather an anticlimax; yet it would be quite wrong to neglect it. In a way, it is as important as anything in *Emile*, because it shows much of Rousseau's thinking about a vital problem which he was unable to solve in his own life. If *Emile* as a whole is an 'art of living', this section deals specifically with the art of living with one's fellows as they are, which is a different matter, although it concerns both the man and the citizen. There is, perhaps, a certain ambiguity about it, in so far as it shows Emile adapting himself to existing social usages which he must obviously regard as being of dubious value; yet it has the merit of posing the inevitable problems of social behaviour at levels which are quite different from the political idealism of the *Contrat Social*. Seen against the whole background of Rousseau's thought, these questions of civility, culture and taste are particularly challenging, but he handles them with a delicacy which is no discredit to the tradition of the French *moralistes*. The first of them is dealt with by means of a fine qualitative distinction between servile imitation and a genuine conformity which can be associated with Self-Interest through a right understanding of the desire to please. As for the embarrassing question of intellectual and artistic culture, Rousseau bows to the inevitable, and allows Emile to learn languages and drink at the classic sources of pure literature. The problem of taste, however, produces an extremely important discussion, which is an essential part of his aesthetic doctrine, and will be examined later in that context.

In general, this final section of Book IV shows that as an educational theorist Rousseau meets his commitments fairly and conscientiously, although one may well wonder how the new stock of knowledge could be acquired in the time available. It is obvious, however, that refined society on the Parisian model is not that for which Emile has been brought up, and it is with undisguised relief that the young man is whisked off to find fulfilment, and a suitable wife, in more rustic surroundings.

Although Rousseau allowed himself the luxury of a story-book ending as though relaxing after a major effort of thought, this must not be taken to imply that he loses his grip on the main educational theory, or fails to work it out to a logical conclusion, or that Book V can be treated less seriously than the rest of *Emile*. In fact, the 'novel' of Emile and

Sophie accounts for barely half of it; and its real structure, consisting of three main sections and a short conclusion, shows him dealing quite methodically with outstanding problems. The first of these sections, 'Sophie ou la Femme', is a necessary and supplementary 'essay' on the upbringing of girls; the second, beneath its old-fashioned fictional surface, is a psychological study of courtship, which is in some respects very sensitive, though it has persuaded some critics that Rousseau did not understand women. The third part, entitled 'Des Voyages', has three main aims: first, to stress the difference between the awakening to love, and readiness for the responsibilities of marriage; secondly, to extend the application of Rousseau's theories of liberty and happiness by subjecting Emile to the test of separation; and thirdly, profiting from this separation, to complete his social education by giving him both an international outlook, and a more specialized sense of civic responsibility which is necessary even in an imperfect world. Only when these have been acquired can the story of Emile be brought to its conventional and provisional happy ending.

Rousseau's ideas on the education of girls are anathema to most liberal thinkers, and to all who have preached the 'emancipation' of women. This is because his practical recommendations, based on the view that Nature intended women for a predominantly domestic function, can be summarized baldly as a good grounding in needlework, a little drawing, a sound general domestic training, and no intellectual pursuits. In the circumstances, it is understandable that critics should conclude that he is an 'antifeminist'; but this label is as irrelevant as the word 'totalitarian' applied to his politics. It is true that his attitude might be traced back to a fear of a minority of clever women encountered in the society of the *salons*, or to psychological causes of a more intimate kind; but common-sense suggests that in assigning a domestic role to women, he is simply expressing the views of most contemporary males, and, perhaps, of most males in all ages.

In any case, there is nothing sinister in his intentions, because he does make the essential concession to feminist principles, in arguing from the outset that in everything not connected with sex, women are the same as men, and have the same right to the happiness and fulfilment which come from a sense of adjustment to the physical and moral order. Far from imputing any intrinsic inferiority to women, he maintains that they are equal to men in what they have in common, and that in the differences, they are just not comparable. In fact, he remains completely faithful to his fundamental doctrine, in claiming that since Nature itself has instituted a sexual differentiation whose effects are bound to extend to other levels than the biological one, it is unreasonable to assume that the happiness or fulfilment of a normal woman can take the same form as those of a normal man. A woman, in short, should *be* a woman, and not a man in skirts; just as the child has the right to *be* a child, and not be treated merely as a miniature adult.

Where Rousseau would fall foul of militant feminism is in his estimate of the actual extent of the effects of sex-differentiation, in social, moral and intellectual matters; and here it must be admitted that a fundamentally liberal view of sex relations as a partnership may be thought to have been sacrificed to a line of logic. The basis of his argument is that although men and women are made for each other, they cannot be conceived as having quite the same independence even in the state of nature, because the consequences of the sexual relationship constitute a greater tie for the female than for the male, not as a matter of right, but as a matter of brute fact. From this natural disparity (he carefully avoids the word inequality), Rousseau concludes that some form of disparity must be expected even in a social state whose merit will lie, after all, in the fact that it reflects as closely as possible the state of nature. Briefly, the woman in Rousseau's society will remain in some respects dependent on the man; and her education is bound to acknowledge the fact in being conditioned by a different system of needs.

In principle, there is no real difference in Rousseau's approach to the education of the two sexes, since in both cases it is orientated to needs, and not wants. In practice, the differences are considerable, because for women greater dependence implies greater relativity. The principle of Self-Interest operates, in fact, in a different way, implying first and foremost an effort to please man, and therefore, an education relative to his needs as well. The extent of the contrast involved can be judged by a single example, namely, the obligation laid upon women to regulate their conduct by reference to the rule of opinion which Emile is trained to reject as the enemy of true moral freedom. It is in developing this idea that Rousseau advocates for women an unquestioning acceptance of religious authority, and seeks to discourage intellectual aspirations.

There is no doubt that if certain passages are judged at face value, and without reference to the whole philosophical context, Rousseau seems to be prescribing a subservient role for women; but this is so foreign to the general spirit of his teaching, that it cannot be taken seriously as his real meaning. What he desires primarily is to re-establish the ideal of marriage as a partnership, and as the creation of a new 'moral

person' analogous to the Public Person of his political society. In this
partnership, the woman is to be a companion and not—as he says
explicitly—a slave; and he goes to great lengths to point out that in
endowing the sex with certain compensations, and in particular the gift
of *coquetterie*, nature has ensured that woman shall not become the slave
of man. Indeed, the contrary is more likely to happen, in Rousseau's
opinion; and there is perhaps a certain resentment and sense of injustice
in his reflections on the desire of some women to 'usurp' positions
which Nature intended for men, when they already have ample resources to meet the requirements of Self-Interest. So far as he is concerned, the average woman can manage very well by preserving and
developing her natural *coquetterie* at various levels of behaviour; and
most of his practical suggestions for the education of girls can be related
to this rather pleasing application of the principle of doing what comes
naturally.

Briefly, then, the strong reactions to which this part of *Emile* is
bound to give rise can be reduced to three major criticisms, the first
of which is that it suggests no scope for women outside domestic life.
This criticism is just, although in the context there is no reason why he
should go further into the question, since he is dealing with what he
calls a 'general law'. The second, which is that Rousseau puts women
into a position of inequality, is not justified if it disregards the compensations which he postulates, or the distinction between inequality and
disparity. The third criticism, that he denies the intellectual rights of
women, is justifiable up to a point; but it must be understood that he is
suspicious of 'intellectuals' of both sexes, and also that he does not say
that women should not or cannot think. On the contrary, he says explicitly that the one really disastrous situation in marriage is where the
man thinks and the woman does not, because then there is no basis for
communication. What he means is that women require a capacity for
sound practical reasoning on the lines of his concept of a *raison sensitive*,
and beyond that, will be happier if they leave logic-chopping to men,
and trust to their intuition. His point may not be palatable, and is
certainly out of date; but it is at least comprehensible within the system.

On the positive side, however, Rousseau is as sincerely concerned for
what he considers the real happiness of women, as he is for that of the
child and the man; and it seems hard when the same critics praise him
for wanting children to be children, and condemn him for wanting
women to be women. Moreover, his intentions are unimpeachable
from a moral standpoint. What he aims to do, and what he must do at

this stage of *Emile*, is to emphasize the sanctity of marriage and the mutual obligations of love and respect, by which the good son may become the good husband, and so, in time, the good father and the good citizen. For thus it is that this 'treatise of original goodness' must be brought to its conclusion.

It is with the laying of the right sentimental foundations for family life that the long section on courtship and the brief conclusion on marriage are chiefly concerned; but with regard to the development of Emile himself as it relates to Rousseau's whole system, the main emphasis of Book V is that placed on the problem of civic responsibility, in the section 'Des Voyages', the lessons of which are linked explicitly with the themes of the *Contrat Social*. The sequence in which they are handled is explained by Rousseau's belief that the family is a *petite patrie*, a belief which appears to run counter to the opinion expressed in the *Contrat Social*, that the State cannot be derived from the natural society of the family. He does not, however, repudiate the distinction between natural society and conventional political society, but re-emphasizes the complementary nature of his political theory and the natural morality of *Emile*, by pointing out that the realization of the New State calls for feelings of attachment of the kind which grow more naturally in family life than through political institutions as such. Family and civic responsibility interact, in short, at the level of sensibility, and it can be assumed that the rational inducements to political association will be 'perfected' by the sentimental experiences of the family-man.

Emile's initiation into civic responsibility is linked with the experience of travel, one intention of which is to take up again the question of 'man' and 'citizen' which could not be settled at the beginning of the book. Rousseau can now reconsider this on the assumption that the pupil is on the verge of moral maturity, for which one of the final preparations is the actual interruption of his courtship, imposed quite ruthlessly by the Tutor. It becomes clear, at this stage, that while the educational programme has been directed so far to the formation of a 'man', Rousseau's intention is that the man shall of his own freewill make the further step to citizenship. Assuming, however, that he is ready to do so, a new problem now arises. Where, in an imperfect world, is the society in which an Emile can integrate himself?—or, as it is posed in the text, *où est la patrie?*

The exploration of this problem requires, on one hand, the subjection of Emile to abstract discussion of political principles, including not only the programme of the *Contrat Social*, but also the prospects for a federal system which would be the logical extension of it. On the other hand, Emile must make his own authentic and first-hand observations of the existing political systems of Europe, and draw his own conclusions from the contrast between the ideal and the real. Not surprisingly, his immediate reaction (which also shows, unquestionably, one side of Rousseau's own feelings,) is a negative 'cosmopolitanism', or urge to political disengagement, which would find its happiness and wisdom in a retreat with the beloved Sophie to a purely private life in some rustic sanctuary. From the social standpoint, however, this is a mere evasion, which cannot be allowed to stand as the final answer; and so, in an impassioned appeal which expresses the last major doctrinal point of *Emile*, Rousseau argues that although the ideal state or *patrie* does not exist, each man has at least a native land to which he owes the most precious things in human life—the morality of his actions, and the love of virtue. In exceptional circumstances, the acceptance of exile may be the best way of serving one's country; but for the average man, willing integration is the clear line of responsibility, and also of contentment. It is *because* existing society is imperfect that the naturally virtuous man must not contract out of it, since to do so would be to forgo a satisfaction of Self-Interest on the highest moral plane, deriving from the conscientious accomplishment of social duties.

This need not, however, involve the sacrifice of all other satisfactions; and Rousseau's last move is (as so often proves to be the case) to suggest a practical compromise, allowing for a peaceful, rustic and domestic life within the state, and the willing performance of such civic duties as may be required, but no seeking after glory or political domination. This is obviously intended to create for Emile conditions comparable to those of the hypothetical Golden Age; but it can also be interpreted as an attempt to harmonize or synthesize the claims of what would be, in Rousseau's political terminology, the General Will and the particular will of Emile.

After this, there is nothing more to be done for the young man, except to permit him to resume his courtship of Sophie, and move through the contract of marriage towards the realization of domestic happiness. With the prospect of the birth of a child, Emile is left to shoulder the direct responsibility for the next generation, while the Tutor assumes the special status of a background 'presence' or standard of reference, as must, presumably, the Lawgiver of the *Contrat Social*.

So ends one of the richest and most stimulating books of the eighteenth century; but no review of its doctrine can stand without some final comments on its value, and, in the first place, its importance for modern educational thought.

It is generally agreed that in spite of the derivative elements in his system, the development of pedagogical theories has been profoundly and decisively influenced by Rousseau, particularly in respect of all child-centred methods which assume a difference between the child's and the adult's view of the world; and stress the value of first-hand experience or learning by doing, and the child's right to enjoy his childhood. The line of historical influence is visible at least in the principles of most educational reformers since Rousseau, from Basedow or Campe in eighteenth-century Germany to Pestalozzi in Switzerland; and on through the nineteenth century to Froebel, and thence to Maria Montessori. And it is still reasonable to argue that one current of educational idealism, which preaches individualism and freedom, owes much to certain parts of Rousseau's teaching. Whether the later theorists have always understood the whole of his thinking with regard to individual liberty, is less certain. For example, Pestalozzi's opinion that Rousseau unwisely separated liberty and obedience, and failed to remember the limits of liberty, would hardly pass now for an accurate interpretation (especially since the one condition on which the Tutor insists from the outset is, in fact, obedience). Similar doubts are stimulated by the shocked bewilderment often provoked by the admittedly startling treatment of women in Book V. A nineteenth-century critic such as Lord Morley may have felt justified in calling this 'oriental'; but his contention that Rousseau here reverses every principle which he has followed in the case of Emile himself is just not strictly true.

In spite of certain misconceptions, however, the applicability of Rousseau's ideas in modern education is limited by practical rather than theoretical considerations, which he himself would be the first to admit. Whether his principles are right or wrong, social pressures and the sheer tempo of life prevent the range of direct application from extending much beyond the kindergarten stage. Nevertheless, reflection on the apparently increasing disparity between man's intellectual achievements and moral development suggests that Rousseau's principles are sane, and should never be lost sight of, in spite of the difficulties of implementation.

The second concluding comment concerns, once again, the relation of *Emile* to the rest of Rousseau's thought; and is, simply, that the social implications of Book V must on no account be forgotten in the inevitable arguments about the literary technique, or the education of women, or the alleged inconsistencies of principle. The 'individualism' of *Emile* does not imply that men in general can find personal fulfilment outside society. Emile is not a primitive, but an artificially-produced natural man for an artificially-produced natural society. He would not be balanced or happy without social experience; but conversely, he would not be balanced or happy in a society which was not at least evolving on the lines of the *Contrat Social*, and to which he could not contribute by personal participation. In this sense, the consistency of the two books is indisputable; and all we need to understand this is the awareness that Rousseau is talking about dynamic processes, in which the individuals of succeeding generations must engage themselves, if they are to work out. By accepting civic responsibility even in an imperfect society, Emile makes what Rousseau calls a 'tacit confirmation' of the Social Contract; and it may be said that irrespective of pedagogical matters, this is what the whole book is really about.

There remains, however, the vital question of what, if anything, lies outside or beyond the Social Contract; and *Emile* poses this problem in two ways. In the first place, the projected sequel *Les Solitaires* is intended deliberately to destroy Emile's civic and domestic security and satisfaction, and throw him back on his own moral resources; and secondly, there is the *Profession de foi du vicaire savoyard*, which raises again the whole question of religion. The first of these aspects will come up later in connection with Rousseau's autobiographical enterprises; but the second must be dealt with now, because it not only supplements the doctrine of the *Contrat Social* and *Emile*, but is indispensable for the examination of the *Nouvelle Héloïse*.

CHAPTER VI

From Social Contract to Enlightened Cult:
Profession de foi du vicaire savoyard

*

WITH the convergence of his political theory and his moral and educational doctrines, it might now be asserted that Rousseau has outlined a complete social philosophy, capable of replacing a religious conception of life; and that henceforward he need hardly concern himself with religion as such. In fact, he is led back to the problem of religion partly through the logic of Self-Interest in his system, and partly through an intuitive conviction that religion is an integral and meaningful part of human experience, however questionable it may be in some of its manifestations. And despite the reluctance of some readers to take his religious thought very seriously, the fact remains that one of the striking resemblances between the *Contrat Social* and *Emile* is the inclusion in each of an element of religious discussion and a profession of faith.

It is sometimes suggested that the creed of his *vicaire savoyard* and the *profession de foi purement civile* of the *Contrat Social* point in opposite directions, and fail to reconcile the 'religion of man' and 'the religion of the citizen'; but it is difficult to accept this in view of Rousseau's obvious anxiety over the existence of a religious attitude which is simply incompatible with the new society. Because of this, it is safe to say that whatever the shortcomings of his actual discussions, his fundamental aim must be to reconcile the public and private aspects of religion; and that the *Profession de foi du vicaire savoyard* is an attempt to show the kind of thinking which would make possible the *sincere* acceptance of the state religion, and with it full integration in the society proposed by the *Contrat Social*. On the other hand, it is also meant to indicate the kind and degree of private and positive religious fulfilment which would be compatible with the state religion, and, indeed, actually favoured by it. And so, before examining the theory of the *Profession de foi*, it may be useful to review the main points which emerge at the end of the *Contrat Social*, and by which it is to some extent conditioned.

Although Rousseau's state, as an instrument of regeneration, is con-

RH   105

ceived as taking over, through the operation of Self-Interest, some of the moral functions and loyalties which in the existing order are associated with religious institutions, it is assumed that religion will continue to play a part in the private life of the citizens, and consequently in the direction of their particular wills. The problem is to prevent particular wills so motivated from interfering with the General Will, and therefore with the liberty of other citizens, especially through the formation of an intolerant association or church within the state; and it becomes a political issue because, as Rousseau says, it is incompatible with people's own love of God to live in peace with men whom they believe to be condemned by God for not adhering to some particular form of faith. Potentially, the resulting conflict between social and religious obligations is so deep that, as we have seen, the whole theory of contract and General Will may be seriously obstructed by intransigent minds dedicated to a distorted conception of their own good, and of the cause of God.

The only political solution conceivable by Rousseau is the institution of the 'minimum' citizens' creed, which should be compatible with any reasonable private belief, and comprises, as we know, the existence of a powerful, intelligent, beneficent, foreseeing and provident God; a life to come; the happiness of the just; the punishment of the wicked; the sanctity of the Contract and the Laws; and the condemnation of intolerance. Any additional or more precise belief is a private matter, and is of no interest to the community, provided that it has no disruptive social consequences.

In theory, all this is liberal and reasonable. The conciliatory intention is shown by the careful avoidance of absolute terms in the description of the divine attributes; and the desire to reduce conflict by encouraging mental attitudes comparable to those of the pre-rational state of nature appears in Rousseau's proposal to regard these articles as 'sentiments of sociability' rather than as dogmas. In practice, however, this civic religion is open to abuse, and might well produce a mere façade of conformity, which would certainly not satisfy Rousseau, with his strong views on être and paraître and insistence upon authenticity and integrity. By itself, the creed would still make no impression on the 'conscientious' bigot or atheist, and it offers no real defence against hypocrisy, which is conceived as an evasion of the General Will. All it does, in fact, is to indicate a conciliatory political gesture on the part of the Sovereign, which must be complemented by a corresponding moral gesture or effort on the part of the individual. And clearly the individual who can make this effort is he whose private religious thinking has been directed by Self-Interest, unlike that of the bigot, the atheist or the hypocrite, who are all motivated by Selfish Interest, to which they are subordinating the good of the community and their own ultimate good.

It can be seen why Rousseau, already preoccupied by inner conflicts arising from encounters with Calvinism, Catholicism, Quietism and Deism, is also impelled inexorably by his own system to show how private religious experience ought to evolve, if it is to take a legitimate form. The scope of what he refers to later as the 'arduous researches' leading to the *Profession de foi* is naturally very wide, but the ultimate aims can be stated simply enough. One of them is negative, and consists of an attempt to show that there is really no such thing as a conscientious bigot or conscientious atheist. The others are positive, and include the extension of the range of operation of Self-Interest from the political to the religious plane; and the adumbration of a religious contract, transcending, yet compatible with, the Social Contract.

Because these aims go beyond the purely pedagogical horizon of *Emile*, there is some argument as to how far the *Profession de foi* is really integrated in the book of which it is nominally a part. For the present discussion, it is enough to say that it was probably conceived separately, and that it was certainly modified for polemical reasons connected less with educational theory than with Rousseau's deepening hostility towards the anti-religious Encyclopedists; but that it fits naturally into an educational system which is itself based on Self-Interest. Moreover, the actual form of the work is almost certainly influenced by its setting, and by the need to relate religious teaching to a particular phase of adolescence. The result of this is Rousseau's decision to resort to a fiction drawing on his own youthful discussions of spiritual problems, but using as a representative figure and spokesman the humble 'Vicaire savoyard'. This is a composite character known to have been inspired by the abbé Gaime and the abbé Gâtier, whom Rousseau met during his early wanderings, at Turin and Annecy; but the religious views themselves are his own speculations in their most mature form, as he tells us in the *Rêveries*.

As it stands in the context of *Emile*, the work is designed to impress the adolescent by a judicious combination of appeals to sentiment and to reason; and by a shrewd exploitation of dramatic narrative to indicate that religion is not an abstract matter, but a vital problem of common experience. It begins with a prologue introducing a young man (who is, of course, Rousseau himself) discussing religion with his Mentor, whose characteristics are derived from Gaime, Gâtier and an older Rousseau.

The effect of this prologue is to reproduce at one remove the Tutor-pupil relationship on which the whole of *Emile* is founded; and it is followed by a main text in two phases, containing respectively the Vicaire's philosophical enquiries and movements of enthusiasm leading to natural religion; and a defence of this position through a rational criticism of revealed religion. Certain conclusions as to conduct and suitable religious attitudes appear at the end of the whole text, but most of the major points of positive doctrine occur towards the middle, at the end of the first part. This arrangement is explained partly by the fact that Rousseau cannot present philosophical and historical criticism simultaneously; but the structure of the whole is determined by emotional considerations as much as by logic. The emotional impact itself depends upon the contrast between the order of Nature and the chaos of human affairs and beliefs; and this is emphasized at the outset by the spectacular natural setting in which Rousseau carefully stages this declaration of religious principles.

The influence of emotional factors on the form of the *Profession de foi* may be indicated most simply by observing that it is, almost literally, a 'sermon on a mount', in which the magnificence of the Po valley is used as a kind of living text, to be exploited by Rousseau's eloquence. Among the resources at his disposal, one of the most important is the dramatic value of the idea of Fall and Redemption, which is used twice in a direct manner. It appears first in the prologue, where Rousseau himself figures as a frustrated and tormented youth being rescued from degradation by the sagacity and sympathy of the Vicaire; and then in the recollections of the Vicaire himself, whose own career is sketched in similar terms of a fall into, and emergence from, a situation of conflict and ambiguity.

This is, of course, no accident, nor is it merely an external device of literature. On the contrary, it is one of many examples of what is perhaps the dominating pattern in Rousseau's works; and is closely bound up with the underlying structure of his religious theory as a whole. This structure may not be apparent at a first reading of the *Profession de foi*, because in relating his ideas to the particular context, Rousseau has modified the usual order of exposition and made the main body of constructive thought precede the main body of criticism. Consequently, for the reader who wishes to trace the central current of religious ideas and relate them to his philosophy as a whole, the simplest procedure is to reverse the order and consider the first phase of the text as the outcome of the second. If this is done, the entire work falls into place as a

further exercise in the familiar fall-and-redemption perspective, modified by the sense of human evolution towards enlightenment.

Rousseau's enquiry begins, characteristically, from the 'fallen' position
symbolized in this case by the misfortunes of the Vicaire, who tells how,
in spite of his training for priesthood and commitment to celibacy, he
found himself unable to overcome normal sexual instincts. Forbidden
to marry, and left with a choice between the corrupt (i.e. 'civilized')
way of adultery, or a free natural union, he took the latter course; and,
on being revealed as the father of an illegitimate child, was exposed to a
disgrace which he would probably have avoided if he had chosen to
mask his weakness by the morally inferior alternative of adultery. His
subsequent despair, his sense of paradox and perverted values, and his
conviction of the utter incompatibility of the dictates of Nature and
established human conventions, provide the pretext for Rousseau to
embark upon a criticism of religious beliefs and institutions which is, in
fact, a variation on the themes of the early discourses.

The starting-point of this profession of doubts, much of which is in
the second part of the *Profession de foi*, is the assumption that if man has
degenerated socially on the lines suggested by the discourses, his religious
behaviour is no more exempt from the effects of this degeneration than
is any other activity, and is probably less so, because it is so heavily
institutionalized and ritualized. This assumption immediately poses the
question of the nature of the primitive religion which is deemed to have
degenerated; and in considering this, Rousseau's thoughts follow inevitably the hypotheses of the *Discours sur l'origine de l'inégalité*.

In the beginning, God created the world as a system of universal
harmony in which man could not create any perceptible dissonance,
because of the extreme limitation of his faculties. In this state, prior to
the development of rational powers and 'ideas', the only conceivable
basis for religion would be some response of instinct or feeling to the
order of Nature: probably a vague acknowledgment of the power
behind the spectacle, in the form of inarticulate awe. Just as, in the discourse, Rousseau postulates primitive instincts of self-preservation and
compassion, so, in the *Profession de foi*, he gives a slightly more elaborate
account of man's early sentimental equipment, in which the instinct of
self-preservation is analysed into the components of love of self, fear of
pain, horror of death and desire for well-being. A significant point here·
is the inclusion of the horror of death, which indicates that Rousseau is
not pushing his hypothesis quite so far back as in the discourse; and that

in his view, the possibility of a specifically religious sensibility arises as soon as man is distinguished from the mass of the animal creation.

As for the instinct of compassion, this is allowed to develop, in the *Profession de foi*, into a collection of unspecified 'innate sentiments relative to the species', which not only form the basis of sociability, but will also give rise later to the active force which we call conscience, and whose infallibility will be proclaimed by Rousseau in one of the most famous passages of the work.

These sentiments, which show what he has in mind when he presents the articles of his state religion as 'sentiments of sociability', are the source of all the moral potentialities of man, including the moral aspect of religion itself; but they do not in themselves offer much explanation of the ritualistic aspect of religious cults. At this point, Rousseau might be expected to explain this in terms of propitiation, based on the fear of pain and death which he has introduced into his theory; but this is ruled out by his conception of the attributes of God. Instead, therefore, of basing the first specifically religious development upon an irrational fear of the unknown, he chooses to associate it with a response of feeling of the *known*, deriving from the first rational judgment postulated in the *Discours sur l'origine de l'inégalité*: namely, that which convinces man of his superiority over the animals, and awakens the sense of intellectual power. In the Vicaire's simple words, man is king of the earth which he inhabits; and the movement of comparison and judgment which reveals this fact to him produces a feeling of gratitude and 'benediction' directed to the Creator of the superior species.

This is the effective beginning of religion, or 'first homage to the beneficent Divinity'; and it raises two points of great importance for the subsequent stages of Rousseau's religious theory. One is that after an initial response of awe to the sheer spectacle of Nature, the first contact between man and God is a more or less rational act of glorification, and not the making of a request. This has a bearing on Rousseau's ultimate view of prayer as meditation rather than supplication for special favours. The second point is that the satisfaction which is involved in this homage is not a particular but a general one, in which, theoretically, all individual men share equally. This is the cult which, in Rousseau's opinion, is dictated by Nature itself, and it comes as no surprise to find him linking it specifically with the concept of Self-Interest; for, as his Vicaire puts it, 'is it not a natural consequence of Self-Interest, to honour that which protects us, and to love that which wills our good?'

Hypothetically, and in default of adequate historical evidence,

Rousseau sees the origin of religion as being coeval with man's earliest social and moral development, occurring at a time when Self-Interest has not yet degenerated into Selfish Interest, although men are beginning to make the value-judgments which will lead ultimately to their downfall, as they are applied increasingly between one individual and another. He does not indicate precisely the beginnings of ritual; but if his religious theory is compared with the master-hypothesis of the second discourse, it is fairly safe to assume that he would link them with the development of aesthetic sensibility, or communal activities such as singing and dancing.

While he does not say so explicitly, it is evident that he regards religion as having been a positive factor in human affairs from the time of the Golden Age; and his predilection for this phase can be inferred from his enthusiasm for both the patriarchal society of old Testament times and the sublime simplicity of the Gospels, which play in his religious thought a part like that of classical antiquity in other fields. Although in anything to do with primitive times and the Bible, Rousseau's thinking is highly impressionistic, it is fair to say that from the human point of view, with respect to simple morality and emphasis on charity, the Gospels represent his religious ideal. As for the element of special revelation, he is already committed, more or less, to the rejection of literal belief; and it is inevitable that this should become the dominating issue in the next phase of his theory, concerning the degeneration since the Golden Age.

Some of his ideas concerning this can be seen in the political discussion of religion in the *Contrat Social*, but most of them appear in the densely-argued second half of the *Profession de foi*. Briefly, they are an extension of the second discourse, and a further catalogue of the ravages of Selfish Interest in a particular sector of human life. Following the Golden Age, when all cults are conceived as being substantially the same, and when it is possible to speak of a 'religion of man', Rousseau sketches the effects of Selfish Interest in terms of the gradual breakdown of the sense of community, and a corresponding particularization of religious awareness and behaviour, going hand in hand with political divisions and the growth of specific cults all claiming special revelation and some form of exclusive and privileged relationship with the Deity. This occurs when acquired ideas become more important than the original human sentiments, and when particular interests become strong enough to interfere with the general order; and it need hardly be said that in tracing the process, he makes no concessions to the doctrine of Original Sin. Once again, it is seen as the outcome of conflicts inherent in society, plus an element of chance. Like any freethinker of his own and earlier centuries, Rousseau maintains that the spread of different religions throughout the world has made belief largely a matter of geography; and that once the notion of special revelation has established itself, there is no stopping it. Thus, in Europe alone, there is a choice of faiths involving one, two or three revelations, all of which have become inextricably entangled with particular social and political institutions, although their function is supposed to be purely spiritual. He does not deny that revealed religions have valuable common ground in their moral teaching; his complaint is that their most striking common factor is mutual exclusiveness and intolerance; and that even if their political role is left out of account, the good which they propose is a pandering to the illegitimate form of self-love.

What is particularly repugnant to him is the thought that not even the concept of the Deity can remain immune from the perverting influence of society; and that with the progressive debasement of religion, the fall of man can be said, in a sense, to have involved the fall of God. Instead of being founded on admiration and gratitude for the power and love manifested in the Creation, religion has become a matter of fear, because competing sectional interests have destroyed the image of an all-powerful, beneficent God of peace, or universal Father, and substituted a series of world-pictures in which God can only figure as a tyrant. In fact, the general sense of Rousseau's criticism of revealed religion is that in the existing order of Despotism, God himself must emerge, sooner or later, through the various cults, as the Super-Despot, or arbitrary and capricious Will, served by an assortment of institutions dedicated to the maintenance of an unjust society, not only on earth but, apparently, in Heaven too.

This assault upon the unjust religious system of competing cults and sects rests upon the belief that truth is one; but it cannot be assumed that Rousseau objects to the actual multiplicity of religions. He is, indeed, hardly in a position to do so, because the conciliatory aim of his own philosophy itself depends on the belief that conflicting doctrines may simply express particular appearances of the same general truth. He would certainly concede that all religions may contain some truth, particularly in relation to a universal moral code; but what he cannot concede is that any religion claiming special revelation has the right to persecute outsiders, or that there is an obligation on any individual to believe this or that revealed religion, including Christianity. This is because, as a true child of his century, and notwithstanding the short-comings of his own performances, Rousseau believes that clarity is the measure of truth, and that if any single revealed religion holds the absolute truth and the right to condemn the dissenter, the fact must be manifest to all men in all places and in all ages. If it is not, he argues, we cannot make sense of God or man, since, in view of the complexity of rival traditions, it is virtually impossible for any individual to sort out the conflicting evidence, historical and textual. The ignorant have not the means, the learned have not the time; and even if the most learned man imaginable could perform the task in his lifetime, it would only be at the cost of all the other functions, social, intellectual or artistic, for which he is equipped by Nature.

In these circumstances, a God who condemns the creatures for not embracing one specific cult can only be thought of as unjust, and as acting inconsistently with the goodness implied in the original Creation. In other words, the existing religious order contrives to put not only men, but God himself, into a position of 'contradiction'. The alternative explanation, that the situation is part of the punishment of mankind, is of course ruled out by Rousseau's rejection of Original Sin; and all that he can see in the doctrines of the dogmatic religions is absurdity, such as is already condemned, for example, in the rule of celibacy which led to the downfall of his Vicaire.

It is not necessary to follow in further detail Rousseau's specific criticisms of revealed religion, most of which are in any case part of the stock-in-trade of all eighteenth-century deists and freethinkers. The essential point, which is now clear enough, is that this extension of his critical thought is entirely in keeping with the general pattern of all his attacks on the existing order, and (as he says himself in the *Rêveries*)[16] carries the same 'revolutionary' implication. At the end of it, there is a situation entirely analogous to that which we have seen arising from the *Discours sur l'origine de l'inégalité*. In the existing and degraded state of human affairs, in which intellectual and moral evolution have got out of step, religion, like everything else, has fallen into contradiction and absurdity, and has become tainted, both morally and politically. The problem, as before, is to resolve the contradictions; and again, the choice is between going back to primitive simplicity, or completing an evolutionary process of enlightenment. As it happens, the *Profession de foi* explores both these possibilities, and so combines the advantage of offering a complete range of thought with the disadvantage of apparent ambiguity.

Ideally, Rousseau would like to look backwards for the solution of his problem, and the final injunction of the Vicaire to his young disciple is, in fact, to return to the simple rustic life and the religion of his fathers, which would be the Calvinism of Geneva. This is a gesture which Rousseau tried to carry out in his own life; and in the text of the *Profession de foi* it is justified on the grounds that in the existing confusion of faiths, it is an inexcusable presumption to reject the religious traditions of one's own people. So far as it goes, this recommendation is clear enough, and points to a 'primitive' faith or *religion de l'homme*, with little ritual and no theological pedantry, but stressing above all practical charity, and the need to love God and one's neighbour as oneself. This is indeed the religion of sentiment to which Rousseau's doctrines have often been reduced by his commentators; but whatever force it retains as an ideal, it can hardly be regarded as the central doctrine of the *Profession de foi*. What we have to remember, here as elsewhere, is that while Rousseau is serious in proposing the conservation of the surviving pockets of simple life and simple faith, he is not so naïve as to think that in the society of the Enlightenment, any general solution of the religious problem is likely to be achieved by inviting man to disregard his intellectual development.

The alternative is to apply the resources of reason to a religious reconstruction; and this is why the *Profession de foi* is not just a sentimental effusion in defence of natural religion, but is also and even more a sustained effort of reasoning, which proposes, as the practical and general solution, an artificial *equivalent* of the original religion of the heart, in which there will be no clash between reason and feeling, but an opportunity for man to use all his faculties for the glory of God, the good of society and the advantage of the individual. In this sense, the *Profession de foi* is a dynamic and forward-looking work like the *Contrat Social*, with a movement of constructive thought beginning once more from the 'fallen' position, and making up the first part of it.

Here, the initial situation is again the Vicaire's mental confusion, resulting this time not from the conflicting claims of revealed religions, but from the mutually destructive traditions of philosophy; and with this confusion, a recognition that his first task is to review the whole philosophical basis of his life. The beginning of this process is an application of the methodic doubt commonly associated with Descartes, who is invoked in the text, presumably as a guarantee of the philosophical respectability of what is to follow: namely, an attempt to arrive at a practical morality, and to use reason as far as it can be used, in opening up a metaphysical perspective in which the affairs of this world make more sense than they do according to the existing religious order. One of the main considerations is, naturally, the restoration of man's sense of the goodness of God, and the destruction of the arbitrary Despot-Deity whom Rousseau associates with all intolerant revealed religions, and whom, he thinks, nobody could love. The deity which it will be possible for the enlightened man to love can only be a God of Justice, presiding over a system which is demonstrably an *order*, and whose relations with men must be conceivable in rational terms. Sooner or later, of course, reason must arrive at a barrier, but this will not matter provided that it is a barrier of 'legitimate' mystery, with the chance of a reasonable gesture of faith, and not a barrier of absurdity leading to despair.

Rousseau's Vicaire embarks upon his painful efforts of reasoning towards a 'more enlightened cult' by writing off the traditional philosophies as manifestations of the Selfish Interest of their authors, and as having merely a negative or destructive efficacity. The study of these philosophies, like that of revealed religions, leaves men floating helplessly on a sea of opinion, without any sure guide; and all that the individual can do is to trust his own 'inner light', and work out his own personal philosophy and religion. The objection which might be made here, that in doing so he automatically qualifies as a meditator and a 'depraved animal', or that he is guilty of the inexcusable presumption mentioned in the other part of the *Profession de foi*, is countered in advance by Rousseau's assertion that in circumstances which already necessitate radical re-thinking, one is less depraved if one makes one's own mistakes and follows one's own illusions, than if one merely accepts the lies of others. The important point here is not the risk of error, but the spirit of the Vicaire's enterprise, which, by relying on the 'inner light', without reference to other men and their thought, is an attempt to put all subsequent mental processes under the direction of Self-Interest. The inner light is, indeed, the alternative to the 'reflection' which has already been stigmatized as the type of mental activity associated with the play of Selfish Interest, and the desire of philosophers for personal prestige.

The programme which Rousseau follows in the constructive thought of his Vicaire appears to be conceived in four stages, corresponding roughly to the system of *Emile*, and the underlying theory of knowledge. The first of them is a consideration of our sensory knowledge of 'objects'; the second, an account of the causes of objects which are experienced through the senses and revealed by an intuitive judgment; the third is a deduction of the principal truths which matter in the practical business of living; and the fourth is the establishment of rules of conduct, which may help the Vicaire to carry out God's intentions for him on this earth, and so complete a movement from speculation to action. These outlines become somewhat blurred in the subsequent development, but the text follows them in general, taking, for example, as its first object, the Self which claims to know and experience.

I exist, says the Vicaire, and have senses by which I am affected; but whether it is possible to conceive a Self apart from sensation is an un-answerable and pointless question, which is best left alone. Secondly, there exist objects which are not me, but by which my senses are affected. These are 'matter'; but further arguments about the nature and appearance of matter are futile, and should also be left alone. Thirdly, the possibility of comparing the objects of sensation implies in the self an *active* force which judges, and which, according to Rousseau, judges better through sentiment than through reason. In fact, reason itself confirms that feeling is a better guide than reason, because the 'truth' is in things, and not in the mind which judges.

Given this active 'intelligence', however (and this means, apparently, a power to judge which includes both reason and intuition), deductions can be made concerning the properties of matter and the causes of phenomena; and the first of these deductions, arising from the com-parison of matter in motion and at rest, is that of the existence of a Free Will. From this comes the Vicaire's first dogma or article of faith: that there is a Will which animates Nature, and must be regarded as a First Cause, no matter what system of physics is followed thereafter.

After this use of the traditional first-cause argument, the second article is equally simple and familiar, consisting of the assertion of a Supreme Intelligence, based on the evidence of design and law in the movement of matter. Sweeping aside the counter-argument from Chance, of which he is well aware and which he is, as we know, prepared to accept up to a point in connection with human affairs, Rousseau now brings together sense-data, intuitions and deductions, and combines them in an enthusiasm of enlightenment, to proclaim that the universe is a single whole, governed according to a unified purpose (which is simply that of its conservation) by a single intelligence and powerful will. And thus, from the consideration of the Self and its environment, Rousseau moves to the author of both, who emerges from his thinking, not as the Despot-God of the revealed religions, but as a substantive Being in whom are combined what men think of as intelligence, power, will and goodness. He does not, however, believe that these attributes can be discussed rationally and meaningfully in a way which would lead to any absolute conclusions, but leaves the statement of them at a 'relative' level consistent with the terms of the state-religion of the *Contrat Social*.

Returning now to the Self, and to the human aspect of the discussion, as the only one which can be fruitfully pursued, Rousseau confronts the problem of the place of the Self in the order of the Creation; and here the questing mind of his Vicaire encounters a dichotomy. On the one hand, the human individual recognizes the collective superiority of his species, and this authorizes a first expression of gratitude to the Deity, as a response of Self-Interest. But on the other hand, the spectacle of relationships within the human community is one of disorder, contrasting violently with the order of Nature; and so, from the problem of evil in human affairs, Rousseau is brought to the next set of 'causes', i.e. to a discussion of the nature of man.

This he sees in the traditional terms of a dualism, suggesting the co-existence and conflict of two principles, one of which is orientated towards the eternal truths, justice, and the highest moral and intellectual values; while the other, i.e. the empire of the senses and the passions, is of an inward and selfish tendency. What we have here is a development of Rousseau's constant theme of contradiction; and from the conflict of these tendencies and the choices which they impose he derives the third of his Vicaire's articles of faith: namely, that man also has freewill, and is therefore activated by an immaterial substance or soul.

This belief in freewill is, of course, an essential article, but it must be observed that his conception of human liberty concerns *actions*, and is limited by a controlling love of self, according to which we are not free to will that which is against our interest, although we may err in our calculation of interest, and heed the promptings of the flesh and the passions rather than those of our 'higher' principle. If this in fact happens, we stifle the liberty within us and become in effect the slaves of vices.

The views which Rousseau develops here through his intermediary the Vicaire, are complicated in detail, but clear in their general sense, namely, that men are only 'free' when they are willing in accordance with their highest moral insight, which is inseparable from, if not actually synonymous with, self-interest properly appreciated. And with the setting-up of this principle, it becomes more obvious than ever that his systems of political and moral thought are interdependent; and that now, having manœuvred into a position where he can postulate an immortal soul, Rousseau is ready to press his theory of Self-Interest to the spiritual consummation which is its logical outcome. It is this phase of his thought which constitutes the doctrinal centre-piece of the whole *Profession de foi*, and its relative orthodoxy can be seen in the following summary.

Because man has freewill (subject to the limitation already indicated), he can abuse it, and is therefore responsible for evil, or what appears to be evil in his picture of the world; although on the other hand, his real power is so limited that this evil is in any case not sufficient to disturb the order of Nature as a whole, and as it must appear to God. This liberty is given to him for the sake of morality, so that in choosing the good, man shall acquire virtue and nobility; but at the same time, the knowledge of having made the good choice brings a satisfaction and a 'supreme enjoyment' which marks the ultimate degree of Self-Interest. To the question of how and when this moral bliss will be enjoyed, the answer can only be: in some after-life or state of spiritual survival. As far as the ordinary human perspective extends, evil exists and apparently triumphs, giving easy arguments to those who deny Providence; but given the factor of the immortal soul and the possibility of indemnity for suffering in this life, it is Rousseau's belief that Providence is justified.

This line of thought may seem naïve, but in following it, he remains completely faithful to his original, and traditional, conception of evil as an appearance of things caused by the limitations of the human point of view; and if he is asked how he knows that evil is a temporary phenomenon, his answer will be to invoke the concept of divine *justice*. Because of the shocking dissonance which would exist in the scheme of universal harmony if the injustices of the existing and visible order were not compensated in some future state, Rousseau's Vicaire can proclaim with complete confidence that if we have deserved happiness, we shall receive it; and he does so in the famous formula, *Sois juste et tu seras heureux*.[17]

These words are, as he says, 'inscribed in his soul', and may therefore be considered as the animating force in a primitive religion of sentiment. They are often quoted, of course, as evidence of Rousseau's alleged naïvety; but what is really important about the formula, when it is seen in the whole context of his exposition, is that it represents his application of the idea of contract, in the religious field. It expresses not merely an intuitive certainty, but also a rational conviction that over and above the

Social Contract, which it is man's responsibility to realize, there is also a contract between individual men and God, by which God is committed to giving the creatures a happiness and well-being which was a promise implied in the original creation. In face of the objection that the Creator owes nothing to the creature, Rousseau insists that God can be thought of as being under some kind of obligation, provided that it is also conceivable as an obligation to Himself, as part of what may be termed Divine Self-Interest; just as the obligation of each to all in the Social Contract is inseparable from the obligation of each to himself. Thus, in order that God too may not be exposed to the accusation of contradictory behaviour, He must conserve through Justice the general order which He has created through Goodness; and the two things together constitute a 'perpetual act of power', which must necessarily transcend human values and all human dimensions, including that of time.

It is with these thoughts that the Vicaire comes to the end of deductions concerning the 'truths' which matter to him, and, indeed, almost to the end of metaphysics as such. The last act of human reason in the face of the eternal, the infinite and the absolute, is to capitulate and abase itself, not in fear and anguish, as might happen in a harsher religion, but in accordance with newer forms of sensibility, to the accompaniment of feelings of *ravissement* and *charme*. Thereafter, all that remains for him to do, is to seek out the maxims which must guide him in daily conduct, if he is to carry out God's purpose for him in *this* life; and these, he claims, are written by nature within the heart, and do not depend upon pretentious philosophy.

The principles on which Rousseau would base the answer to all problems of conduct are worked out in his famous doctrine of the Conscience, and summarized with disarming simplicity in the classic phrase 'tout ce que je sens être bien est bien; tout ce que je sens être mal est mal'. These formulas, which apparently imply a moral instinct or intuition, are frequently seized upon by those who seek to ridicule him for simple-mindedness, or condemn him for a dangerously irrational and subjective approach to ethics; and it is true that much of what he says exposes him to this kind of attack. It is also true, however, that in the development of his doctrine, the terminology becomes unusually involved even for Rousseau. Consequently, the sense of his teaching has been obscured in some interpretations, with regrettable results, the worst of which is a tendency to assume, from the existence of a subjective element, that he is encouraging a kind of moral anarchy.

The best corrective to such misinterpretations is to keep in mind the total context, and remember that however confusing his expression may be, he *cannot*, in that context, be intending to divorce reason and morality or postulate a moral sense which is entirely subjective and arbitrary. On the face of it, and out of context, the phrase 'tout ce que je sens être bien est bien' can, no doubt, be invoked to justify even murder if it 'feels right'; but Rousseau obviously does not intend anything so perverse, because it thwarts one of the fundamental aims of his own religious theory, which is, as we have seen, to destroy the claims of religious persecutors to special authority of conscience, and to a special place in Heaven.

What Rousseau does contend, in the face of the moral relativism which he himself ascribes to Montaigne and to some contemporary thinkers, is that by and large the promptings of conscience are universal, and that the existence of all kinds of deviations does not invalidate the universal moral code. The existence of this latter is believed in by Rousseau as a 'general truth', and the exceptions only serve to prove the rule, which is itself the necessary complement to a theory of moral intuition.

The operation of this insight is, no doubt, an individual matter based initially on feeling, but it is his firm conviction that all consciences will react in the same way, provided that there is no unnatural interference. The primitive, for example, not having learned the ways of competitive and selfish interest, will automatically do what is 'right' because that is the logic of Original Innocence. And since, even in his degenerate state, man has not lost irrevocably the capacity to love the good, there must be some way of describing this capacity as a constant, irrespective of degrees of intellectual development. What Rousseau means by Conscience, therefore, is an innate and indestructible tendency to choose the good; he does not mean an actual innate *knowledge* of good and evil, for this is something which depends upon the development of powers of reason.

This is a vital point, because it means that Rousseau's moral doctrine is not a matter of pure emotionalism and arbitrary feeling. His theory of Conscience relates to man in his evolved or enlightened state, and cannot therefore (in spite of some misleading expressions) be reduced entirely to natural sentiments in a primitive sense. The reason why this has not always been understood, is that he says categorically that the acts of the conscience are feelings and not judgments. These feelings, however, have in themselves nothing to do with actual rightness or wrongness, but, as the text shows, are deemed to have been given us as a means whereby we may commit ourselves positively to actions which have *already* been judged right by *reason*.

> Connaître le bien, ce n'est pas l'aimer: l'homme n'en a pas la con-
> naissance innée, mais sitôt que sa raison le lui fait connaître, sa con-
> science le porte à l'aimer: c'est ce sentiment qui est inné.[18]

This passage, which is sometimes overlooked, is of crucial importance as an indication that even when he seems to be at his most emotional, and concerned with some vague transcendentalism of pure sentiment, Rousseau does not wish men to deny their own evolution and throw reason overboard in anything to do with the practical business of living. His doctrine of conscience may be confused, but it is linked with the rational advance to virtue, involving what he calls *nouvelles lumières*, which turn out to be a further application of the concept of Self-Interest, and a rejection of the Selfish Interest which can find satisfaction only at the expense of others. In short, it is through a combination of original, intact feeling and evolved reason, that Rousseau completes his moral theory and advances to the religious plane, pushing the ultimate fulfilment of Self-Interest beyond time and space, to some paradise where Selfish Interest will finally be overcome.

The precise nature and organization of the Vicaire's paradise are of necessity left to the imagination; but the principles are worked out logically enough, as combining a blissful sense of willing integration in a system where all is ordered for the best, with an exquisite consciousness of individuality, wholeness and freedom from 'contradiction'. There is, indeed, such an obvious continuity of principle between the artificial and provisional political paradise of the *Contrat Social* and the ultimate religious paradise of the Vicaire, that it is worth looking at certain other aspects of the doctrine of Conscience which gives access to it.

One of these is the notion of *infallibility* implied in the alignment of reason with an objective and universal moral law; another is the idea of *indestructibility*, which is bound up with continuity of feeling from the primitive state to the enlightened state; and a third is Rousseau's conception of the innate feelings of conscience as an intermediate stage between knowing the good and doing it, which suggests something in the nature of an 'enlightened will'. In the text of the *Profession de foi*, he juggles with this idea in a most confusing way, but it is evident that the attributes of the individual conscience are almost identical to those already postulated in connection with the General Will. There are, in fact, good grounds for arguing that the General Will of the political

R I

theory is the collective version of the conscience or *lumière intérieure*; and that it could as well be called a Public Conscience as a General Will.

Because of these correspondences, it seems quite natural to find that Rousseau's paradise is conceived on egalitarian lines, with no privilege and no *dependence*, although one possibility of a heavenly hierarchy is allowed for by certain references to the angels, whose status is, apparently, lower than that of the virtuous man. The final relationship of the individual soul to God, the *Etre juste*, is, of course, not specified, because it is not conceivable; but one thing which is proclaimed as the hope of the Vicaire is that the individual soul will no longer be dependent upon anything external to itself for its *happiness*. The bliss of paradise will, it seems, be a mixture of moral and aesthetic satisfactions related to the general order of the universe, and not to particular status, as would be, presumably, the kind of satisfaction sought by the intolerant and persecuting bigot whom Rousseau sees as a stumbling-block to the Social Contract. The key to this general satisfaction cannot, of course, be the granting of special requests, which is a privilege hoped for when prayer is corrupted by Selfish Interest; it can only be the sense of participation in a General Will which is also the Will of God, as the peroration of Rousseau's Vicaire makes clear.

> Source de justice et de vérité, Dieu clément et bon! dans ma confiance en toi, le suprême vœu de mon cœur est que ta volonté soit faite. En y joignant la mienne, je fais ce que tu fais, j'acquiesce à ta bonté; je crois partager d'avance la suprême félicité qui en est le prix.[19]

The outcome of the Vicaire's doctrine is, therefore, an act of will which is a surrender of will; and so, with the 'enlightened' acquiescence involved in the phrase 'Thy will be done', the effort of constructive thought in the *Profession de foi* reaches a conclusion which gives meaning and coherence to the whole of Rousseau's public philosophy; and which seems to require for its understanding only that the rest of the sentence of the Lord's Prayer—'On earth as it is in Heaven',—be invoked and applied to the interpretation of his political and moral thought.

This conclusion requires us to believe, of course, that the processes of evolution, regeneration or enlightenment indicated in the *Contrat Social* and the main body of *Emile* are simply the social beginning of a total process whose consummation is spiritual; and one of the most important consequences of this is that the General Will, which emerges first as a political concept, capable of generating all kinds of logical and psychological arguments, now begins to appear as an attempt to describe the presence of the Divine Will in human society, or to propose a meeting-point between Man and God, in the concept of Law, which emanates from the 'democratic' operation of a collection of consciences. From this, it would indeed seem that the voice of the People is the Will of God —but only if the people are really kept free from the taint of Selfish Interest by their consciences, or, putting it the other way, by their appreciation of where their ultimate interest lies. It also appears that a collection of Emiles whose education includes religious enlightenment on the lines of the *Profession de foi*, must produce, logically, the society of the *Contrat Social*, which may be described simply as the Kingdom of God on earth.

Without arguing about the practical difficulties of realizing the New Jerusalem, it can at least be said of this vision that it completes the enterprise of offering a 'rational' re-statement of the religious tradition, in the hope of reconciling religious authority and the current philosophies of Rousseau's time. And it is supremely ironic that this conciliatory work, which, trying to appeal to the simple and the sophisticated, offers senti-ment for the sentimental and reason for the rationalists, should be the chief cause of Rousseau's persecution, and the miseries of his later years.

The reasons for this are obvious enough. In trying to reconcile the two sides, Rousseau pleased neither; and while, by the time of the pub-lication of *Emile*, thoroughgoing materialists of the Diderot type had already gone far beyond the Deism or Theism of the Vicaire, the Christian apologists and authorities could hardly be expected to accept this presentation of the idea of Redemption. For it is in the *Profession de foi* that the ultimate consequences of the *Discours sur l'origine de l'inégalité* can be seen, in the great question-mark which Rousseau leaves hanging over the historical figure of Christ.

If Fall and Redemption become, as they do in Rousseau, simply the idea of a social maladjustment and a subsequent readjustment which, as he undoubtedly tries to suggest, is within the capacity of evolving or 'enlightened' man, it follows that the revealed truths of Christianity have at most a pragmatic value; and that the Christian scheme of Redemption must join the Genesis account of human origins as a species of myth, true, perhaps, in a general sense, but no longer true—or no longer relevant—in a particular or literal sense.

In the *Profession de foi*, Rousseau does not say this in so many words, although he does venture upon a cautious discussion of the question. His Vicaire, in fact, is inclined to accept the divinity of Christ, at least at the level of emotional assent, and on the basis of a comparison between the Crucifixion and the 'philosophical' death of Socrates. Moreover, it seems perfectly possible for Rousseau himself to accept the historicity of Christ, if not exactly as the Son of God, at least as *a* son of God in the special category suggested by his own doctrine of Genius. This, however, would not affect the general significance of his thinking, which it is difficult to interpret as meaning anything except that in the 'historic' future of enlightened man Redemption means simply the full development and application of *all* human faculties of feeling, reason, conscience and will, for the restoration and maintenance of the harmony of the Creation. This explains why, when faced with Christian revelation, Rousseau's Vicaire is inclined to accept it emotionally and, as it were, in spirit, while remaining, rationally, in a state of involuntary but *respectful* scepticism. This is probably Rousseau's own position; and it leaves as the final, unspoken implication of his teaching, the view (which some commentators would compare with the old Pelagian heresy) that henceforth every man must be, in some sense, his own Christ.

But in what sense? And if there is sense in it, how is this doctrine to be brought home to the urbane and sophisticated society of the mid-eighteenth century? These are complicated questions, but they concern, in one way or another, Rousseau's later autobiographical writings, and also the novel, already published, of *Julie, ou la Nouvelle Héloïse*.

CHAPTER VII

A Symbolic Fiction:
Julie ou La Nouvelle Héloïse

★

In a first introduction to Rousseau, there are three main reasons for dis-regarding chronology and postponing until this point the discussion of the *Nouvelle Héloïse*. The first is that although its publication preceded that of the *Contrat Social* and *Emile* by more than a year, it provides, by part of its content and by its very form, as an epistolary novel, the way of transition from the discursive works of public doctrine to the more sub-jective writings. The others are that a knowledge of Rousseau's key-ideas makes it much easier to grasp the sense of the novel; and conversely, that it offers, within a single text, the most complete reflection of the range of his thought, and so helps to draw together the philosophical threads which, so far, have had to be examined separately. The indis-pensable prelude to discussion is, therefore, to outline the plot of a narrative which, while it is inspired by the medieval example of Héloïse and Abelard, has a realistic and contemporary setting on and around Lake Geneva, which Rousseau knew so well.

In its final form, consisting of six parts, it expresses the conflict of Nature and existing society in the frustrated love of Julie d'Etange, daughter of the Baron d'Etange, and her tutor Saint-Preux, and follows this with an account of her subsequent marriage to M. de Wolmar, the man of her father's choice. As his name implies, Saint-Preux is a young man of intrinsically noble character, but one condemned to unhappiness because of his inferior social status. At the opening of the story, he has been accepted as an unpaid tutor by Julie's mother, during the Baron's absence with his regiment; and conceives for his pupil a passion which is gradually reciprocated by Julie, until it finds expression in a celebrated kiss, bestowed in the appropriate setting of the groves of Clarens. This episode is followed by the return of the disapproving Baron, and the withdrawal of Saint-Preux on a journey into the Valais region; but his absence is ended when, in consideration of Julie's unhappiness, her cousin and confidante, Claire, urges his return. After this, however, temptation becomes so strong that Julie finally surrenders to him, during a temporary removal of Claire's restraining influence. Julie's subsequent remorse leads to another withdrawal of Saint-Preux, but further absences of the parents and other chance circumstances bring about a repetition of her surrender. At this point, there intervenes in the story an English nobleman, Lord Edouard Bomston, who is an acquaintance of the Baron, but who, after first quarrelling with Saint-Preux, becomes his friend and 'conscience', and tries to persuade the Baron to allow the marriage of the young lovers. These efforts are rejected because of the Baron's social prejudices, and his wish to marry Julie to M. de Wolmar, to whom in fact he owes his life. In face of the Baron's anger, arrangements are made by Claire's fiancé and Bomston for another departure of Saint-Preux, this time to Paris.

The second part of the novel is concerned largely with Saint-Preux's accounts of life in Paris, and Julie's reactions to them; but there are slight developments in the plot, as Julie declares that she will not marry Saint-Preux without her father's consent, and conversely, that she will not marry another without Saint-Preux's consent. In the meantime, her cousin marries a M. d'Orbe, and this event leads indirectly to the discovery by Julie's mother of the letters from Saint-Preux, and the full revelation of their relationship.

In Part III, Rousseau completes a picture of frustration and despair. The Baroness dies, in circumstances of unhappiness for which Julie feels responsible; Saint-Preux renounces Julie, under pressure from the Baron; Julie falls ill (and is visited briefly by Saint-Preux); the household is completely disrupted; and Julie herself is brought to the point of considering, as a way out of the misery of conflicting loyalties, an adulterous union with Saint-Preux as an accompaniment to the now inevitable marriage of convenience with Wolmar. Finally, however, in a moment of emotional exaltation associated with the solemnity of the marriage-ceremony itself, she lays hold on virtue, professes to have recovered serenity of mind, and accepts by an act of will all the implications of marriage to Wolmar. Saint-Preux is left in a state of suicidal despair, from which he is rescued by Bomston, who arranges for him to join the expedition of Admiral Anson around the world, so bringing to an end the first half of the novel.

The events of the second half, or last three parts, take place some years later, when Saint-Preux, having returned from his adventures, is invited by Julie and her atheist-husband Wolmar to their estate at Clarens, where the now widowed Claire is also to make her home. Letters from

Saint-Preux to Bomston give an account of the enlightened administration of the Clarens property on the shores of Lake Geneva, and of Julie's situation as a model wife and mother. This fourth part of the text has direct links with earlier events; and is so devised as to allow Wolmar, who, it now appears, is well aware of them, to undertake a sort of psychological cure of Saint-Preux, the principles of which are related to an important but unrealized project of Rousseau's, entitled *La Morale sensitive ou le matérialisme du Sage*. The experiences recounted in this section include a second scene in the *bosquet* or grove of Clarens, and a final ordeal for Julie and Saint-Preux when, in the absence of Wolmar, they go for a boating excursion on the lake. Obliged by a storm to shelter on the opposite shore, the former lovers are exposed to all the emotional stresses of memory and association; but again, thanks mainly to the will-power of Julie, accept their separation, at least in a physical sense, and return to Clarens. This moving and famous passage is the final crisis for Saint-Preux; and there is evidence to suggest that Rousseau originally planned to end his story here, with some kind of tragic denouement.

In the event, he continued it with two further sections, one of which— i.e. Part V—prolongs the account of life on the Clarens estate, with such things as the description of the festivity of the wine-harvest, and discussions of the education of Julie's children, for whom Saint-Preux is designated as tutor, in accordance with principles enunciated at greater length in *Emile*. In the meantime, however, Saint-Preux departs for Rome with Bomston, who is involved in a love-affair which necessitates the advice of his friend; and the section ends with the departure of Claire also, and a project by Julie for the marriage of Saint-Preux and her widowed cousin.

The sixth and last part is devoted mainly to the death of Julie, which takes place in Saint-Preux's absence, from an illness occasioned by her jumping into the lake to rescue one of her children. This is a 'providential' denouement, in that it occurs at a point where there is a hint of a possible relapse by Julie into passionate feeling for Saint-Preux. It is described in great detail in a letter to him from Wolmar, and transfers the story to the religious plane. The book ends with Claire refusing to marry Saint-Preux, but urging him to return to Clarens and assume the responsibilities of tutor to the children of Julie and Wolmar. There is a strong suggestion that Wolmar himself will renounce his atheism through the impact of his wife's death, but no precise indication of the ultimate destiny of Saint-Preux.

If it is considered purely in terms of this central plot, the *Nouvelle Héloïse* appears as a relatively simple work, especially by contrast with the typical adventure-novels of its century. One would hardly expect it to produce great argument; but it has to be remembered that through Rousseau's multi-dimensional treatment, which is made possible largely by the epistolary form, this simple story expands into a text of some seven hundred pages; and that the analysis of group-relations, sentimental states, moral attitudes and social or religious problems is so complex that it has produced much controversy and an extensive critical literature. To complicate matters further, all interpretations of the book have to take into account Rousseau's relations with various women, including, of course, Mme de Warens; and in particular the romantic passion which he conceived for Sophie d'Houdetot during the actual period of its composition. In each of these sentimental relationships, there is some sort of manifestation of the idea of the *ménage à trois*, which has a bearing on the second half of the novel. Because of this, and the knowledge that it was much modified during Rousseau's association with Mme d'Houdetot and her official and faithful lover Saint-Lambert, arguments arise as to whether and to what extent the book is simply a reflection of his own sentimental experiences and aspirations; or, conversely, whether his relations with Mme d'Houdetot were an attempt to live the novel, and translate imagination into reality.

The ramifications of these arguments go beyond the scope of the present study, which is concerned primarily with the relationship of the *Nouvelle Héloïse* to the rest of Rousseau's major writings. The essential points to remember are that this is an exceptional creation which can be approached quite legitimately at very different levels; and that while much of its historical importance derives from its status simply as a novel (and, more precisely, from the first half, where it appears as a subjective novel of passion), it is at the same time something more than a novel: namely, a kind of allegory. It is, in fact, one of those rare and profound works in which an author distils the essence of his experience and aspirations, and which require from the reader a certain effort of understanding, as well as sympathy. If these are not forthcoming, the book may well be written off as a monumental bore; if they are forthcoming, on the other hand, it will be seen to be a great and unified work of art, expressing a highly individual but thoroughly systematic philosophy.

Looking at it first of all purely as a novel, it may be observed that while it must have merits to account for the enthusiasm which greeted its publication, and the esteem in which it is still held by a minority, it

must also have defects to explain its loss of popular appeal. One merit
which has already been noted is the relative simplicity of plot, and
freedom from the worst extravagances of its age. This economy of
action puts the emphasis upon mental events and the analysis of feeling,
and allows Rousseau to present situations from different points of view
by the skilful use of the epistolary technique. The directness of this form
is in itself appropriate for the expression of the passion and strong
emotions which the arid-seeming eighteenth century found singularly
refreshing. It allows also a flexibility and variety of style which can be
recognized retrospectively as a major contribution to the liberation of
the literary language of France from some of the constraints imposed
upon it in the previous century. To these qualities must be added the
descriptive element, and the relative novelty of the enthusiastic depiction
of Alpine scenery; and more particularly, the rhythmic and musical
values of Rousseau's prose, which even now retain the power to enchant,
even though the emotional ardour has lost its appeal.

On the debit side, it must be admitted that the sentimentality, which
found a ready response in its own day, is now almost intolerable to many
readers; and that the slow movement of the actual plot exposes Rousseau
to the charge of long-windedness. Similarly, the philosophical discussions on which the lovers embark at every pretext are apt to appear
as useless digressions on what are no longer living issues. The epistolary
form also suffers, of course, from related drawbacks; it may allow a
direct style, and a treatment in depth of evolving situations, but it can
be repetitive and tedious when associated with interminable moralizing,
which most readers would regard as the novel's gravest aesthetic flaw.
As a novel of passion, the *Nouvelle Héloïse* achieved a remarkable success,
but the didactic element in it seems to have been accepted with reserve
even by contemporary readers, and certainly accounts for much of its
decline in popularity with succeeding generations. It is, indeed, so unlikely that the book will ever regain popular favour as a novel, that the
best chance of understanding its real greatness lies in taking the alternative approach, and treating it frankly as an allegory, expressing not
merely the experience of an individual, but the conflicts and aspirations
of an age.

One advantage of doing so is that in emphasizing the seriousness and
urgency of Rousseau's moral aim, it makes the didacticism more
tolerable; another is that it throws into greater relief the symbolic aspect
of the book, and enhances the psychological and philosophical interest,
by displaying as integral parts of a whole those elements of discussion

which tend otherwise to appear as digressions. On the other hand, it may be objected that this approach assumes on Rousseau's part a unity of intention which, in the opinion of some commentators, is hardly consistent with known facts relating to the actual composition of the text. Critics holding this view may argue, on good grounds, that the *Nouvelle Héloïse* began as something intensely personal; as the expression of a dream, an escape into a world of ideal love; and a defence against the real-life frustrations of its author; that it was initially a work of pure feeling, without moral or philosophic purpose; and that the conception of the work as an allegory takes insufficient account of the presence in Rousseau's life of Sophie d'Houdetot.

What is ultimately at stake in these arguments is the autonomy of the book as a work of art, and its meaning and integrity as a work of ideas; and there have always been readers prepared to assert that the *Nouvelle Héloïse* is not one work, but two, on the grounds that the second or 'moral' part is the product of a guilty conscience anxious to excuse the spontaneous expression of natural passion in the first part. The short answer to this opinion of the work is to admit that it evolved gradually into its final form, and that the process was affected by the presence of Mme d'Houdetot; but to point out that this is not incompatible with a predetermining influence of a philosophy which was still in process of formation, and incompletely expressed.

Whether Rousseau first conceived the *Nouvelle Héloïse* as a whole or not, it is still a fact that the definitive version in six parts shows, from beginning to end, a remarkable correlation with his system as we have traced it in other works; and that the psychological action evolves in accordance with doctrines already examined. There is, indeed, every chance that the ultimate significance of the novel derives from the application of these doctrines; but it is only rarely that literary historians allow their appreciation of it to rest on this basis. On the contrary, it is certain that its meaning has been distorted through the reluctance of nineteenth-century critics, in particular, to assess it in terms other than those of literary Romanticism and individualistic revolt; or to admit that the work is, after all, a product of the Age of Reason. Because passion, feeling and frustration are apt to be more interesting, from a literary and human standpoint, than the triumph of reason, and because Rousseau knew frustrated passion in his own life, it is easy to assume that these were the things through which he desired above all to gain the interest and sympathy of his readers. It must be observed, however, that while he undoubtedly exploited these elements to arouse interest, and found solace in doing so, it does not follow that he intended his readers' sympathies to lie ultimately or exclusively on the side of frustrated passion. In reading the *Nouvelle Héloïse* we have, in fact, the possibility of seeing it as an exaltation of feeling, or an exaltation of rational morality; or simply as a work of synthesis and conciliation, combining but transcending both these elements; and the varying responses of individual readers depend very much, in practice, upon the relative importance which they are prepared to ascribe to the leading characters. In many respects, the *Nouvelle Héloïse* is the history of a *group*; but the key question is: which character, if any, has the central and most significant role?

On balance, it is probably fair to say that Rousseau's commentators have unduly neglected Wolmar as a significant character in his own right, and reduced him to a utility figure, existing for the sake of the plot, and serving propaganda aims which are incidental to the main theme; and that conversely, the importance of Saint-Preux has been exaggerated over the years. From the literary point of view, this is understandable in so far as the character is a prototype of a line of Romantic heroes presented as victims of their own sensibility. When the book was published, it was undoubtedly Saint-Preux who appealed to the imagination of the public; and the feeling persists that this is the character who contains most of Rousseau's own personality, and therefore represents what is most vital in the novel.

More recently, however, critical studies have tended to restore to Julie the primacy which is, after all, implied by the title; so that while Saint-Preux may still be thought of as a more effective and influential literary creation, it is increasingly difficult to regard him as the central character. The unifying element in the book is undoubtedly the figure of Julie, because it is in her experiences that the themes are worked out in full, and that the book can be appreciated as a whole and coherent structure.

It does not, for example, require much contemplation of the completed work to see that the structure is related fundamentally to the idea of Fall and Redemption. From the standpoint of conventional morality, Julie obviously 'falls' in allowing herself to be seduced by Saint-Preux; and just as obviously is redeemed, or redeems herself, in the marriage to Wolmar. There are, however, certain objections to reducing the book in this way to a simple diptych in black and white. The first is that Rousseau's moral views are not precisely orthodox; the second, is that in the process of rationalization which we have traced elsewhere,

Fall and Redemption is modified by evolutionary doctrines in such a way as to produce an eclectic system of 'revolutions', not unlike the dialectical processes of later philosophies of Hegelian inspiration. It is because of these complications that we must regard the *Nouvelle Héloïse* as a fluid or dynamic work with at least three major phases, the last of them provided by the quasi-religious conclusion, which opens up perspectives of human destiny extending beyond either the novel of passion or the novel of rational domesticity, which are worked out through the agency of Saint-Preux and Wolmar respectively. If this view is taken, it tends, of course, to confirm that despite his literary and human interest, Saint-Preux is no more qualified than Wolmar to carry the philosophical weight of the book; and that it is to the life and death of Julie herself that we must look for an illustration of Rousseau's attempted compromise between theological tradition and the rationalism of his time.

The most straightforward way of grasping the sense of the work *as a whole* is to thrust Sophie d'Houdetot firmly aside and concentrate upon it as a development in novel form of the thesis of Original Innocence, and an expression in popular and emotional terms of Rousseau's central theory of *amour de soi* and *amour-propre*. If this approach is taken, it can be assumed, for example, that while the novel may and must contain contingent evil and unhappiness, it will not present any individual as essentially wicked. Thus, while arguments may arise as to which character is the 'hero', it is clear that this is a book without a villain except the collective one of existing society. Similarly, it is possible for anyone with previous knowledge of Rousseau's thought to predict the general course of events, and explain many of them by simple analogy with his other writings; and it is perfectly legitimate to do this, provided that one refrains from dogmatizing about his conscious intentions.

If the plot of the *Nouvelle Héloïse* is scrutinized on this basis, the first thing that can be expected is some analogy between the 'fall' of Julie and the principles of the *Discours sur l'origine de l'inégalité*. There is, in fact, a striking parallelism between the first three parts of the novel, in which Saint-Preux makes his most positive contribution, and Rousseau's earlier philosophic variation on the theme of Paradise Lost. It can be seen in operation if the relationship of Saint-Preux and Julie prior to her marriage is analysed into three major phases, corresponding closely to the pattern established in the hypothetical history of society. In the first of them, Rousseau depicts a perfectly innocent attraction, explainable, so far as Saint-Preux is concerned, by the spontaneous imperative of instinct, which is, of course, a natural and intrinsically 'good' manifestation of love of self. On Julie's side, it is explained rather by a sentiment of compassion, which, it will be remembered, is for Rousseau an essential part of the pre-rational equipment of man, and lies at the root of all human associations. The text emphasizes the role of pity in the initial response of Julie; but the development of the *particular* relationship between these lovers requires, if it is to be consistent with Rousseau's principles, the presence of another factor. This factor is Chance, and it operates decisively throughout the first half of the novel, from Saint-Preux's original appointment as tutor, in the absence of the Baron. Given appropriate circumstances of propinquity and relative freedom, it does not take long for the attraction of the young couple to assume a more positive form; and Rousseau shows, in famous and inflammatory letters, the awakening of the senses and the beginning of the empire of the passions. This *fol amour* is not, of course, wrong in itself, because its origins are entirely natural; but a situation of potential danger is already developing, in so far as the urge to satisfy sensual desire may appear retrospectively, and in a larger context, as a movement of short-term or selfish interest.

The culminating point of this first phase is reached when, playing with fire in the presence of Claire, Julie kisses Saint-Preux in the grove of Clarens. Quite apart from the historical interest of its impact upon a public with rather astringent literary tastes, this episode stands out as one of the great and significant 'moments' of the book, when a developing situation finally crystallizes. In terms of the analogy with the second discourse, it brings to an accelerated conclusion a 'revolution', and symbolizes in the lovers' relationship a new order, which may well be thought of as its Golden Age. What is 'golden' about it, is that although they do not realize this at the time, it maximizes their happiness by the combination of actual satisfaction and anticipated or potential satisfaction. They now enjoy all the value deriving from awareness of mutual love; but any further move towards consummation of their passion can only lead to an abyss of conflict and remorse, in the social situation in which Rousseau has placed them. In sentimental terms, they have emerged from the blank unconsciousness implied in the original 'state of nature' without having encountered, as yet, the distortion and corruption deriving from a false society; and there is—*mutatis mutandis*—an unmistakeable resemblance between this situation and the precarious equilibrium of those early societies which are presented in the second discourse as being equidistant from primitive and negative innocence and the sophisticated corruption of Selfish Interest.

How far this correlation between the handling of the sexual urge and the general social history of man implies conscious purpose, at this early stage of the *Nouvelle Héloïse*, must remain a matter of argument; but it is worth noting that at the end of this first phase of the novel Rousseau transfers us from the individual plane to the social plane, and allows a breathing space by dispatching Saint-Preux on his visit to the Valais. The letters in which he describes to Julie his reactions to the place and to its inhabitants serve to introduce new dimensions into the work, and initiate a process giving it a social echo or resonance, and establishing a significant link between movements of plot, psychological states and physical setting. The passages which convey the response of his own mood to surrounding nature, and indicate the therapeutic effect of the Alpine landscape and the mountain air are well-known and profoundly interesting from both artistic and philosophical points of view. It is important to note, however, that what lies behind these evocations is not primitivism of an absolute and 'rugged' kind, but, rather, a modified primitivism. The aspect which Saint-Preux savours above all is what he calls 'the astonishing mixture of wild nature and cultivated nature', denoting the presence of man and the integration of humanity in the natural scene. Similarly, the society of the Valaisans is rustic, but not savage; it represents, in fact, a survival from the Golden Age, and the account of it is introduced not merely as 'background', but to indicate a precise relationship between the psychological development of the main characters and the social history of mankind. Moreover, in describing the freedom and simplicity of the private life of these people, Rousseau makes a point of having Saint-Preux relate it to their political behaviour; and so expresses for the first time a principle which illuminates the whole of the novel: namely, that 'the family is the image of the state'.

The second phase in the love of Julie and Saint-Preux is their gradual surrender to passion after the latter's return from the Valais, and in the face of the obstacles set up by the hostility of the Baron. This may be interpreted, in terms of Rousseau's philosophy, as a fall into a situation of conflict or 'contradiction', reproducing exactly, in personal relationships, the processes of social degeneration which follow the Golden Age in the hypothesis of the *Discours sur l'origine de l'inégalité*. What Rousseau is doing here, apart from telling the simple love story as such, is to show the impossibility of maintaining in the existing social context, and with any chance of happiness, forms of innocent natural behaviour which belong to an earlier order of individualism. Obviously, Julie's surrender to Saint-Preux is not presented as a sin in the orthodox sense; and the sympathetic treatment of the lovers might well lead us to suppose that this is a simple case of individuals being right, and society being wrong. This view is not quite accurate, however, because the situation depicted is, on both sides, an ambiguous one, to which the absolute ethical judgments 'right' and 'wrong' are not really applicable. Thus, although Julie and Saint-Preux do not 'sin' in consummating their natural union, and although Rousseau does everything in his power to extenuate guilt, notably through the operation of Chance in the arrangement of circumstances which make it difficult to resist the pressure of natural instincts, their conduct is presented, nevertheless, as an error or miscalculation in terms of the doctrine of Self Interest.

This is made clear by an observation occurring in Part I, letter 32, where, in reply to the justificatory arguments of Saint-Preux, Julie recognizes that while they have sought pleasure, happiness has fled from them. In other words, the gratification of the passions is seen by Julie immediately after her fall as representing no more than a short-term and debased form of self-love, or *amour-propre*, and offering nothing permanent in place of lost innocence. And this recognition of the principles of the doctrine of Self-Interest, combined with the somewhat confused promptings of a more orthodox moral sense, shows that Julie is already more 'evolved' and enlightened than her lover, who is still, to all intents and purposes, little more than a 'natural' man caught in a false environment.

In Rousseau's text, this idea of miscalculated self-interest tends to be obscured by the surrounding pages of passionate outpourings and complicated moralizing; but it is the key to a situation which, in all essentials, corresponds to that stage of social development indicated in the *Discours sur l'origine de l'inégalité*, as a Second Revolution. The main features of this phase of social history are, it will be recalled, the corruption of the community through the ravages of Selfish Interest, and the entrenchment of injustice and inequality through the institution of private property, which is its symbol. These are unquestionably the social themes which affect the course of Rousseau's love-story at this point; for while, on the one hand, social and economic inequality is a major obstacle to the legitimate union of Saint-Preux and Julie, on the other, the property-theme is echoed in the whole concept of the marriage of convenience, and the right of the Baron, deriving from the false values of an inauthentic society, to dispose of his daughter against her inclinations.

Given these correspondences, it is not difficult to imagine the course of the third major phase in the history of Julie d'Etange and Saint-Preux; and, in fact, the misery of Julie, the revolt of daughter against father, the assaulting of daughter by father, the distress and death of the mother, and the general collapse of family solidarity, make up a situation which no-one who is familiar with the early discourse can fail to recognize as a State of War. Moreover, the pattern of these external events is completed as, we feel, it must be, by Julie's capitulation to the will of her father, who thus emerges as the 'Despot' of the story. It is, however, characteristic of Rousseau, and completely in accordance with his premises concerning human nature, that he presents this despotic father not as a wicked man, but as one who sincerely believes that he is acting for the best, and who follows his highest principles in honouring his word to Wolmar. These principles are doubtless wrong, but his 'guilt' is really that of society; and he is, as Rousseau shows by having him appeal to her compassion, no less dependent on Julie than she is dependent on him.

These, then, are some of the more obvious stages in the 'fall' of Rousseau's heroine from a Golden Age of love to a state of frustration deriving from the pernicious principles of the unjust society. And it is in accordance with his aim of providing the novel with a social dimension that as these events are taking shape, Saint-Preux, absent once more, has been reporting to Julie his experiences of Parisian life. This account of the manners, morals and culture of the French capital is intended on the whole as a picture of social corruption, contrasting with the earlier picture of life in the Valais. Saint-Preux, it may be added, is no more immune from some aspects of it than Rousseau appears to have been in his own life.

With Saint-Preux experiencing the doubtful benefits of civilization at its most refined, and Julie succumbing to the social pressures put upon her to marry Wolmar, the 'Fall' element in the novel is evidently nearing its conclusion, and the third part brings the first great turning-point of the story, in the actual marriage. Before the significance of this can be fully grasped, however, Rousseau still has to fill in certain details concerning the moral state of Julie, since the fall with which the novel is concerned does not consist simply in her physical surrender to Saint-Preux.

In Rousseau's political philosophy, we have seen that the notion of a fall is equated with a condition of servitude, arising when men seek to escape from the miseries and conflicts of the State of War by renouncing the responsibility of freewill, and accepting the dictates of a despotic will. This is truly the abdication of all human dignity, but it is given a façade of spurious legitimacy by the contract of government, or 'anti-social contract', which looks respectable, but only serves to confirm and perpetuate a situation of ambiguity in which appearance and reality are quite different. In view of the analogies which have already been noted between the *Nouvelle Héloïse* and the second discourse, it is reasonable to expect the state of domestic war described in the novel to be followed by some corresponding, but equally false solution. What Rousseau does, in fact, is to introduce an 'inauthentic' solution, not as an actual situation, but as a possibility conceived in the mind of Julie, and expressed, particularly in the eighteenth letter of Part III, in the form of a projected state of adultery, in which she will be wife of Wolmar and mistress of Saint-Preux. Unable to reject the natural obligation of love to Saint-Preux, or the obligation to her father, which is equally natural and right in principle, although socially corrupted in its requirements, Julie balances precariously on the brink of this final 'precipice' of civilized compromise, which would certainly complete her fall by the implied acquiescence in an equivocal situation which is neither natural nor social, in any real sense.

The moral and sentimental context of the novel may be far removed, technically, from Rousseau's political philosophy, but there is certainly a parallel between this contemplated adultery and the loss of human dignity involved in the false political system; and a reflection, in this immoral compromise, of Rousseau's loathing of the monstrous ambiguity of existing society. To all intents and purposes, therefore, the idea of adultery is the 'anti-social contract' of the *Nouvelle Héloïse*; and if the thought is not translated into reality, it is because at this crucial moment in the story, there occurs a kind of providential intervention, which, like so many things in Rousseau, can be interpreted in different ways according to the susceptibilities of the individual reader.

As Julie enters the church for the marriage ceremony, she is overcome by the solemnity of the moment, the sight of the expectant congregation and the sense of the numinous generated by the place itself. In this state, she experiences what is described variously as a *changement*, a *renaissance* and an *heureuse révolution*, in consequence of which she is able to make her vows and accept the obligations of her union with Wolmar in complete sincerity, and with all the determination of her will.

The passage in which Julie describes this event (and which will be mentioned again in connection with the art of Rousseau) is itself a

R K

masterpiece of ambiguity, although it is designed, presumably, to reconcile the religious and the philosophical attitudes of the century.
From the religious standpoint, it could be seen as the operation of Divine
Grace; from the point of view of the unbeliever, it could be interpreted
as a criticism of religion and the demonstration of a sentimental illusion;
but what it most probably represents is the kind of rational miracle or
sudden expansion of awareness which is encountered in all the constructive and revolutionary aspects of Rousseau's thought. Its interpretation,
like that of almost all the crucial texts in Rousseau, can generate interminable argument; but one thing which can be said without hesitation
is that in the dialectical structure of the *Nouvelle Héloïse*, it plays the part
which we should now expect, and provides, after the spurious 'contract
of adultery', the 'authentic' contract based on Self-Interest, equivalent
to the as yet unpublished Social Contract; and offering also analogies
with the 'pedagogical contract' of *Emile*, and the surrender to the Will
of God involved in the *Profession de foi*.

For anyone prepared to take the extreme view that, in its final form,
the *Nouvelle Héloïse* is more a philosophical allegory than it is a novel,
it is possible to argue that the marriage of Julie *is* the Social Contract,
thinly disguised and symbolized in the only way which Rousseau could
conceive as meeting the requirements of a popular fiction. And even
if one does not go quite so far as that, it must still be admitted that it
represents an *aspect* of the Social Contract, and is in any case one of the
most important of all Rousseau texts, because it applies his basic principle
to domestic life, in addition to holding open the door to a religious consummation. The specifically religious element in Julie's 'revolution' is
something which the reader can take or leave; but the immediate object
of her expanded awareness is not a matter of argument. It is through the
enlightenment of self-interest, or triumph of *amour de soi* over *amour-
propre*, that she recovers her dignity in the exercise of freewill; and she
uses her freewill, as the *Vicaire savoyard* will do, in acquiescing in what she
feels to be the Will of God.

From now on, the conduct of Julie will be governed by conscience, or
by her 'constant will', which is explicitly equated with the Will of God;
and it follows, of course, that in accepting the responsibilities of marriage,
she acts not only for her own good, but for the ultimate good of true
society. Irrespective of the religious sanction, which may or may not be
accepted at this stage, marriage is now presented as a fundamental
institution, and a particular contract between individuals, implying, as
Rousseau puts it, the tacit participation of the whole human race. In

other words (although in writing his novel, Rousseau was not in a position to make use of the term, because he had not completed the theory of the *Contrat Social*), marriage has a social sanctity because it is an institution deriving immediately from the General Will; and adultery, whether it is regarded as a 'sin' or not, is certainly a crime, and an anti-social act. In proclaiming her fidelity to Wolmar, therefore, Julie is in effect linking the Will of God with what is to emerge in the *Contrat Social* as the General Will; and accepting in her own life the Rule of Law which is the object of all Rousseau's political philosophy.

It may be doubted whether Saint-Preux finds much comfort in the arguments which Julie uses to explain her new position; but in order to keep the story open for further developments, he too has to be rescued from complete despair by some corresponding process of enlightenment. If this were genuinely a 'Romantic' work, he would doubtless kill himself; and the *Nouvelle Héloïse* might be more acceptable even today as a novel of the *Werther*-ish type, had its author allowed this to happen. But in the context of Rousseau's philosophy, the contracting out implied by the project of suicide is no more permissible for Saint-Preux than adultery is permissible for Julie. Both would be false solutions, in terms of the doctrine of Self-Interest and the General Will; and the arguments with which Bomston deflects Saint-Preux from his suicidal intent are, fundamentally, much the same as those of Julie, although in Bomston's case, there is an added flavour of Stoicism. Suicide, which may or may not be a 'sin', is both a miscalculation of self-interest, at the stage of moral and intellectual development which Saint-Preux has already attained, and a social crime into the bargain, in that it deprives the human race of a potentially useful life. And so, as the unhappy tutor departs on his travels round the world, it is, we must assume, to broaden his perspective of life, and reflect on the problem of individual happiness and the well-being of mankind as a whole;—in short, to complete the 'revolution' of growing up, so that he may be at least a sympathetic witness to the New Order which is obviously about to emerge from the marriage of Julie and Wolmar.

The study of this marriage, on which the last three parts of the *Nouvelle Héloïse* are based, is, like the love of Julie and Saint-Preux, not really comprehensible without reference to Rousseau's general philo-sophy. Indeed, it is even more dependent on this background, and is consequently more markedly allegorical in character, although, para-doxically, most of the principles involved are to be found in the con-structive works which were not completed when the novel was written.

It must therefore be clearly understood that most of the parallels to be established from now on involve a slight anticipation of history, justified by the assumption that the essentials of Rousseau's doctrines were by now well formulated in his mind, even though they were not all down on paper.

From the principle that 'the family is the image of the state', and the analogy between the psychological revolution involved in the marriage-ceremony and the political revolution of the Social Contract, it follows, with, by this time, slightly depressing inevitability, that the next phase of Julie's experience will consist of a passage through a situation which realizes on the domestic plane the aspirations of Rousseau's political and moral philosophy. This does not mean that marriage to Wolmar suddenly becomes in every respect a better thing than union with Saint-Preux; because after all, the lost paradise of innocent love is a state to which there is no return. What it does mean is that in Julie's married state there is the possibility of creating through reason a tolerable substitute, offering the moral advantages of virtue without, somehow, being quite free from the disadvantages of artifice. The marriage stands, therefore, in relation to the love-affair with Saint-Preux, roughly as the state of the *Contrat Social* stands in relation to the state of nature: not necessarily better or worse, but different and, indeed, unique in that it offers the greatest possible satisfaction of Self-Interest conceivable *in the particular historical circumstances*.

Julie's passage through this state is depicted in the fourth and fifth parts which, while they show many significant and subtle adjustments in personal relationships, also tend inevitably to emphasize the social aspect of the novel, through Saint-Preux's descriptions of life on the Wolmar estate. Apart from their immediate connection with the psychological states of the characters, these accounts complete the pattern of social commentary by adding to the pictures of rustic simplicity in the Valais, and refined corruption in Paris, a vision of the kind of order which could come into being through the initiative of a 'Lawgiver'. In this instance, however, it seems that there is no one Lawgiver, but that the functions attributed elsewhere to this enigmatic figure are exercised jointly by Julie and Wolmar, who form by their union a 'moral person', to which Wolmar contributes understanding, and Julie, will.

The letters describing in detail the functioning of the Clarens estate may seem tedious in comparison with those which keep the book alive sentimentally, by introducing into the relationship of Julie and the returned Saint-Preux a fitful nostalgia for the past. They must not on that account be ignored, because in their blending of realism and idealism they suggest once more that Rousseau's vision is not, as is sometimes thought, entirely Utopian. Some of them are concerned with purely practical matters, such as the training and treatment of the servants and workers, who are the citizens of this welfare state; and it is interesting to note, for example, how the principle of Self-Interest is applied in economic terms, by the introduction of such devices as an incremental system of wages.[20] At the other end of the scale, however, there is a description of Julie's private garden or *Elysée*[21] which is one of the most elaborate pieces of symbolism in the book, illustrating the withdrawal of the governing élite, but also the general principle of 'humanized nature'.

The aim of this society of Clarens, like that of Rousseau's formal theories, is to reconcile order and liberty; but the objection is sometimes made that in spite of the democratic implications of its principles, which involve mutual confidence and respect between morally equal individuals, it is in practice paternalistic, and tends to reduce Rousseau's political theory to the standard enlightened despotism of his age. This is at the most a half-truth, expressing a grossly oversimplified view of a highly complex state which seeks not only to harmonize nature and reason, but includes in its programme of conciliation such formidable undertakings as the synthesizing of the opposing philosophies of Stoics and Epicureans. In the circumstances, he can hardly be expected to please everybody all the time; and we must remember, above all, that he is not just a dealer in abstract ideals, but that his constructive thought starts from historical reality as he sees it. It is inevitable, in the context, that the Clarens society should have a paternalistic appearance, because it is presented from the standpoint of those who are, after all, the proprietors of the estate, and have, as a matter of brute fact, special and immediate powers and responsibilities. The point is that Clarens represents, not a static ideal, but a dynamic vision of an evolving society; and at the stage depicted by Rousseau its legislator-figures must naturally appear as an exceptional group or élite within the wider community for which they have above all a *moral* responsibility. They form, with their personal friends, what Rousseau calls a *société des cœurs*; and this formula is sufficient indication that while superior enlightenment and responsibility may imply particular satisfactions and compensations, they do not imply any form of permanent *political* privilege.

Because the picture of life at Clarens is part of a novel dealing with individuals, many of the pleasures of this highly organized and artificial rusticity are presented in intimate terms at what may be called the Lawgiver-level; but Rousseau is careful to stress the general social significance of this phase by episodes which are shrewdly timed to fit into the total structure of the book, and prolong the alternation of private and public experiences on which it depends for much of its symbolic effect.

At the end of Part IV there occurs, as we have seen in outlining the plot, the famous boating excursion, with its symbolic storm and crisis of nostalgia, after which the sentimental relationship of Saint-Preux and Julie settles into the relative calm of resignation on both sides. This is one of the great and last turning-points of the novel, where a movement of private revolt is abandoned for the sake of the well-being of the group, and where Saint-Preux, after his 'psychological cure', is able at least to go through the motions of surrender to a sort of general will on which the stability of Clarens depends. The logical complement to this episode, according to Rousseau's system, must be some attempt to compensate for the ideal but unattainable satisfaction of a particular relationship, by a more general satisfaction deriving from the sense of integration in a wider community; and Rousseau faithfully carries out this attempt in various accounts of intimate social pleasure. The most notable of these is the so-called *matinée à l'anglaise*, described in the third letter of Part V, which offers a curious picture of silent 'togetherness', contrasting with the frivolous chatter of ordinary society, and in which the feelings of Julie and Saint-Preux can, as it were, dissolve into a wider communion of sensibility.

After this, there is, humanly speaking, little to be done with the Julie Saint-Preux relationship; and it is hardly surprising that the emphasis of Part V is, in the main, a social one, and that this aspect of the book now reaches a climax of its own, representing a similar kind of equilibrium, and noteworthy for its combination of patriarchal forms and egalitarian principles.

This social climax of the *Nouvelle Héloïse* is provided by the seventh letter of Part V, with its celebrated account of the Wine Harvest. It shows, in roughly equal proportions, the sense of human community and the simple enjoyment of the fruits of Nature; and is a statement of Rousseau's faith in the possibility of the evolved, rationally restored, or revolutionary society finding again the happiness of the Golden Age. By virtue of its descriptive power and its combination of realistic detail and nostalgic idealism, it is the most memorable example of the *fête publique* or spectacle of public rejoicing, which is a recurring theme in

Rousseau's writings; and much of its importance lies in the manifestation of the principle of equality, and a community-sense in which even
the lawgivers of Clarens are more or less absorbed.

This episode of the *vendanges* can be appreciated at different levels;
and it is in fact sometimes seen either as mere background, or as a piece
of sentimental primitivism. Its real purpose is, almost certainly, to
synthesize man's historic past and his future prospects; and to combine
with an appearance of Golden-Age rusticity, a symbolic presentation of
the new society of the General Will, in which the attainment of *unanimity* is expressed most clearly in a vision of the women harvesters
singing together in *unison*, after the day's work. At any level of interpretation, it is a fine piece of writing; but like the episodes on the private
sector to which it corresponds in some degree, it poses the problem of
what can happen next. It is evident that this fifth part brings us almost
to the end of the road, leaving Rousseau little choice but to move, in
his denouement, to the metaphysical and religious plane. The result is
the protracted and detailed account of Julie's death, which, because of
the changes in literary taste, rings oddly nowadays as the end of a novel,
but remains remarkably interesting as the conclusion of an allegory.

The simplest thing that can be said of this denouement is that it
describes an exemplary death, and that as an exposition of the 'art of
dying', it is the natural complement to the 'art of living' which runs
through much of this book, as it will run through *Emile*. It records,
moreover, a death free from anguish, a philosophical triumph over the
Last Enemy; and there is, of course, every reason to suppose that it will
be based on the principle of Self-Interest. By itself, however, this gives
little idea of a situation which goes far beyond the marriage of Julie in
its complexity and apparent ambiguity.

Philosophically, its starting-point is the position of maximum earthly
contentment, which assumes the development and use of all human
faculties, and includes sensual pleasure, rational and moral satisfactions,
and the charm of sentimental relationships. The balanced enjoyment of
all these satisfactions clearly requires the ideal social conditions symbolized in Part V of the novel, and constitutes a *bien-être* or state of well-
being, which is described by Julie in the eighth letter of Part VI. Taking
the past and the present together, she admits that she has arrived at the
peak of earthly happiness, and derived the maximum value from life;
and that there is nothing more for her to look forward to, at least in
terms of actual possession. And yet this state of happiness is not enough;
as she now discovers, there is such a thing as the *dégoût du bien-être*, a form

of ennui which afflicts us because, even at the maximum degree of
normal human well-being, desire outruns the possibility of fulfilment.
The requirements of Self-Interest are not met, in fact, by the attainable
satisfactions of a physical, rational or moral nature, since there exists
another human faculty which is not yet fully provided for. This is the
power of imagination, which operates in fact over the whole range of
human desires, partly through memory, but especially through the
pleasure of anticipation. And so, at the point where no further earthly
consummations are conceivable, there remains, for the play of the
imagination, only the land of visions, or *pays des chimères*, offering a
range of mental experiences which explains the striving of mystics,
metaphysicians and religious teachers towards the absolute satisfaction
which this life cannot provide. In the death of Julie, therefore, Rousseau
completes his exposition of human experience in terms of Self-Interest,
by means of a synthesis of philosophical and religious traditions; and
this includes a deathbed profession of faith corresponding in all essentials
to the *Profession de foi du vicaire savoyard*.

It is not possible here to comment in detail on this fascinating product
of Rousseau's eclecticism, but some idea of the kind of synthesis involved
in it can be derived from the twin sources of inspiration, which play a
part also in the *Profession de foi*. On the one hand, this is a serene,
philosophical death, inspired by that of Socrates, especially in the discussion of life, death and the hereafter, which takes place between Julie
and the local pastor. But on the other hand, the whole story of her
departure from this life is clearly influenced by the Crucifixion. It includes, for example, a direct suggestion of redemptive purpose, in that
Julie, who regards herself as morally responsible for her mother's death,
herself dies to save her child, and as a 'martyr to mother love'; and the
inordinate length of the denouement, which has always been a stumbling-block to literary critics, is explained by the fact that the events
surrounding her death constitute a rationalized 'Holy Week', complete
with a Last Supper and even a false Resurrection, when an overwrought
servant believes mistakenly that the corpse of Julie has shown signs of life.

Just how far Rousseau's account of Julie's death is deliberately intended as an evocation of the Gospels is uncertain; because, while the Last
Supper, the Resurrection and references to Gethsemane offer fairly
transparent analogies, the text contains a number of minor points, such
as the division of Julie's wardrobe among the servants, a reference to the
'ninth hour' and so on, which look suspiciously like biblical reflections,
but cannot be proved to be so. What does seem clear, is that Julie,

whose experiences throughout the book could be said to epitomize those of society, is transformed at the end into a Christ-figure, who is at the same time a rationalist upholding the principles of natural religion. In view of this, it is difficult to interpret the final symbolism of the *Nouvelle Héloïse* as anything but an expression of Rousseau's belief that Redemption and Enlightenment are particular appearances of the same general truth. This is, indeed, another and earlier manifestation of the idea which has already been noted as a possible outcome of the *Profession de foi*: namely, that every man can and must be his own Christ. The possibility of this rests on the fact that, as Rousseau sees it, men are not essentially corrupt, but are endowed with resources of feeling, reason and will; and the active principle of a Love of Self which can expand its range of operation with a process of enlightenment, going through and beyond the social phase, until it includes Love of neighbour as the Self, and finally Love of God.

Briefly, therefore, the death of Julie represents again, but in symbolic form, the rationalization of the Redeemer which is necessitated by the rationalization of the Fall; and can be taken as completing the allegorical purpose of the *Nouvelle Héloïse* with an invitation to reconciliation between the extremes of religious and philosophical thought in the eighteenth century.

This exposition of the movement of Rousseau's novel is not, of course, proposed as an exhaustive or definitive interpretation. Its purpose is merely to present the outlines in the way which makes most sense in the whole context of Rousseau's thought; and to demonstrate how the novel can be regarded as his attempt to communicate as much of his doctrine as possible to as many people as possible. Inevitably, it leaves untouched a vast number of problems of detail, of which one or two, at least, must be mentioned. Some of these relate to the characters, including the minor figures of Claire and the stoic Bomston, who are not only confidants, but interesting creations in their own right. The most enigmatic character, however, and the one who tends to suffer most when the interpretation is based on Julie, is undoubtedly Wolmar, the *philosophe* who, as the representative of mature reason (of a sort), has special responsibilities at the social level of the book; but who forfeits sympathy simply because of his function as the intervening husband.

The main difficulty raised by the presence of Wolmar is that as a directing intelligence behind the Clarens society, and instrument of the 'cure' of both Julie and Saint-Preux (so far as they can be said to be cured), he has some claim to be considered as the true Lawgiver of the book. On the other hand, the fact that he is an atheist might be taken as dissociating the function of the Lawgiver from any sort of religious sanction; and it can, if suitably presented, be used to call into question the seriousness of the religious element in Rousseau's system as a whole. The most sensible way of dealing with this very real problem is to remember that in spite of its allegorical aspect, the *Nouvelle Héloïse* is still a novel, based on the complexity of people as they are, and that Rousseau does allow for the ultimate conversion of Wolmar to natural religion. Furthermore, while all the characters illustrate some aspect of man's quest for the fulfilment of his natural potentialities, including religious awareness, all of them, even Julie, must also show something of the limitations of human nature or the human condition, at some point or other. In some ways and at certain stages, Wolmar seems more enlightened than the other characters; but he still has the flaws which Rousseau believed that he saw in the intellectuals of his day, and especially the Encyclopedists. The real grounds for rejecting him as a complete Lawgiver are provided, not by his atheism as such, but by his lack of real moral dignity, which in Rousseau's philosophy, can derive only from the exercise of freewill. Wolmar is doubtless an intelligent man, within the limits imposed by Rousseau's deliberate use of the word *entendement* in his case. He also does good, and sets a high standard of social behaviour. The point is, however, that his well-doing is an example of what the eighteenth century calls *bienfaisance*, rather than of *vertu*; and is the expression not of a genuine moral choice based on 'conscience', but of a sort of determinism of character. As Julie herself puts it, in the eighteenth letter of Part III: 'il fait le bien par goût, et non par choix'; and on this count alone, Wolmar simply does not qualify for the function of leadership in Rousseau's New Order, whose authenticity depends, as we have seen so often, upon freewill. It is Julie, not Wolmar, who reigns supreme in the order of Will, and who therefore represents in the novel the most important element in the concept of the Lawgiver.

The role of Wolmar is certainly one of the most delicate of the particular problems which have to be faced when the general sense of the novel has been understood; and there is one other outstanding question which, by its very nature, forms a natural conclusion to almost any discussion of the work. This is the problem of Saint-Preux, who remains as a sort of loose strand in the otherwise tightly-woven fabric of the story, because from the moment when Julie accepts marriage with

Wolmar, he has no further scope for real initiative. Having played his part as the natural man (and representative of *bonté*, as opposed to the *bienfaisance* of Wolmar and the *vertu* of Julie), he belongs to the *past*, and his function becomes primarily that of spectator or witness. It is true, of course, that he keeps a special place in Julie's heart; that Rousseau uses him as a subject of psychological experiment and further sentimental analysis; and that he attains full moral status as a responsible individual; but he can hardly be said to have a substantive position in the society of Clarens. The only prospect he has of justifying his existence socially is as tutor to Julie's children, i.e. to the next generation; and even this is left as no more than a probability, like the conversion of Wolmar. In this sense, therefore, Saint-Preux belongs to the *future*; and the possibility of limited or vicarious fulfilment in the present, which is opened up by Julie's desire that he should marry the widowed Claire, is destroyed by Claire herself.

In short, Saint-Preux remains, in the last analysis, an unintegrated 'outsider'; and there is every reason to suppose that there is a bitter reflection here of Rousseau's view of his own situation in the world. This explains why the character continues to exercise a special fascination; and why the conclusion of the *Nouvelle Héloïse* can direct us straight towards the autobiographical writings, which are in many ways the most important part of Rousseau's legacy to posterity.

CHAPTER VIII

The Problem of the Philosopher:
Confessions and *Dialogues*

*

WITH the metaphysics of the *Profession de foi* and the symbolism of the death of Julie, Rousseau's public or general philosophy is brought to the limit of its expansion, to complete a system which is at least as self-sufficient as the religious thought from which its structure is mainly derived. There are, of course, other works, published during or after this period, which add detail or emphasis to particular aspects of his scheme. Such are the *Lettre à d'Alembert sur les spectacles*, of 1758, which opposes the establishment of a theatre in Geneva, and marks his open breach with the materialist philosophers of the *Encyclopédie*; and the *Lettre à Christophe de Beaumont*, showing an equally radical conflict with Catholic authorities, after the publication of *Emile*. In the main, however, these are occasional and polemical writings, which do not and cannot extend the scope of his philosophy in any significant way; and two projects which might have done so remained unfulfilled. They are the discussion of a federal scheme in politics, which is envisaged tentatively at the end of *Emile*; and the psychological study entitled *La Morale sensitive*, which has left its mark not only upon certain actions of Wolmar in the *Nouvelle Héloïse*, but also upon Rousseau's last production, the *Rêveries du promeneur solitaire*.

These publications and projects need not be considered in a general introduction, but there remains also the more esoteric side of Rousseau's work, represented by the *Confessions*, the *Dialogues* and the *Rêveries*, which can all be classified loosely as autobiographical writings, although there are great differences between them. No view of Rousseau can be complete without some account of them; but by their very nature, they pose at least two new problems of appreciation, the first of which is, precisely, whether or not they should be put in a special category, quite distinct from the other major works.

This particular problem arises chiefly because Rousseau himself tended to separate them from what he called his 'vrais écrits', and be-

148

cause they contain a number of passages in which he expresses bitter regret over his literary career, and seems to be repudiating his own philosophy. Needless to say, this is an illusion; but in the circumstances, it is not surprising that these works are often treated separately, or used by commentators as mere background to the philosophy. In fact, they offer between them not only the background of experience which produced the system, but also a 'foreground' in which the system, with all its possibilities of conflict and drama, can be seen operating in life, and deliberately applied to the solution of Rousseau's personal difficulties.

Assuming, provisionally, that these works do play an integral part in his whole philosophical enterprise, the second preliminary question is to decide how far appreciation of them depends upon a knowledge of the actual historical circumstances in which they were written, or to which they refer. This is a very real problem, because certain parts of these texts are almost unintelligible without specialized knowledge of events or personalities. The only way of dealing with this difficulty in an introductory survey is to postulate for them a general philosophical significance, distinct from the particular historical significance; and to concentrate upon the former, reducing historical observations to the few really essential points.

Beginning with the *Confessions*, the first of these points must be the fact that they came into being over a period of about fifteen years, most of which was marked by the persecution which seems to have affected the balance of Rousseau's mind, and was bound, in any case, to change the nature of the work as it was composed. The second is that the *Confessions* were not originally conceived under this title, but were thought of simply as memoirs, and undertaken partly in response to suggestions from Rousseau's publisher, Marc-Michel Rey. The third is that before these suggestions were put to him (possibly as early as 1757) he may already have been prompted to write his personal reminiscences by the nostalgic feelings associated with a visit to Geneva in 1754. A fourth and final point to be emphasized is that although most of the text was composed during the years from 1762 to 1765, and 1769 to 1770, in the various refuges which he was compelled to seek in Switzerland, England and France, the outlines were probably determined during the period following the great 'effervescence', between 1756 and 1762.

The important inference to be drawn from these few observations is that while Rousseau abandoned any idea he may have had of publishing his reminiscences in the lifetime of himself and others who figure in them, and while his conscious aims may have varied with changing circumstances, it is reasonable to seek in the *Confessions* certain direct and positive links with the system, which may enable us to cut through the web of biographical detail, with its appeal to mere historical curiosity, and get down to the fundamental *meaning* of the book.

If the *Confessions* are examined from this standpoint, it is clear that they can be related to the major philosophical writings in several ways. In the first place, by showing Rousseau's thought directed back into his own mind and existence, after being allowed to expand upon the world in general, they represent a simple extension of the field of speculation, and the beginning of one of the most remarkable of all explorations of the Self. In the second place, the *Confessions* can be looked upon as part of an attempt to deal with the problem of the outsider, as it is seen in the situation of Saint-Preux at the end of the *Nouvelle Héloïse*. It is evident that Rousseau has been offering to the world a philosophy of integration and reconciliation; but can the 'witness' to the philosophy, whether he be thought of as natural man, or as Tutor or Lawgiver, himself fit into it? Must he work out his own salvation? Can he do so? What manner of man is he, in any case? All these questions, posed by the uncertain future of Saint-Preux, can open up ways into the 'labyrinth' of the *Confessions*, and the other subjective writings; and all of them show how the problem of personal integration in society is a source of real anguish for Rousseau.

The third approach to the meaning of the *Confessions* is to consider them as an answer to the problem of justifying both the system and the outsider who has created it. To some extent, such justification is necessitated for Rousseau by his own moral failings, by the misunderstanding between himself and his former friends such as Diderot, and by the public condemnation and persecution resulting from the appearance of *Emile*. On the other hand, he does not confuse confession and justification, at the personal level; and there is reason to think that the effort of justification is imposed, in the beginning, by the system itself as much as by the misfortunes, failings or guilt-complexes of its author. For it is obvious that even if the system is admitted to be complete and coherent, and worked out logically from the premise of man's essential goodness, the mere fact that it starts from a hypothesis and ends with gestures of faith involving the possibility of some purely spiritual experience, means that men are bound to seek more satisfying answers to the questions: is it *true*? or: can it be *realized*?

Contemplation of these questions suggests that whatever influence particular historical factors such as a nostalgia for the past, or the prompt-

ings of a publisher, may have exerted upon him, the real issue in Rousseau's autobiographical enterprise is a philosophical one: namely, the
break-through from thought to reality, which calls for a first-hand
demonstration of the facts and potentialities of human nature as he has
described them. In practice, this implies first a demonstration of the
basic humanity of the *homme de la nature*; but it will also mean, sooner or
later, a demonstration of the evolved humanity enshrined in the concept
of the Lawgiver, or even the Christ-figure. In either case, Rousseau's
resource, in order to anchor his system in reality and history, is to fall
back upon himself and draw a portrait which is unique, yet representative or symbolic. In other words (to adapt from a religious context a
phrase which seems entirely appropriate), Rousseau's Word must be
made Flesh, and seen to dwell among the scoffers and the persecutors.
This is what the *Confessions* are really *about*, at least to begin with; and a
great deal can be learned about his intentions from a careful reading of
his preamble, and some associated passages in the first pages. For example,
the aim of bridging the gap between hypothesis and truth appears clearly
enough in the famous opening phrases.

> Je forme une entreprise qui n'eut jamais d'exemple, et dont l'exécution
> n'aura point d'imitateur. Je veux montrer à mes semblables un homme
> dans toute la vérité de la nature; et cet homme, ce sera moi.
>
> Moi seul. Je sens mon cœur et je connais les hommes. Je ne suis fait
> comme aucun de ceux que j'ai vus; j'ose croire n'être fait comme
> aucun de ceux qui existent. Si je ne vaux pas mieux, au moins je suis
> autre. Si la nature a bien ou mal fait de briser le moule dans lequel elle
> m'a jeté, c'est ce dont on ne peut juger qu'après m'avoir lu.[22]

At first sight, this may seem no more than the posturing of romantic
individualism; but there exists a note, written later,[23] which shows that
the aim is not merely to impress by an exhibition of uniqueness, but to
make of the *Confessions* a work of general utility, in providing a *standard
of comparison*, the lack of which is a major obstacle to men's understanding of themselves, and hence of their true interest. The urge to
truth includes, in fact, not only the particular and unique truth about
Rousseau, but an attempt to induce all men to arrive at a saner view of
themselves by means of a comparison and value-judgment which, for
once, is supposed not to involve the invidious operation of *amour-propre*
or Selfish Interest, but is designed to create a sympathy based on a recognition of moral equality, which can be related to Self-Interest. Rousseau
may seem to be indulging in ostentatious egotism; what he is really
proposing, in effect, is to offer himself, through the sacrifice of his own

amour-propre, as a kind of mediator, not between Man and God, but between Man and Man. And it is because of this that the subsequent narrative of the *Confessions* has a general as well as a particular import, comparable in some respects with the symbolism of the *Nouvelle Héloïse*, and suggesting an analogy between the personal history of Rousseau and the general history of mankind.

This desire to present the 'natural man' is orientated mainly to the *past*, since it involves the stripping-off of the accretions making up the social façade; and its effect can be seen when Rousseau's autobiography is considered purely as a descriptive narrative. It is clear, however, that the provision of a mere corroborative statement is not and cannot be his sole aim, because it leaves out of account such things as the enlightened conscience, or the power of initiation vested, for example, in the figure of the Lawgiver. It omits, in fact, all those elements in Rousseau's thinking which relate to a hypothetical *future*. But if the autobiography is a direct application of the philosophy, we are obliged to ask what becomes of these elements, and of the revolutionary implications of his doctrine.

The answer to this question is very simple, and is to be sought in the plain historical fact that at some point, Rousseau ceased to think of writing *memoirs*, and began to conceive his autobiography in terms of *confession*. When this happened, the projected narrative was no longer a mere description or book, but became instead an *act*, having an evident moral purpose and, again (though in a different way), a public as well as a private significance. In other words, simply because they *are* confessions and not memoirs, the *Confessions* of Rousseau combine an evocation of fundamental human nature with an exemplary and highly 'evolved' moral gesture, of great psychological as well as social interest.

Since Rousseau's intentions are somewhat blurred in the actual execution, this aspect of the work is sometimes neglected; there is, however, no doubt that confession is not only a personal need for Rousseau, but is also a vitally important idea in his system as a whole. The best evidence of this is provided by the *Nouvelle Héloïse*, where it is a recurring theme, and where the New Order symbolized by the marriage of Julie and the society of Clarens cannot, as it were, be ratified until there has taken place a general clearing of consciences, in which Julie confesses to Wolmar her earlier relationship with Saint-Preux, and Wolmar confesses in turn that he has known all about it. What is so important about this theme, considered in the light of the symbolism of the novel, is that it makes of confession a corollary of the Social

Contract, and the way to both the recovery of personal contentment and the realization of the General Will in the new society, which are private and public aspects of the doctrine of Self-Interest.

This analogy should not be pushed too far, but it does throw a great deal of light on one of the most significant passages of the preamble to Rousseau's own *Confessions*, which runs thus:

> Que la trompette du jugement dernier sonne quand elle voudra; je viendrai ce livre à la main me présenter devant le souverain juge. Je dirai hautement: voilà ce que j'ai fait, ce que j'ai pensé, ce que je fus. J'ai dit le bien et le mal avec la même franchise. Je n'ai rien tu de mauvais, rien ajouté de bon, et s'il m'est arrivé d'employer quelque ornement indifférent, ce n'a jamais été que pour remplir un vide occasionné par mon défaut de mémoire; j'ai pu supposer vrai ce que je savais avoir pu l'être, jamais ce que je savais être faux. Je me suis montré tel que je fus, méprisable et vil quand je l'ai été, bon, généreux, sublime, quand je l'ai été: j'ai dévoilé mon intérieur tel que tu l'as vu toi-même. Etre éternel, rassemble autour de moi l'innombrable foule de mes semblables: qu'ils écoutent mes confessions, qu'ils gémissent de mes indignités, qu'ils rougissent de mes misères. Que chacun d'eux découvre à son tour son cœur aux pieds de ton trône avec la même sincérité; et puis qu'un seul te dise, s'il l'ose: *je fus meilleur que cet homme-là.*[24]

With this typical rhetoric, Rousseau does not only set up at once the metaphysical and religious perspective of the *Profession de foi* and the *Nouvelle Héloïse*, invoke the presence of the whole human race, and announce his own public and total confession: he also invites a *reciprocal* gesture in the consciences of all men. It must, indeed, be a tacit gesture, but theoretically, it is as valid in terms of the doctrine of the conscience, as is, for example, the 'tacit participation of the human race' which is involved in Julie's conception of the sanctity of marriage.

Considerations of taste may incline us to dismiss this preamble as a piece of empty spellbinding; but it is wiser to recognize that with this passage, the *Confessions* are integrated into the body of Rousseau's philosophy; and that the reciprocal act of conscience which is demanded here is analogous to the reciprocal submission proposed in the theory of the *Contrat Social*. And it can now be argued that we have here Rousseau's own attempt to initiate the New Order and realize the Contract through the public purification of a private conscience, as a first step to the creation of a Public Conscience, which is, as we have seen, one of the possible ways of describing the General Will.

R L

The psychology of confession in Rousseau is a complicated subject, but it can be said without hesitation that like almost every major feature of his doctrine, it is completely bound up with the central theory of Self-Interest and Selfish Interest; that in this way it has both private and public significance; and that it shows again the secularization of a religious tradition which we have encountered throughout.

From the individual standpoint, for example, the act is a substitute for private confession in a religious context, and as such is completely in the logic of the system. Psychologically, moreover, it is consistent with the tendency of Rousseau's political thought, in that confession to the public offers an escape from the humiliating submission to an individual. He may genuinely desire to clear his conscience of certain feelings of personal guilt, connected, for example, with the abandonment of his children, or the unjust dismissal of a servant-girl, but he cannot do so through the established (and therefore corrupt) religious institutions. He can, however, submit to the judgment of society because ultimately, on his own hypothesis, his guilt is the guilt of society; and in writing his confessions, he is in effect gambling on the willingness of society to admit this, to absolve him, and thus allow him his own measure of social salvation.

More interesting than this, however, are the implications of his confessions at the public level. What he appears to intend, when the *Confessions* are finally revealed, is that through his mediation men shall acknowledge their moral equality, and be enabled to recover their moral dignity through the act of will required for the casting-out, not of 'sin', but of Selfish Interest. And this is not all, for what is also at stake in the *Confessions* is the creation of a state of *confidence* between Rousseau and the public, which will give him the moral authority associated with a heroic gesture, and allow him to be accepted not only as the representative of the old natural man, but as the first New Man—the 'homme naturel éclairé par la raison'. To put it simply, this act of public confession fulfils the immediate requirements of Self-Interest, in enabling Rousseau to live at peace with himself. But it would also enable him to claim personally the status of moral leadership which is the common attribute of his Lawgiver, his Tutor and his Genius, and which is indispensable for the realization of his system. He does not, of course, actually say this in so many words, but examination of the *Dialogues* and *Rêveries* tends to confirm that this is what is in his mind.

The text of the *Confessions* resulting from this remarkable gesture is much too long and complex to be considered in anything more than outline, but fortunately, this outline can be conveyed in familiar terms. The work consists of twelve books, covering Rousseau's life down to 1765, and his ill-fated attempt to find refuge and peace in England. There is increasing evidence of his mental torment in the second half, where the growing conviction that his persecution is the result of a plot involving his former friends leads to a rather confusing use of actual documents, and an obscuring of the main theme by the urge to immediate personal justification. This main theme is the 'innocent fall' of Rousseau, from the relative simplicity of his childhood in Switzerland, into the conflicts and frustrations of life in a sophisticated society, where a veneer of refinement barely conceals the squalid play of passions and selfish interest; and, very broadly speaking, its development follows a pattern similar to that established in the second discourse, and applied in the first half of the *Nouvelle Héloïse*. Obviously, the tissue of particular personal recollections, and the digressions caused by the vagaries of memory, cannot be expected to conform exactly to the scheme of 'revolutions' to be found in Rousseau's hypothesis of social degeneration; but he does convey brilliantly, by an accumulation of detail, the kind of continuous processes which finally crystallize in the mind, and allow us to organize our memories into general impressions of phases of past experience.

The first four books, for example, containing his recollections down to the return from his earliest visit to Paris in 1731, provide a picture of first youth or *première jeunesse*. They cover his childhood in Geneva, his first encounters with Mme de Warens, and many adventures and wanderings, and the account remains as fresh today as when it was written. In terms of historical particularities and facts, this is clearly a period of many vicissitudes, containing good times and bad, pleasure and pain, some corruption, but also the beginnings of morality. It includes one of the major 'crimes' of Rousseau: the theft of a ribbon, leading to the dismissal of the servant-girl in Turin; yet the general impression is one of innocent insouciance, akin to Self-Interest in the primitive sense, which makes it possible to see this phase as Rousseau's own 'first state of nature'. In a similar way, Books V and VI, in which the highlights are provided by his ambiguous relations with Mme de Warens at Chambéry, and the variations on the theme of the *ménage à trois* involving Claude Anet and Winzenried, become, chiefly by virtue of the idyll of Les Charmettes in 1735 or 1736, an evocation of Rousseau's Golden Age. It is in fact the *précieux intervalle* preceding the inevitable fall; and this time it ends with a real revolution or *bouleversement*, as he realizes that he is supplanted in Mme de Warens's affections by the inferior Winzenried.

From this point, Rousseau's interpretation of his past can almost be predicted, in the same way as the general movements of the *Nouvelle Héloïse*. Thus, in Book VII, he leaves for Paris, full of personal ambition and confidence, ready for the competition of *talents*, and trusting to his musical system to make his way in a society which he sees retrospectively as being based on Selfish Interest. He cultivates such of the right people as he can find—writers, intellectuals and social figures; but he soon discovers, in the disastrous experience with the French ambassador Montaigu, in Venice, that he has fallen into a state of humiliating dependence on the tyrannical will of a fool, whose social status has nothing to do with merit or justice. It is this episode which sows the seed of his subsequent indignation against the stupidity of existing institutions, by which the sanction of authority is added to a mere simulacrum of social order. It does not, however, prevent him from following the path of ambition in music and letters; or from imitating the examples around him, and abandoning the children of his union with Thérèse Levasseur; although on the other hand, most of his observations on the inauthentic society of Paris have the critical edge of the comparable passages in the *Nouvelle Héloïse* and other diatribes.

As the narrative moves on, in the eighth book, to the revelation of Vincennes, the era of the Discourses, and Rousseau's first celebrity, it is evident that the predominant theme is now that of 'contradiction' or moral warfare, expressed in his alternating desires to flee from this society, or to dominate and reform it, and, either way, to recover his moral freedom by 'breaking the chains of opinion' forged by passion and Selfish Interest. Above all, the personal tragedy becomes increasingly apparent in the breakdown of communication between Rousseau and the society around him, including Diderot and his friends; and the incomprehension which meets his attempts to resolve the contradictions by bringing his conduct into alignment with his principles. His rejection of luxury, or the adoption of music-copying as a steady and useful occupation, may have struck some of his contemporaries as absurd affectations; but as, in the last four books, the record moves to its climax, with the impossible passion for Sophie d'Houdetot, the famous quarrels, the flight from France and the stoning of the house at Môtiers, it can hardly be denied that this is indeed a tragedy—the tragedy of the outsider, rejected of men and (to use Rousseau's characteristic description of his plight) shipwrecked on a sea of misfortunes.

Without labouring this systematization unduly, it must be observed that the existence beneath the rich detail of the *Confessions* of a structure recalling so clearly the previous uses of the idea of the rationalized Fall, is bound to raise the question of how far he really does tell the truth about himself in his autobiography; and whether the book is a 'monument of innocence', as he would claim, or a monument of humbug, as his detractors are apt to think. And this is clearly a vital question for any evaluation of it, because of the prime importance which Rousseau attaches to the issue of truth and sincerity.

There is no doubt that the narrative does contain 'inaccuracies' (though fewer, perhaps, than has sometimes been thought); and that it offers examples of what may be regarded as nauseating casuistry, such as the Platonic defence of the abandonment of the children, which occurs in Book VIII. Nevertheless, the problem of these inaccuracies is not one which can be dealt with summarily on simple moral grounds. The answer to it depends partly on an understanding of Rousseau's position as an artist (to which we shall come later), and more immediately upon his conception of truth. The most succinct statement of his view of truth is to be found in the fourth Promenade of the *Rêveries*; and it must be mentioned here because it involves a distinction between *general* truth, which is a matter of public concern, and *particular* truth, which is not. This is to all intents and purposes a theory of pragmatism, and it suggests that there are two points to bear in mind as one reads the *Confessions*. The first is that Rousseau must be thought of as being fundamentally sincere, if only because of the importance of the autobiography as a means to the realization of his philosophy. The second, is that he is concerned with extracting *general* truth from his experiences, and not simply with the recording of raw historical facts. It may be argued, indeed, that the transcendental and intuitive element in his thought implies almost inevitably a distinction of this kind between truth and facts. Thus, although the tracking down of discrepancies between Rousseau's accounts of particular situations, and the facts which can be established from other sources, has been a source of harmless pleasure to countless critics and biographers, it is not indispensable for our general appreciation of the *Confessions*.

It may well be that the book presents the 'hypothetical' Rousseau necessary for the confirmation of the philosophy, but the hypothesis can still be considered to possess a sentimental or pragmatic truth. He is not really trying to present the raw facts of his *existence*; and it is significant that when, in the last books, he does resort to precise documentation, the interest of the narrative evaporates almost completely. What he is trying to do is to evoke the 'chain of sentiments' to which the facts give rise in himself, and which, by their continuity, allow him and his reader to obtain an intuitive grasp of the *essence* of Rousseau. Without resorting to existentialist jargon, this process can be described in Rousseau's own terminology, as the presentation of a 'general truth' which may be useful to society, rather than a succession of 'particular truths' which would have no public significance or utility.

The sincerity of Rousseau is a complicated matter, and it certainly varies according to the point of view. In the long run, the change of appearance can be shown to depend on whether he is being judged in the light of *amour de soi*, or of *amour-propre*; but to cut a long story short, it means in practice that to the dispassionate observer of 'facts', an episode such as the liaison with Mme de Warens may seem more than a little sordid, whereas to Rousseau himself, judging his past in accordance with the principle of Self-Interest, it is genuinely a Golden Age idyll. In his mind, this *is* the truth; and it is, moreover, the source of the permanent value of the episode to his system, which is, after all, what he is trying to communicate to the reader. Similarly, it is doubtful whether the ambassador Montaigu was such a knave or fool as Rousseau's account suggests, but the permanent feelings which their association inspired in him have undoubtedly a truth of their own, and consequently a value in relation to his system.

The outcome of the perennial controversy about the truth of the *Confessions* can be summed up by saying that there is little point in reading them simply for the sake of the facts; and that the most sensible approach is to adopt a frame of mind like that which, in an amusing passage of the sixth book, Rousseau ascribes to Mme de Warens, in her attitude to Catholic belief. She admitted sincerely all the Creed, he tells us, but when discussion arose on each article, it turned out that her belief was different from that of the Church, to which, nevertheless, she submitted![25] Theoretically, it would seem that the proper spirit in which to experience Rousseau's autobiography is to 'submit' to the whole, even while one may contest the accuracy of the parts; because only thus can there take place the communication of sympathy and feeling which is necessary if the *Confessions* are to play their part in the conversion implied by the philosophy.

It will be seen that the relationship between author and reader which is required by this work is a very special one; and that in so far as it assumes on the part of the reader a willingness to allow the effacement or adaptation of particular truths for the sake of establishing a general or average truth—i.e. the 'sense' of Rousseau's life, it offers an obvious analogy with the superseding of particular wills by the General Will, as part of man's advance towards Justice. From Rousseau's point of view, it could be argued, indeed, that anyone who reads the *Confessions* and then produces some document tending to show that he is a liar, a rogue or a hypocrite, is just not *playing the game*; but in judging Jean-Jacques in the light of *amour-propre*, is condemning himself at the same time, since the Rousseau of the *Confessions* is a representative and symbolic figure! Needless to say, this has not prevented many readers with less complicated minds, and in every subsequent generation, from judging Rousseau to be all of these things; and it is precisely with this question of judgment following confession, that we come to a final appraisal of the autobiography.

Considered purely as a literary phenomenon, the *Confessions* must be rated a great success, with a remarkable posterity to prove it, in the realm of subjective and introspective literature from the Romantic period onwards; but for Rousseau himself, and considered as a philosophic gesture, they must have seemed a failure. He could not publish them, and when, in 1770 and 1771, he finally gave readings of them in various Parisian circles, they were received, not surprisingly, with the silence of disapproval and incomprehension. His gamble had failed, and he was, as he saw it, still the Outsider, and the object of persecution, with little hope of an equitable judgment, at least from his contemporaries. In these circumstances, the only recourse left to him was to prepare an exemplary judgment of himself; and this is what we find in the next 'monument of innocence'—the *Dialogues* or, *Rousseau juge de Jean-Jacques*.

Among the major works of Rousseau, the *Dialogues* are probably the most neglected and least appreciated. This is partly because they are difficult to digest, being both dense and long; but mostly because they are considered to show definite abnormalities connected with their author's persecution-mania, and to a degree which tends to put them outside the ordinary philosophical or literary categories. This is extremely regrettable since, whatever mental state Rousseau may have been in when he wrote them, they provide the indispensable link between the relatively popular *Confessions* and *Rêveries*, both as an exercise in introspective psychology, and in terms of dialectical positions. They were composed very slowly from 1772 to 1776, when, follow-

ing events such as the moves made by Mme d'Epinay to bring about an
official prohibition of readings of the *Confessions*, Rousseau was becoming more and more convinced that there was a plot against him.
His references to them as a painful undertaking indicate that he was in a
state of considerable distress; but we must be careful not to over-
dramatize his situation, because while he was writing them, he was also
occupying himself quite methodically with musical and botanical interests which are far from suggesting that his mind was unhinged.

The *Dialogues* are, in fact, his supreme effort to justify the essential
claim to goodness, after the failure of the *Confessions*; and the basis of his
argument is, of course, that the existing state of public opinion concerning him represents a miscarriage of justice which must, sooner or later,
be put right. For fifteen years, since the publication of *Emile*, he has,
he maintains, been ostracized and treated by society as a sort of monster,
partly because of the attitude of religious bodies, but above all through
the machinations of the philosophical party. These, he says, have gained
such a hold on opinion, that if d'Alembert or Diderot were to assert
that he had two heads, the public would rush to support them, as actual
eye-witnesses to the fact. Rousseau has therefore to demonstrate all over
again that the monster is in reality a man, by creating artificially an
'objective' point of view; and to do this, he resorts to a device which
involves him in the bitterest and most ironic of all his paradoxes. By
dividing himself into 'Rousseau' and 'Jean-Jacques', he assumes, as it
were, a second head, in order to prove that he has but one. The effect
of this doubling is to make possible a discussion of the nature of the
essential 'Jean-Jacques', between 'Rousseau' and 'le Français'. This latter
is a hypothetical figure representing the misguided public; and he is
invoked partly to be converted to Rousseau's judgment of himself,
and partly to initiate, at least in imagination, the restoration of the normal
human contacts and confidence of which he feels himself to have been
deprived.

This discussion takes the form of three dialogues, designed to analyse
and then to rectify the existing situation. The first of them, entitled
rather discouragingly 'Du système de conduite envers Jean-Jacques
adopté par l'administration avec l'approbation du public', presents the
public attitude in terms of a reaction of horror against the profession
and publication of virtuous principles by a person whose private conduct
is believed to be wicked. Following the line of the last books of the
Confessions, it then offers, as the most probable explanation of the
apparent unanimity with which this attitude is maintained, the hypo-

thesis of a conspiracy, whose methods are considered at great length. At the end of it, as a means of confirming the hypothesis, the Frenchman is put through a preliminary 'revolution', in being prevailed upon to study carefully works which he has previously condemned unread, and on hearsay. This means that his future attitude to Jean-Jacques's books will at least be based upon personal and authentic experience; just as, for example, the enlightenment of Emile is derived from first-hand knowledge. In the meantime, as a complement to this move, 'Rousseau' undertakes to visit Jean-Jacques, and report upon his character and conduct.

The second dialogue, 'Du naturel de Jean-Jacques et de ses habitudes', gives this report, with the subsequent discussion of it by the two interlocutors, and contains a brilliant self-portrait which is justly famous in the annals of introspective literature. In the third section, entitled 'De l'esprit de ses livres', the Frenchman, having examined the books, is brought to agree that they are consistent with the character of their author as reported by 'Rousseau', and also that they are consistent among themselves, forming a coherent system deriving from the principle of Original Innocence. Finally, the movement of the whole series of dialogues culminates, characteristically, in a definitive 'revolution' in the mind of the Frenchman, who now admits the malignity of Rousseau's critics, concurs in a favourable judgment of him, and agrees to associate with him. He does not, it is true, commit himself to any sort of present action which would embroil him with the rest of society; but he does make the appropriate moral gesture, in undertaking to do what he can to transmit the works, and hence the message, to posterity, from whom Rousseau confidently expects a *general* revolution of opinion.

Considered objectively and on its own merits as a framework for a dialectical exercise, this scheme is simple and straightforward; and notwithstanding the density and complexity of the actual development, there is no indication in the dialogues that Rousseau ever loses his grip on the main themes, or falls into incoherence, or does any of the obvious things which might suggest madness or abnormality. But since the comparative neglect of the work stems partly from the belief that it *is* abnormal, there is clearly a problem which calls for consideration before we can sum up its meaning and importance.

The principal reasons for regarding the *Dialogues* as the product of an unbalanced mind are of a historical nature; and there is good evidence, including his correspondence, that at the relevant period, Rousseau had been reduced to a state of general suspicion, through brooding on his earlier persecution. This seems to have led him to question the motives and behaviour of everyone he encountered, including innocent passers-by in the streets. It does not, however, necessarily follow from this that the *Dialogues* have to be singled out for abnormality, because recent research into the subject tends to confirm rather than invalidate his belief in an association of interests spying upon him, and working to discredit him; and suggests that he was right in thinking that governmental circles were involved. All that history tells us, in short, is that Rousseau was in a state which, today, would probably be thought to warrant psychiatric treatment, and that there are fairly good reasons for this. To arrive at a balanced view of the problem as it concerns the *Dialogues*, we still have to consult the text itself for direct internal evidence; and here, the argument turns almost exclusively on the idea of the conspiracy or *complot* developed in the first dialogue.

There is fairly widespread agreement that this dialogue does in fact postulate a 'universal conspiracy', with the result that rather more than a third of the whole work is often written off as delusional, as though Rousseau believed firmly and literally that the human race had entered into a sort of compact to destroy him. One reason for this view is that he uses rather loosely such terms as *complot*, *ligue* and *accord universel*; and it is easy for us to telescope these mentally into *complot universel*, and so lose the drift of the argument. We must remember, however, that in the text, he does after all use the idea of a conspiracy as a *hypothesis* for dialectical purposes; and that the dialogue contains a good deal of evidence to suggest that what he is really proposing is a *limited* conspiracy and a universal *error*. From Rousseau's point of view, and seen against the whole philosophical background, this is not the same thing as a universal conspiracy, because as far as the general public is concerned it does not involve a positive and authentic act of will, but, at most, a negative and unenlightened acquiescence. This essential point is actually implied in the title, and is made explicit at the end of the dialogue, after a long and cogent discussion of the ways in which minority interests can delude and manipulate public opinion. And it is enough, in itself, to teach us to be very wary in approaching the *Dialogues*, especially where notions of madness or delusion are concerned. The fact is that, like the *Confessions*, the *Dialogues* can be examined at different levels, and have not only a historical interest, but a philosophical and artistic significance which transcends all arguments about Rousseau's persecution-mania. If they retain their fascination, it is not because they are delusional, but because they are developed on the very frontier between imagination and delusion, and are thus, apart from anything else, a valid work of art.

What the reader embarking upon this curious work for the first time really needs to know, is precisely what is at stake for Rousseau; and the easiest way to find out is to go back to the beginning of the *Confessions*, recalling at the same time the outline of his political thought. The intentions of the *Confessions* are, as we have seen, partly to justify the concept of the innocent Natural Man by an appropriate interpretation of Rousseau's own past life, and partly to initiate a new order of enlightened Self-Interest through confession, considered as an exemplary act of virtue. This act puts Rousseau into a position of moral leadership akin to that of his imagined Lawgiver, and the public are invited to judge him, and to respond to this gesture by a reciprocal act. But the hostility which he continues to encounter, and the reception given to the readings of the *Confessions*, demonstrate clearly that the required communication has not taken place; and thus the first step to an understanding of the *Dialogues* is to see that Rousseau is now regarding himself more than ever as being in the position of a Lawgiver or 'minority of one', in conflict with the society around him, and the values by which it is motivated. He has been misjudged by existing society because, inevitably, that society is so conditioned by Selfish Interest as to be incapable of a just verdict, without another great labour of explanation. Most of this painful labour goes into the famous self-portrait of the second dialogue, which shows Jean-Jacques as a surviving natural man or *vieux enfant*, and is so rich in psychological nuances that it defies any attempt at brief summary; but the relationship of the whole work to the philosophical system is brought out by a restatement in the first dialogue of the whole central theory of *amour de soi* and *amour-propre*.

The immediate aim of this is to show that society's verdict is based upon the short-term interest of individuals and associations, including the Government itself, who are in a position to exploit the ignorance of the mass, and make of the presence and doctrine of Rousseau a public scandal. The techniques of exploitation and the attendant contagion of error are analysed in detail as a general 'jaundice of the mind'; and at the end of it all, we are left with the notion of Rousseau right and the world wrong, and the idea of the so-called conspiracy. In terms of facts or 'particular truths', this may indeed seem a crazy spectacle; but from Rousseau's point of view it can be understood as the same kind of 'general truth' as those involved in the earlier narrative of the *Confessions*.

What is particularly interesting in all this is that although he does not actually put it thus, it represents the application to a particular phase of his own life, of certain aspects of the political as well as the moral theory; and creates through imagination a situation which can be interpreted quite easily in terms of the General Will and the Will of All. If Rousseau is, as has been suggested, putting himself into a position analagous to that of the Lawgiver, it follows that his is the single conscience in which the indestructible General Will of society provisionally resides, pending a general revolution or enlightenment. By the same token, the famous *complot*, which makes little sense historically, makes much more sense philosophically, as the manifestation of a broad agreement which is exactly analogous to the Will of All, in that it derives from the accumulation of particular interests, and the despotic influence of a few minds over a sheep-like herd. And this, it will be recalled, is how Rousseau conceives existing society from the very beginning.

From this point of view, it can be seen how the movement of ideas in the *Dialogues* represents a rationalization of Rousseau's situation in accordance with his philosophy. It can also be understood why this extremely interesting process can hardly be expected to appear in the eyes of the world as anything but an expression of madness. But if it is madness, there is certainly method in it; and not the least disconcerting aspect of this text is the rigorous, and at times almost dispassionate way in which the logic of the system is applied to life. In view of the historical evidence relating to Rousseau's condition, one can hardly assert categorically that the *Dialogues* are not in some respects abnormal; but in reading them, it is possible, and infinitely more rewarding, to lay aside 'particular truths' such as persecution-mania, and, taking the alternative view of their abnormality, accept them simply as the brilliant dialectics of misunderstood genius.

There is just one way in which this remarkable effort of rationalization might be thought to show a serious deviation from its author's abstract principles, and, in particular, from the doctrine of Self-Interest; and that is, paradoxically, in the fact that the *Dialogues* exist at all as an attempt at personal justification. Theoretically, it can be argued that having put himself into the Lawgiver-situation, Rousseau has no right to assume judicial functions at all, much less to be judge in his own cause. This is because the Lawgiver is deemed, after all, to be 'an extraordinary man in the state', who is neither sovereign nor magistrate, and whose concern is simply with the enunciation of laws and principles. In the *Dialogues*, however, he does depart from the position of the Lawgiver, in so far as he actually fights public opinion at a *personal* level, and tries to force a favourable judgment on his contemporaries, even while claiming to be concerned with the opinion of posterity.

As a dialectical point, this may seem trivial and excessively delicate, but it is important for two reasons. The first is that Rousseau himself comes to think of his actions more or less in this way, and tries, as we shall see in the *Rêveries*, to rectify his position by cultivating an attitude of complete resignation. The second is that this is the pointer to the fundamental human tragedy of the outsider, which the *Dialogues* express so poignantly. In these long-drawn-out arguments, Rousseau keeps on fighting what he conceives to be the public attitude towards him, partly because in terms of his system a Lawgiver is right by definition, and the public must be shown to be wrong; but also because, being flesh and blood and not a creature of logic like the Lawgiver, he still cannot bear his isolation. In defending himself rather than his doctrine, therefore, he is yielding to what he calls elsewhere the Rule of Opinion; and in fighting the public with its own polemical weapons, is himself stumbling into the trap of Selfish Interest. This is why the unhappiness which permeates the *Dialogues* can be taken as the sign of Rousseau's real Fall, as well as of the fact that in trying to solve the problems of the world by his philosophy, he has not yet solved the problem of the philosopher, and accepted in his own life the remoteness and loneliness implied by his doctrine.

CHAPTER IX

The Final Adjustment:
Les Rêveries du promeneur solitaire

*

THE *Rêveries*, which Rousseau calls a 'formless journal', contain an intimate record of his states of mind during the last two years of his life, expressed in ten so-called Promenades, the last of which is a mere fragment, begun and apparently abandoned less than three months before his death.

Unlike the *Dialogues*, they have exerted considerable influence on later literature, and for fairly obvious reasons. One of these is that being among the most intensely subjective of Rousseau's works, they have profited greatly from the changes in taste which are part of the legacy of the Romantic movement. Another is that through the play of imagination and the exploiting of sensory experience, they open up new ranges of sensibility and new styles of writing, and can be regarded, for example, as part of the background not only for Romanticism, but for the later Symbolist movement in literature. A third and more mundane reason for their impact, is that consisting as they do of short and self-contained passages of prose, they are easier to read and have a more immediate attraction than most of the other works.

This relative popularity carries with it, however, certain disadvantages. It means that they are often studied in the general perspective of literary history, as a convenient starting-point for various tendencies; or considered out of context in a rather abstract way, as a stock example of the reaction against the drier side of eighteenth-century literature, without very much thought for their special significance in the whole series of Rousseau's writings. Parts of them can certainly be appreciated and enjoyed in this way, for their intrinsic literary interest, but they cannot be understood as a whole without general knowledge of the *Dialogues*, and particular reference to certain historical circumstances relating to them.

One of the facts revealed by the *Dialogues* is Rousseau's increasing preoccupation with the need to ensure the survival of his autobiographical writings, so that posterity, at least, may have a portrait of the 'true' Rousseau on which to base its judgment, and be prevented from rejecting the doctrine through misunderstanding of its author. The measures taken to this end are the subject of an appendix to the *Dialogues* entitled *Histoire du précédent écrit*,[26] which records the placing of manuscript copies in the hands of the philosopher Condillac, and of one of Rousseau's English acquaintances, Brooke Boothby. More important than this, however, is the account in the same fragment of an incident which occurred on 24 February 1776, during a severe crisis of Rousseau's anguish.

On that day, acting in accordance with his belief in Providence, he tried to deposit the manuscript of the *Dialogues* on the High Altar of the cathedral of Notre-Dame. By doing this, he hoped that it would escape from his enemies, find an equitable judge, and be brought ultimately to the notice of the King himself. Part of the logic behind this action is, of course, that if Louis XVI, as the despotic head of the established society, could be moved to deliver a favourable judgment like that expressed in the text by the representative Frenchman, the conversion of the public would follow automatically on this act of royal will. In the event, Rousseau found the gates of the cathedral choir closed, barring him from the altar; and in a poignant passage he tells how, in the first moments of shock, he interpreted this discovery as a sign that God also was on the side of his enemies, until calmer reflection revealed to him that he had been expecting a personal miracle, against the principles of his own religious doctrine.

In itself, this famous incident, which is the last great 'revolution' in Rousseau's own career, may no doubt be thought of simply as part of a case-history of abnormality, and a subject for the alienist; but the psychological processes involved in it are the essential prelude to the *Rêveries*, because it is through them that he is at last brought face to face with the inevitability of resigning himself to the state of non-integration in existing society. It is this historical event, in short, which raises the problem of the general purpose of the *Rêveries*; and this must be dealt with before they can be appreciated in detail.

Part of the answer to this question is quite clear, and is expressed in the opening sentences of the first Promenade, where Rousseau registers his isolation from society as a simple fact, and goes on to say that all he can now do is to consider what he himself *is*, in this curious state of detachment. To this extent, therefore, we can say that the *Rêveries* have a declared and conscious purpose, as a study of the Self outside the social context. In this respect they are a supplement to the *descriptive* element in both the *Confessions* and the *Dialogues*, and another extension of actual philosophical enquiry, involving what Rousseau calls 'applying the barometer to his soul'.

Nevertheless, this does not show the whole of his intention, and does not explain, for example, the significance of the *form* of this allegedly formless work, or, indeed, the meaning of its title, except for the word 'solitaire'. It is evident that the title is chosen to introduce a record of experiences outside society, but why 'promeneur' and why 'reveries'? Briefly, the explanation is that these two terms express Rousseau's double view of himself in isolation, as representing natural man in both the 'primitive' and the 'evolved' sense. We know from other passages of his writings that walking was an occupation which tended to stimulate the free play of his mental faculties; but in this case, it has an additional significance as a mechanical activity orientated to the physical and sensory level of existence, whereas reverie involves much higher levels of existence and consciousness. Reverie, in fact, is not, as might be thought, a vague word denoting simply a passive surrender to feeling. It may be used in this way, but a passage of the *Dialogues* reveals that Rousseau also uses the term in a very precise and active sense, to indicate the deliberate use of the imagination under the direction of the principle of Self-Interest.[27] This is a way of attaining true individual satisfaction, in contrast to the more normal use of imagination in the social context, where, tending to serve the ends of Selfish Interest, it encourages the competitive spirit and feeds harmful passions such as jealousy. In other words, the conception of a 'solitaire' who is both 'promeneur' and 'rêveur' means that in this work we may expect to find not just a record of experience outside the social context, but an expression in personal terms of the *whole range* of experience guided by Self-Interest, which Rousseau has already indicated as lying outside the pale of existing and degenerate society; and including that of the primitive, that of the Lawgiver, and even, perhaps, that of the Christ-figure of the *Nouvelle Héloïse*.

What is particularly important about this aspect of reverie as the play of imagination directed by Self-Interest, is that it provides a key to the rest of Rousseau's intentions, which are not declared so explicitly at the beginning of the series of Promenades, but which include, besides the descriptive aim, a search for consolation through the favourable interpretation of given circumstances, and processes of mental adjustment to these circumstances. This suggests that once again Rousseau will be found rationalizing his position; and there is some evidence in his manuscript notes that he does so partly, at least, in accordance with the principles of psychological control in the abandoned project of *La Morale sensitive*.

From this point of view, the *Rêveries* can be considered as an exercise in practical Wisdom or *Sagesse*, resembling at the 'evolved' level the resignation shown in the attitude of the dying Julie, in the *Nouvelle Héloïse*; but corresponding also to the attitude of the primitive described in the *Discours sur l'origine de l'inégalité*, who, when he is the victim of aggression, does not struggle to fight back, but merely seeks a new refuge, which is readily available in the state of nature. Rousseau himself, faced, as he thinks, with the aggression of society, will seek such a refuge partly in the play of memory and imagination, including thoughts of some unspecified paradise of his own, and partly in reorganizing his mental world as a 'state of nature', in which he can reduce himself to a primitive and childlike state of moral neutrality. In this way, the whole range of his evolutionary thought is drawn upon in an attempt at mental evasion which constitutes his last systematic application of the principle of Self-Interest.

Before we examine more closely the product of these multiple aims, there is one other question which bears on the appreciation of the *Rêveries* as a whole. This is the problem of structure, and it arises because we are predisposed to think of them as a work which, by definition, has no coherent structure or plan. This opinion has several sources, the first of which is, obviously, Rousseau's own description of the work as an *informe journal*. The others are a natural tendency to think of reverie as a passive state contrasting with processes of conscious ratiocination, and the fact that in some cases, there was a considerable lapse of time between the composition of successive Promenades.

This view of the *Rêveries* as a work without a general structure is acceptable up to a point; but it is not the whole truth, and there is no reason why it should be, considering the ambiguity of Rousseau's intentions, and the way in which he himself uses the term reverie. Nobody would deny, for example, that he does allow his thoughts to meander; and that the taking of 'barometric readings' of the soul implies a kind of passivity. It is incontestable, moreover, that the literary and artistic importance of the *Rêveries* derives mainly from certain passages in which he is clearly attempting to liberate himself from the constraints of intellectual organization, in order to arrive at, and express, a state which is little more than pure consciousness of existence. Nevertheless, it must be pointed out that the conception of reverie as imagination directed by

Self-Interest does not rule out the possibility of a recognizable structure. So far is it from doing so, indeed, that even the most obviously systematic of Rousseau's writings, such as the political theory, can be, and often are, looked upon as reveries—usually, of course, in a pejorative sense.

The fact is, that while the *Rêveries* are not planned as a series, their undeclared tendency, which is to bring Rousseau to terms with the circumstances of his life as he sees them, results in a kind of undercurrent of logical relationships in the positions through which his mind wanders. This undercurrent runs through the whole set of Promenades, and while a grasp of it is not absolutely essential for an appreciation of Rousseau's art, it is by following its movement that we can most easily understand the relationship of the *Rêveries* to his other works. This movement does not, it must be added, imply a regular progression; what it does involve, throughout the series, is a pattern of changing emphasis on three or four leading themes or problems, some of which carry on directly from the *Dialogues*, and all of which, since they may disappear and reappear at almost any point, tend constantly to overlap.

The first of these themes, which gives an idea of what is most important to Rousseau in the first few Promenades, is provided by what may be called the problem of resignation. This is a recurring element in his philosophy, closely connected with the concept of Self-Interest, and offering the key to contentment, which is the nearest approach to absolute happiness in this life. Now, however, it has become the great practical and personal problem for Rousseau himself, left over, as it were, from the *Dialogues*; and it can be stated thus: Society has rejected him, and he must accept his state of isolation; but is he to accept it *de facto* or *de jure*? The principle of Self-Interest requires him to submit, since submission is a happier state than the continuation of futile struggling; but is he submitting, as does his primitive man, to the 'yoke of necessity', or, as does his enlightened man, to the 'yoke of reason'? In the event, he contrives, as we shall see, to have it both ways, a fact which illustrates what has been said already about the complete range of extra-social activity which is involved in the *Rêveries*.

What is really at issue, here as in the *Dialogues*, is whether Rousseau can accept society's rejection of him as an individual without repudiating a social philosophy which he has based upon himself. Previously he has been incapable of doing this; but now he can be seen reconciling the two things by a series of mental adjustments which, like the *Dialogues*, can be understood most easily in terms of the analogy of the General Will and the Lawgiver.

In the *Dialogues*, we have seen that he refuses the judgment of contemporary society, because he conceives it as something like a Will of All, or unanimous error, with himself as a kind of Lawgiver, willing and expressing the true interest of society through his philosophy, and representing also, presumably, the design of Providence. The reason why the incident of Notre-Dame is such an appalling shock to Rousseau, is that it seems a sign that God endorses the popular verdict on him. In his hypersensitive condition, the interpretation which his own system forces him to place upon this is that the *complot* is the expression not of a Will of All but of a General Will, in opposing which he has been mistaken as to his own ultimate good. He has, in fact, surrendered to Selfish Interest in expecting a special and personal miracle, and this, moreover, despite the fact that he is in the situation of a Lawgiver, and right by definition. Now we cannot, of course, claim to know exactly the thoughts of this tortured mind; but it seems clear that at this stage of his career, Rousseau is caught in a logical noose of his own making; and that while he is prepared, on reflection, to make the necessary adjustment of resignation, this inevitably puts him back, after all the effort of the *Confessions* and the *Dialogues*, into a position corresponding to that of the 'unintegrated' Saint-Preux, at the end of the *Nouvelle Héloïse*. The idea that for him there is no hope of integration in existing society, and little prospect of a favourable verdict from posterity, is an extremely bitter pill for Rousseau; and one of the most fascinating aspects of the earlier *Rêveries* is the light they throw on the stages of thought by which he finally brings himself to swallow it.

In the first Promenade, for example, where he attempts to take up a position of complete impassivity, he continues his ironical references to himself as a 'monster', and conceives his enemies as a whole misguided generation, determined unanimously to spit upon him and 'bury him alive'. In this, it would seem that he is still regarding the will of his generation as a Will of All; but in the same Promenade, following a line of thought in the *Dialogues*,[28] he also begins to look upon himself as a sacrifice to particular associations and influential groups within the 'generation', such as those of doctors and ecclesiastics, which he calls 'the associations which have conceived an aversion for me'. The thought that he is capitulating to groups of this kind is slightly less unpalatable, because having, as collective bodies, a continuity which individuals cannot have, they will transmit their hostility to subsequent generations of their own kind, so that there is less point in struggling against them.

At the end of the second Promenade, however, after allowing his mind to wander to completely different matters, Rousseau returns to this theme, and makes a further mental adjustment. He now chooses to regard his condemnation as an expression of the corporate will of the most powerful body within the community, i.e. the Government itself, which includes, apparently, all those who hold high office or direct public opinion. But this time, although he still considers the universal agreement as something too incredible to be fortuitous, he drops his original hypothesis of a purely human conspiracy, and accepts the whole situation as a manifestation of the Will of God, or, as he puts it, 'one of the secrets of Heaven, impenetrable to human reason'.

This process, which brings in successively the whole community or 'generation', the collective bodies, the Government and finally God, obviously sets up a hierarchy of wills, to which Rousseau contemplates the possibility of surrender; and in choosing to regard himself as bowing to the Divine Will, he just as clearly selects the mental position which is least offensive to his ego. This psychological manœuvre is an excellent example of what is involved in the direction of imagination by Self-Interest, which is essential to the concept of reverie; but the particular reasons why he can submit calmly to the Will of God are that, humanly speaking, submission is thereby completely 'depersonalized', and that the justice of God is a guarantee of indemnification in a life to come.

At this point, Rousseau is following the ways of consolation which are opened up by the *Profession de foi*; and as if to confirm this, there now follows a remarkable passage in which he makes a partial comparison between himself and Saint Augustine, who 'would gladly accept damnation if such were the will of God'. The point of this is that Rousseau who obviously cannot accept the idea of damnation in the ordinary hellfire sense, is here accepting instead the 'social damnation' which is, after all, a logical possibility in a scheme of thought which, from the beginning, has been concerned with an idea of 'social salvation'. What these passages show, in fact, is that far from having any thought of repudiating his philosophy (in spite of regrets over his literary career), Rousseau is now seeking to confirm it by making the supreme sacrifice of his hopes of present and normal integration; thus completing, as it were, the General Will of the society which has rejected him, in addition to acquiescing in the Will of God.

It is with thoughts of this kind that Rousseau's attempt to 'live' his philosophy passes beyond the stages of Confession and Judgment to a new phase, which commentators sometimes describe as martyrdom, but which might be more properly thought of as a pseudo-Crucifixion. In dealing with a scheme of fantasies as complex as those of the *Rêveries*, it is naturally difficult to say exactly what mental images or comparisons are involved; but there are certain textual indications, especially in the first Promenade, that Rousseau is now going through an imaginative process implying a mental identification with Christ. For example, the vision of himself being mocked, spat upon and buried alive by a whole generation (a generation of vipers?) may well be an adaptation of the Gospels; and some of his phraseology elsewhere—e.g. his 'Tout est fini pour moi sur la terre'—is probably inspired by Saint John's Gospel. In particular, the sentence 'Les hommes auraient beau revenir à moi, ils ne me retrouveraient pas' following upon the entombment theme already mentioned, is almost certainly inspired by the empty tomb of the Gospels, and by the passage in Saint John, chapter VII: 'Ye shall seek me, and shall not find me; and where I am, thither ye cannot come.'

The evidence on this point is not, indeed, conclusive; but it must be observed that a Rousseau-Christ analogy is completely in accordance with the Julie-Christ analogy in the *Nouvelle Héloïse*, and that it realizes a possibility which has been in Rousseau's system ever since his first attempt to re-think the Fall-and-Redemption tradition. It seems that sooner or later Rousseau must appear to himself as the incarnation of a new conception of Redemption; and this is certainly one of the most important of the ideas which are woven into the earlier *Rêveries*.

It is probably in accordance with this trend of thought that in the third Promenade, he goes on to review quite systematically his whole moral life, with the object of defending his moral philosophy, and recalling anew that the *Profession de foi* is its climax and ultimate gospel. And it is significant that whereas, following the line of the *Dialogues*, he has previously been proclaiming his *innocence*, he now reaffirms his *virtue*, thereby safeguarding his claim to morality and to its reward hereafter; and preparing the way to another phase of this spiritual adventure, which is the subject of a well-known passage at the end of the fifth Promenade. This passage, in which he describes his urge to communion with the 'celestial intelligences', is indicative of a kind of Ascension on the wings of imagination, and, as a complement to the entombment-theme of the first Promenade, has an obvious bearing on the Crucifixion analogy.

These four Promenades contain, of course, many other trains of thought, as Rousseau lets his mind wander; but if they are taken together on the basis of this theme of resignation and its consequences, they can be said to show the culmination of his social philosophy as it is worked out in his own life. As Lawgiver-Tutor, he has proclaimed the principles of the new society; as a 'Christ-figure', he has suffered a social death or crucifixion to establish the New Order; and the only duty which he now has left is that of abstention from further social activity. And whereas, up to this point, the thought of the *Rêveries* has been orientated mainly to the future, and ultimately to the paradise of integrity and fulfilment envisaged, for example, by the *vicaire savoyard*, it can now begin to move back towards the original state of nature.

This change of direction emphasizes once more the polarity which was noted at the very beginning of Rousseau's work; and brings us to the second major theme of the *Rêveries*, namely, that of Abstention and Disengagement. This is not always stated explicitly, but it serves to link together a number of Promenades which, on the surface, are quite independent. What happens is that following the only logical course which is open to him if he is to go on existing without suffering, he now goes through another series of meditations and mental adjustments, which tend to release him gradually from the various obligations and responsibilities of the social state. In the course of these changes of mental position, he appears to reduce himself deliberately to a kind of second childhood, becoming in effect the *vieux enfant* which he has already claimed to be in the self-portrait of the *Dialogues*; and as might be expected, this process resembles the movement of *Emile*, and, to some extent, of the *Discours sur l'origine de l'inégalité*, but this time in *reverse*.

Rousseau's idea that because of his rejection by society, he has no further obligation except to abstain from positive social action or thinking, appears as early as the first Promenade; but it is not until the fourth one that it can be seen in full operation. This is the well-known text containing the discussion of truth and falsehood, which has already been mentioned as a valuable guide to the appreciation of his autobiographical writings as a whole. By its distinction between General Truths and Particular Truths, and its insistence on the criterion of utility, it is a pragmatic theory bearing not only upon the *Confessions*, which Rousseau himself now seems to regard as a useful fiction or *fable* of his life, but also upon the play of public and private interest in his political theory. Its implications obviously extend far beyond the thought of the *Rêveries*, explaining, for example, the dangerous idea to be found in the *Contrat Social*, that the Lawgiver may occasionally deceive the public for its own good; but the discussion arises in the *Rêveries* because of

Rousseau's preoccupation with certain specific lies of his own. In the context, it is an aspect of his personal escape from the order of raw facts to that of imagination; and in so far as it tends to release him from a sense of guilt born of a conception of truth which he would claim to be purely social in origin, it can be considered as the initiation, on the *moral* plane, of the process of disengagement.

The next important manifestation of this urge to withdrawal occurs in the sixth Promenade, where Rousseau drifts into a comparable discussion of charity and almsgiving, to which he claims a natural inclination, but which he now begins to find intolerable, because in the social context, it is transformed into a kind of duty. This is a particularly interesting text, since it contains his last explicit use of the idea of contract. In this instance, the contract in question is the tacit understanding which, according to Rousseau, comes into being between the benefactor and the beneficiary when charity has once been bestowed; and which leads the beneficiary into a legitimate expectation that the benefaction will be repeated in the future. In other words, it is the benefactor rather than the beneficiary who finds himself gradually assuming the burden of obligation, so that in giving alms, he finds that he is no longer acting freely, or enjoying the satisfaction which is to be found in a natural and spontaneous act of charity. This passage is one of the most curious in the whole work, and can stand alone as a minor moral discussion of an aspect of the theme of social corruption; but, like the theory of truth, it has immediate relevance to the process of disengagement, since at the end of it we find that Rousseau has withdrawn from certain practical implications of the social tie, and taken up formally the position of 'abstention'. It contains, incidentally, the last reference to the Social Contract itself, and can be interpreted symbolically as a step towards Rousseau's definitive and formal withdrawal from the major engagement.

At first sight, there seems little common ground between this discussion of a specific social and moral question and the seventh Promenade which follows it, and where he writes of the pleasures of botanizing. These pleasures, he says, are so absorbing that they are tending to take the place of reverie itself, so that the collection of *rêves* is not likely to go on much longer.

This seventh Promenade is among the more rambling and complex ones, and is related to more than one of the major themes. Its first links with the movement of abstention and disengagement can be seen chiefly in a certain critical element, whereby Rousseau gradually develops a broad attack on the exploitation of nature for purposes connected with the Selfish Interest which is generated in society. Almost all the positions taken up in this criticism can be traced back directly to the early discourses; they include, for example, a condemnation of the excessive preoccupation with the medicinal properties of flowers and herbs; of the use of minerals for the production of superfluities; and especially, of the role of vanity and the competitive spirit in the cultivation of the sciences. It is this last element of criticism which reveals what Rousseau is really concerned with in this Promenade: namely, the fact that he is 'forced to abstain from *thinking*'. What he is now doing, in effect, is to follow up his withdrawal from *moral* commitments with a statement of his emancipation from the *intellectual* commitments of social life, in favour of the pure contemplation of nature for its own sake, and for the satisfaction of Self-Interest rather than Selfish Interest.

At this stage it is becoming increasingly clear that the dominating idea in his mind is simply that of his own return, mentally, to the state of nature and the original rule of Self-Interest, with its independence of conventional opinions. This process, however, is by no means complete; there is at least one other major social commitment which still has to be broken: namely, the tie of conscious *religious* obligation. We are not surprised, therefore, to find that Rousseau now moves on with inexorable logic (even in this 'unplanned' work) to a mental position which annuls this commitment and, in addition to carrying forward the theme of disengagement, completes at the same time the previous theme of resignation.

In the eighth Promenade, starting from a meditation on the disproportion which he has experienced in life between the outward signs of wellbeing and the actual inner feelings of well-being, he concludes that his ability to find consolation in adversity comes from having learned to be self-sufficient, and to bear the 'yoke of necessity' without complaint. His views on this subject are, in fact, simply a restatement of the interpretation of Self-Interest which provides the guiding principle in the first books of *Emile*; and he goes on, inevitably, to apply this principle to his own present state of isolation. And whereas in the first Promenades he has gradually brought himself to submit to Providence or the will of heaven, which is the act of an enlightened and *moral* being, he now takes the final logical step. Making the only move remaining open to one who has in the meantime contracted out of the social and moral state, he chooses to regard his submission not as being made to the Will of God, but as a resignation to 'blind necessity'. In other words, having

previously capitulated *de jure*, as an enlightened leader, he now puts his
capitulation on a purely *de facto* basis, as a 'primitive'. And when this
happens, rather more than three-quarters of the way through the
Rêveries, we can say that his mental world is becoming almost void of
any social or moral content.

Nevertheless, he is still in the world, and surrounded physically by
other men who, he would claim, have broken the Social Contract with
him; and the question arises: what is he to do about them? The answer
is short, simple, and completely logical; as a measure of self-defence,
Rousseau 'depersonalizes' them, and chooses to regard them from now
on not as men, but as 'mechanical beings' or mere physical masses,
moving about in different ways, but deprived of any moral nature, so
far as he is concerned. From this moment, with the reduction of the rest
of humanity to the status of physical phenomena only, the Social Contract is at an end for Jean-Jacques Rousseau, and with it, all its moral,
intellectual and religious implications. Having previously asserted his
superior enlightenment as Lawgiver and even as Christ-figure, he has
now become in imagination the natural primitive, living, or rather
existing, at the level of pure *sensation*.

Even this, however, is not quite the end of this process of mental
adjustment; and the eighth Promenade brings up yet another problem
facing Rousseau in his effort to accept voluntarily the conditions of
isolation or 'living death'. In spite of his attempt to reduce the human
beings around him to moral nullity, society still has a last hold on him
through the senses themselves. Dominated, as he now claims to be, by
the senses, he cannot escape entirely from the inward effect of physical
gestures or appearances indicating hostility. Even at the level of sensation, a 'sinister' look or a 'venomous' tone of speech are enough to upset
his equilibrium. His only defences against this kind of unwelcome
sensation are, first, to escape from human contacts and into the paradise
of nature, whenever this is possible; and secondly, to use the body itself
as a sort of combined shock-absorber and safety-valve, by allowing
himself the luxury of *emportements*: i.e. by giving free *physical* rein to
feelings of anger and indignation, until physiological processes themselves bring about a restoration to a state of calm.

This ultimate technique of self-preservation is obviously related to
some of Rousseau's views on infant behaviour in the first book of
Emile[29]; and so we can say that by the end of the eighth Promenade, he
has in thought 'become as little children'—a point which may well, of
course, prompt some interesting reflections on his views on entry into

the Kingdom of Heaven. And it is almost as a direct confirmation of this urge towards the childlike state that in the ninth Promenade, Rousseau's thoughts begin to run on the subject of children; although the immediate cause of this is doubtless the desire to exorcize the remaining socially-inspired feelings of guilt over the abandonment of his own offspring. The main effort of this reverie is directed almost inevitably, it would seem, to persuading the reader that he has never really been an 'unnatural father', and that his works show him to be essentially a lover of children. This leads him to efface the memory of the Foundling Hospital with recollections of acts of natural benevolence to children; to proclaim twice his own childlike condition; and to make a last attempt at restoring his sense of human contact at the child's level by the remembrance of an impromptu scene of festivity, when he had caused wafers to be distributed to a crowd of little girls, to their general and uninhibited joy. This is Rousseau's last and curiously pathetic application of the theme of public rejoicing—the *fête publique* which recurs throughout his work, and which we have seen, for example, in the wine-harvest of the *Nouvelle Héloïse*.

Now although there are, as has been said, many other currents of thought in the *Rêveries*, there can be little doubt that in examining the themes of resignation and disengagement we have seen the two main trends of the whole series, one of which shows Rousseau aiming, as it were, beyond the Social Contract, and claiming his place among the celestial intelligences; while the other shows him contracting out of a society in which he has no further function to perform, and aspiring to complete his earthly existence at a childlike or primitive level, in his mental 'state of nature'. As it stands, however, this second train of thought would leave him in a neutral state of abstention; and it is at this point that we must take account of the third major movement of the *Rêveries*, which is concerned above all with active and positive integration in nature. The difference between this and what has gone before, is that the negative contracting-out of society is superseded by a more positive attempt to lose all sense of personal identity, and to merge into the system of nature through the deliberate exploitation of sensory experience in a process of self-hypnotism. In so far as this implies some deliberate act of the will, it can be considered as Rousseau's final attempt to contract in to nature; although looked at from another point of view, it is at the same time a substitute for what, in a more orthodox religious context, would be mystical contemplation.

The main reason why this third movement is so important, is that it involves direct linguistic transcription of states of feeling at different levels of consciousness. It cannot, in fact, be thought of as a 'theme' in any strict sense, because it is made up of unconnected passages in which Rousseau is no longer rationalizing his position, or, indeed, thinking 'about' anything at all. What he is doing is to record his attempts to transcend the normal limits of mental experience, and synthesize in one comprehensive state of feeling the antithetical movements of the other themes, with their respective tendency towards the celestial and the primitively physical states. It is, needless to say, because of this expression of abnormal awareness that the *Rêveries* are a landmark, from both the literary and psychological points of view.

In the series as a whole, the movement can be traced back to the second Promenade where, having described an accidental collision with a dog, in which he was knocked down and rendered unconscious, Rousseau records, in a famous passage, the delicious sensations which accompanied his return to consciousness. He tells how, aware only of the sky, a few stars and some foliage, he seemed to fill these things with his own floating existence, without any precise sense of time, place, or personal identity. This particular experience is, of course, an involuntary one, but in the text of the *Rêveries*, it is the prelude to accounts of deliberate attempts to induce artificially a comparable trance-like condition, of which the best-known is in the fifth Promenade. In this text, Rousseau recalls his short stay on the island of Saint-Pierre, on the Lake of Bienne, during the early days of his persecution and wandering; and tells how he would take a boat, allow it to drift on the lake, and, lying back with his eyes on the sky, gradually lose himself in a delicious reverie; or how, alternatively, he would sit on the bank and let the lapping of the water induce a similar state, from which he would awaken, not to raw reality, but to a mingled experience of reality and imagination.

It is with recollections of such *extases*, which give a new depth to the notion of reverie, and which are based initially upon sense-experience, that Rousseau develops in this work the possibility of identification with, and absorption in the whole system of nature. There is a striking expression of this aspiration in the seventh Promenade, and one which could provide also, incidentally, an interesting comment on the tendencies of his political thought.

Plus un contemplateur a l'âme sensible, plus il se livre aux extases qu'excite en lui cet accord. Une rêverie douce et profonde s'empare alors de ses sens, et il se perd avec une délicieuse ivresse dans l'immensité de ce beau système avec lequel il se sent identifié. Alors tous les objets particuliers lui échappent; il ne voit et ne sent rien que dans le tout.[30]

The eighth Promenade also continues this train of thought, as Rousseau writes of his ability to find an earthly paradise in escaping from his fellow-men and abandoning himself to the sensuous enjoyment of nature. It seems, however, that this level of awareness cannot be sustained; for there is already, in the seventh Promenade, an admission that with age he is becoming incapable of his former ecstasies, and that as his ideas are reduced more and more to pure sensations (this again reversing the theory of development in *Emile*), so the sphere of awareness tends to be reduced to the immediate environment. For this reason, just as the movement of disengagement breaks down to some extent in the ninth Promenade, with the regretful and pathetic recollection of the children's *fête*, the effort to transcend or lose the sense of personal identity also seems to weaken, after producing some of the most remarkable passages of writing to be found in eighteenth-century literature.

These, then, are the three main currents, or undercurrents, which enable us to obtain some sense of direction in these complex *Rêveries*: the resignation of a potential 'celestial intelligence' to the Will of God; the withdrawal of an intact 'primitive' to his state of nature; and the seeking and enjoyment of a new and synthetic form of experience, in a kind of sensual mysticism. And at this point it is difficult to see what else there is left for Rousseau to say in the *Rêveries*, since he has now finally rationalized his position, done what he can to 'redeem' himself, in terms of his own doctrine, and recorded the essentials of his extra-social experience. In the circumstances, it is hardly surprising that the impending breakdown of the *Rêveries*, which is mentioned at the beginning of the seventh Promenade, should now take place in the fragmentary tenth; leaving us to consider, as a final problem, whether Rousseau actually intended the work to end as it does.

On this point, the only evidence is that of the text itself; but analysis of it suggests that its apparently 'unfinished' state is, after all, the logical outcome of the complex process, involving life and thought, which has been going on since the beginning of the *Confessions*. In this last text, Rousseau seems to confirm his inability to maintain himself at any extreme of the positions which he has taken up on the preceding Promenades. He may wish to exist at the level of pure sensation, or at some transcendental level of enlightenment, or to combine the two; but he has always to contend with certain ineffacable memories of his real past. In this situation, the logic of Self-Interest requires that he should select what can be safely remembered without suffering; and it is no doubt in accordance with his guiding principle, that in this Promenade he returns through imagination and memory to his youth, and to his Golden Age with Mme de Warens, now fifty years behind him. Rousseau's farewell to writing is, therefore, a last evocation of his stay at Les Charmettes, when he was, as he says, more than free; and when, having both love and innocence, he was in a state of maximum earthly happiness.

The story might end here, with Rousseau safe at last in the haven of his happier memories; and it is, in fact, sometimes made to end thus, in a dream of golden days with *Maman*. Possibly, however, this is not quite the end; because unfortunately, even in imagination and memory, it seems that he cannot 'fix' himself firmly in his Golden Age. The processes of memory tend to lead him, inevitably, to experience again in the mind the collapse of the relationship, and of the idyll which his imagination had woven around Les Charmettes. It is significant, therefore, that the ultimate train of thought in the *Rêveries* peters out, precisely, at the very brink of a relapse into unhappy memories, which, if he were to follow them, could only lead him back again into his Fall, and over the ground already covered in the *Confessions*.

Technically, there is more than one way of interpreting the last mental position of Rousseau. It may indicate simply a drawing back from a new Fall in imagination; or it may, on the other hand, express the breaking of another and most powerful social tie, namely, that of remembered love. This latter interpretation is supported, on the whole, by the last sentence, where Rousseau can be found thinking in terms of the reciprocal obligation which even the relationship with Mme de Warens had imposed upon him, and which he had hoped to fulfil, he says, by making his fortune. But in any case, and whichever technical interpretation we may put upon it, the tenth Promenade undoubtedly stops at the point where the logic of Self-Interest is worked out. Consequently, it may be suggested (making a point which will come up again in connection with the art of Rousseau) that the last act of disengagement in the *Rêveries* is the abstention even from thinking of the past, and certainly from writing about it. The last paradox in Rousseau's works is, indeed, that they end without being 'concluded', leaving the reader with the uncanny conviction that their author is allowing himself to be 'extinguished', like the primitive man conceived so long before in the second of the discourses.

This is why it is difficult to conclude an exposition of his major writings otherwise than by saying that Rousseau has *lived out* the problem of the philosopher, which for him is, of course, the problem of the Outsider; and that in doing so he completes his public doctrine of Self-Interest by exemplary personal action of a kind which fulfils both the *naturel ardent* and the *naturel indolent* which this ambulating dreamer distinguishes within himself.

CHAPTER X

The Problem of the Artist

*

THE *Rêveries* must, by any standards, rank among the most significant works of their century. Not only do they reveal in a most intimate way the last stages of a dynamic process involving the thinker and the man, but, in offering a new kind of literary experience, they lead naturally into what may be called the third dimension of Rousseau studies—that of art. And here, new questions arise, which must be thought about before one can have anything like a rounded view of him.

There are two ways of approaching Rousseau as an artist. The first is to relate him to the general tendencies of his age, and to pick out certain obvious characteristics like the subjective element or the feeling for nature, on the strength of which he can be consigned to some appropriate category of literary history, which usually turns out to be the one labelled *Pre-romanticism*. The other way is to look at his work from the inside, and try to see *why* he displays these characteristics: to enquire, in fact, how the form of his writings is conditioned by his ideas and experiences.

This second approach is infinitely preferable, because for Rousseau himself art is a problem—an acute personal problem, which he has 'lived', not only as a writer, but as a composer, seeking to express himself in music. It is, moreover, an urgent philosophical problem, because almost at the outset of his career he takes up a Platonic position involving a theoretical condemnation of art, as an important factor in the process of social degeneration, if not, indeed, as an intrinsically worthless or 'inauthentic' activity. These facts alone suggest that the question of Rousseau as artist is highly complex; and that it must include at least two major issues: namely, the social justification of art, and the quest for personal fulfilment. Everything points, indeed, to the likelihood of discovering in this connection a double orientation, similar to the public and private aspects of his philosophy in general; yet this dualism is not always recognized. This is probably because his aesthetic doctrines are not easily assimilated as a whole, being scattered in various works, including secondary ones such as the *Essai sur l'origine des langues*, the *Lettre sur les spectacles*, and articles in his *Dictionnaire de musique*. Before considering Rousseau as a writer, it may, therefore, be useful to trace briefly the development of his critical and constructive ideas on art and aesthetics in general.

The premise from which all his discussion of the subject derives is the premise of Deism, that the Creation is not only good but beautiful, in that it is an *order*, revealing harmony and proportion. This thesis is expressed by Saint-Preux, in the twelfth letter of the *Nouvelle Héloïse*.

> J'ai toujours cru que le bon n'était que le beau mis en action, que l'un tenait intimement à l'autre, et qu'ils avaient tous deux une source commune dans la nature bien ordonnée.[31]

In consideration of this idea, it is almost inevitable that, preaching conformity to nature, Rousseau will at some point appeal to aesthetic as well as moral feeling. The other fundamental element in his public doctrine is the thoroughly 'classical' belief that art is imitation; and if the two principles are juxtaposed, it follows for Rousseau that if art can be good at all, its goodness will be in the imitation of nature; and this he affirms in Book IV of *Emile*.[32] On the other hand, his interpretation of the Fall of Man as a rejection of nature implies, amongst other things, that men have turned their backs on beauty, and that the arts cannot be exempted from the general charge of corruption. In terms of the typical vicious circle, they both corrupt and are corrupted by society; and this idea is the basis of a critical doctrine which offers close parallels to the religious thought. It is developed in general terms in the two early discourses; and particularized with reference to the theatre, in the *Lettre sur les spectacles*, and to language and music in the *Essai sur l'origine des langues*. Like most of Rousseau's critical thought, this phase of his philosophy of art can be set out in the quasi-historical framework established by the *Discours sur l'origine de l'inégalité*.

The first stage relates, of course, to the original state of nature. Here, there is no art as such, since life is passive and art is active; but what can be postulated are four factors providing the conditions for aesthetic experience and artistic expression. The first is sensory experience, which allows an immediate response to the environment, although reason and imagination are not yet operating. The second is the existence of prerational instincts. In his discourse, Rousseau mentions only those of self-preservation and compassion; but in the *Lettres sur les spectacles*, he maintains that 'the love of beauty is as natural to the human heart as the love of oneself'; and later, in *Emile*, he will formalize this into a 'natural taste'. Even in man's most primitive response to his environment there is, it seems, a vague awareness of beauty. The third factor, which is also noted in Book IV of *Emile*, is the capacity for imitation, seen in animals as well as in man; and the fourth is the instinct of communication, described in such terms as 'the cry of nature'. All these factors will appear in a 'rationalized' form in the constructive phase of Rousseau's aesthetics.

The next stage relates to the Golden Age, when the arts begin to develop in step with man's evolving social consciousness. The factors now coming into play include the sense of time, which is measured initially (according to the *Origine des langues*[33]) in terms of boredom and amusement; and then a rudimentary sense of values, moral and aesthetic, based upon the comparisons which are inevitable in the social state. As he puts it in the second discourse, men acquire, without being aware of it, ideas of merit and beauty which give rise to feelings of preference; and this is the beginning of Taste as a social phenomenon.

As for art itself as a creative activity, Rousseau's ideas on its origin are not absolutely clear, but he seems to ascribe a priority to visual art. In his *Origine des langues*, painting is said to be nearer to nature,[34] and to be more individual than music, which is conceived as more 'human' and certainly more social in its operation. Rousseau's personal interest in music reveals itself in the second discourse, through the idyllic evocation of simple gatherings round a tree, when 'singing and dancing, true children of love and leisure, became the amusement, or rather the occupation of men and women brought together in idleness'.[35] This primitive use of the theme of the *fête publique* and vision of collective hedonism is particularly noteworthy for the distinction between *amusement* and *occupation*, which, as we shall see, may have some bearing on the concluding phase of Rousseau's own activity as a writer; and there are two other points of interest. One is that in such evocations of the past, although the mood seems to be conditioned by a joyful response to the beauty of nature, there may already be a conventional and arbitrary element tending to break away from imitation. The other is that the pleasure involved is communal and reciprocal; and this implies that while the entertainment factor in art is beginning to emerge, it has not yet become a specialized activity on the basis of individual skill.

Now all this is highly speculative, but Rousseau is approaching a point in his doctrine where he can expect more criticism, and where his readers may well demand less hypothesis and more history. What he now does, consciously or unconsciously, is to graft on to the stock of

RN

Golden Age philosophies which he has been exploiting, a newer body of opinion, and work on under the protection of the defenders of antiquity in the famous controversy of the Ancients and Moderns. He does, of course, sincerely admire the simplicity and sublimity of classical art, as he admires what he conceives to be the spirit of Sparta or the virtue of republican Rome; but at the same time, he contrives to exploit existing sympathies, in the awkward transition from hypothesis to history.

The third stage of Rousseau's criticism of the arts covers their degeneration in the social or pseudo-social state, as an accompaniment of social, political and economic distinctions, and as a form of *luxury*, which again enables him to exploit the feelings stirred up by another of the great controversies of his century. In a note to the second discourse, he sums up bluntly the whole process, observing that from society and the luxury it engenders are born the liberal and mechanical arts, commerce, letters and other useless things, which, by encouraging industry, first enrich, but finally destroy states. At this point, the arts are seen as deviating from the utilitarian function, discernible in the Golden Age, of providing a *general* satisfaction; and the entertainment factor is conceived as being directed towards the few rather than the whole community. Moreover, the artist, in becoming a 'specialist', is deemed to have lost some awareness of his basic humanity; and this leads Rousseau to emphasize the distinction between agreeable arts and useful arts, i.e. fundamental skills such as agriculture, which minister to the real needs of the whole community, and are more or less legitimate, in that they involve the principle of Self-Interest in the original sense of subsistence. From a rational point of view, it is to such necessary skills that public esteem ought to be accorded; and it is an indication of perversity that existing society does not distribute rewards on this basis, but favours the 'useless' arts.

Part of Rousseau's doctrine, to be found in *Emile*,[36] goes on to deal with reasons for this discrepancy, and it may seem that he is sacrificing the discussion of art to other considerations; but in fact, it leads him to certain ideas which are very relevant, and make up what may be called for convenience a Theory of Talent. This concerns the application of particular artistic skills, not for subsistence or for genuine aesthetic pleasure, but for the acquisition and storing of surplus value, on the basis of scarcity—in other words, as 'business', which substitutes for the artist's free enjoyment of his art a servile dependence upon the opinion of others. Rousseau's objection to contemporary artistic culture rests largely on the belief that it is the product of Talent, giving a corrupt public what it wants and operating competitively for reasons of vanity or gain. And the way to achieve these ends in the inauthentic society is to flatter the rich, the powerful, and the patronizing class generally. If these people approve, the rest will follow like sheep.

Although he is held back by his hedonism from the outright rejection of all art, he does castigate artists in general for misapplying their talents in the service of a despotic society, for adding useless ornament to the façade of legitimacy, and, as he expresses it in the first Discourse, for spreading garlands of flowers over the iron chains with which men are loaded.[37] In this process, art has become a profession, and cleverness and technique have replaced true integrity of vision as a source of esteem. The art of antiquity may seem relatively pure; but as society moves further from nature, so art degenerates into artifice, and acts increasingly as a screen between men and nature, offering only what Rousseau calls, in the same discourse, 'images of all the aberrations of the heart and of reason'.[38]

These opinions, most of which can be found in the discourses, are expanded and applied in various ways, notably in the *Origine des langues*,[39] and polemical works attacking the conventions of French music, and extolling natural melody at the expense of arbitrary and 'intellectual' harmonic systems. The observations on the Paris opera in Part II of the *Nouvelle Héloïse*[40] are a typical sample of Rousseau's criticism; and it is in Book IV of *Emile* that he finds a formula to sum up the sense of his doctrine. What he now finds in the arts, he says, is not the beauty of nature, but a *beau de fantaisie, sujet au caprice et à l'autorité*,[41] which is merely that which pleases those who guide us; and what he finds particularly galling is the protection and encouragement given to bad taste through 'political' institutions such as the *Académie Française*, the *Académie des Inscriptions*, and the Opera itself. And so, with observations of this kind, his critical doctrine comes to a conclusion which can be seen to tally exactly with the moral and political thought at the corresponding stage, and to pose the same kind of problems.

One of these clearly concerns the empirical value of his criticism; and few people, presumably, would endorse all of his pronouncements: for example, his views on the art of antiquity, or the implication of a steady degeneration. On the other hand, it is possible to sympathize with his dislike of academic art, or the system of patronage; and there are some specific aspects of the art, and particularly the literature of the period, such as the pornographic novel, or the licentious fantasies of *conteurs* of the Crébillon type, which might allow us to go part of the way with Rousseau, if his criticism is fairly presented in its historical context.

The real test of sympathy is imposed, however, by the implications with regard to artists, literary or otherwise, whose genius is confirmed by common consent, but who are exposed to censure by the logical application of Rousseau's doctrine. For example, he does not hesitate, when occasion demands, to criticize not only contemporary figures like the composer Rameau, or Voltaire, but also Molière, Racine and La Fontaine. In *Emile*, La Fontaine's *Fables* incur disapproval because the moral element is obscured by the art; and in the *Lettre sur les spectacles*, two of France's greatest playwrights are accused of compromising their genius by giving a false moral emphasis, the one in *Le Misanthrope*, and the other in *Bérénice*.[42] While not actually denying the great gifts of these writers, Rousseau does imply, in his *Discours sur les sciences et les arts*, that they have sought to satisfy short-term ambition rather than long-term interest, preferring present applause to lasting glory.[43]

Since posterity has not sided with him, it is usual to gloss over these opinions as pure paradox-mongering, or as the aberrations of a humourless and hypersensitive misfit with no sense of proportion; but they are certainly consistent, and have at least a negative value in posing anew some genuine problems: e.g. that of art as entertainment; and the question of how far and in what circumstances the artist can meet the public without sacrificing his integrity. Furthermore, Rousseau's criticism is of considerable interest in suggesting, in aesthetics as well as politics, the possibility of 'unanimous error'; and the belief that immediate public acclaim is not in itself a criterion of value. There are, obviously, some absurdities in the doctrine; but it is not wholly vitiated even by the ill-advised singling-out of a Molière or a La Fontaine for criticism; and it has at least that challenging and radical quality which is apt to lead, sooner or later, to a genuine renewal. The manner of renewal depends, however, on the constructive thought which follows the criticism; and it is this phase of Rousseau's philosophy of art that we must now consider, bearing in mind that his own writings must be deeply affected by it.

At this turning-point in his thought, Rousseau is confronted in this field as elsewhere by two possibilities in the application of the principle of returning to nature. One is to turn back in the direction of primitive life; the other is to press on and complete an aesthetic development comparable to the moral and political developments envisaged in other aspects of the system. In this instance, he does, in fact, contrive some sort of outlet for primitivism even in his public doctrine, by insisting that his Emile should be taught a manual skill, rather than be allowed to dabble prematurely in the arts.[44] This absorbs some implications of that part of his critical doctrine which concerns useful arts and agreeable arts; but it also leaves him free to deal with the future of the latter on the assumption that, like society itself, they have come to stay.

What can now be expected is some attempt to purify art of its in-authenticities born of Selfish Interest, and to move through the mech-anism of contract, in the direction of a true love of beauty or *amour du beau*, which in this context is the appropriate variant of *amour de soi*. But can art be treated thus? It may be argued that it is too personal in all aspects, whether of creation or communication, to be capable of this kind of rationalization; and with this view, Rousseau himself would certainly sympathize. Nevertheless, art is also a social phenomenon, and since its future is to some extent a social matter, its regeneration must take account of those factors which have developed in the social state— for example, reason, morality or imagination. The problem is, in fact, to restore art to its true function, which is to give pleasure—but it must be an appropriate *kind* of pleasure. From the social standpoint imposed by history, there cannot be a simple rejection of all moral con-tent, and a return to a 'primitive' and purely sensuous pleasure; what is required is a social equivalent, involving the satisfaction of all our developed faculties, intellectual and moral, as well as physical, and to which Rousseau gives the rather confusing name of *volupté*. This highly evolved form of pleasure is an individual response, but it meets the re-quirements of the situation in so far as it draws upon man's accumulated social experience. Without probing too deeply into the concept of *volupté* (which obviously 'expands' according to the degree of enlighten-ment), it is enough, for the moment, to say that Rousseau now confronts a question calling for exploration from two sides. With regard to the general public, it poses the problem of *appreciation*; with regard to the individual artist, it poses that of *creation*. What they share, however, is a need of liberation from the constraints of the false society; and it is this common need which could lead in the direction of 'contract'. It is not surprising, therefore, that from this point, Rousseau's thought bifurcates again to produce, in his scattered writings on the subject, two main lines of constructive thought, dealing respectively with *Taste* and *Genius*.

Rousseau's reflections on taste, the best of which are in the article 'Goût' in his *Dictionnaire de Musique*, and in the fourth book of *Emile*, rest partly on a vague belief in eternal aesthetic values; more particularly on the view that if art is a social phenomenon, society has a right, if not to dictate to the artist, at least to judge his works; and also on the utilitarian notion that such judgments must express the greatest pleasure of the greatest number. This last aspect is discussed in the article 'Goût', where, recognizing that tastes differ, Rousseau makes a characteristic distinction between the particular and the general. Particular tastes reflect the diversity of temperament and physical organization in individuals; but in any collection of normally sensitive and reasonably educated people, there will emerge a general agreement as to the relative value of works of art; and it is to this consensus of opinion that he gives the name of Taste. It is not absolute, of course, in any logical sense, but is determinable by the counting of votes. Taste, in fact, is a majority opinion, and as such can be deemed to reflect the satisfaction of the greatest number. But the question now turns on whether it expresses the *greatest* satisfaction of the greatest number; and this, of course, means for Rousseau that it must involve the right *sort* of satisfaction.

That part of his critical doctrine which includes disapproval of Molière and Racine implies, as we have seen, a mistaken majority opinion amounting virtually to unanimous error; and it is in dealing with this problem that, in Book IV of *Emile*,[45] he finally and formally differentiates the possible kinds of satisfaction as *volupté* and *vanité*, in order to distinguish between a valid and an invalid majority vote. That which is based on *volupté* is Good Taste; the other is merely Fashion (*la mode*); and while the first reflects a genuine and durable pleasure, the second, i.e. the response of vanity, is by its nature transitory and self-defeating. There always has to be a latest fashion.

Rousseau believes that either kind of satisfaction may determine the public response to art; and that the predominance of one or the other depends largely, though not exclusively, upon the social organization. Thus, in the conditions of inequality associated with the false or despotic society, it is Fashion which prevails, on a basis of social prestige; and a majority verdict thus obtained, apart from defeating its own ends, has no more aesthetic validity than the Will of All, to which it obviously bears strong resemblance, has political validity. It is evident, indeed, that at this stage Rousseau's doctrine is on the point of producing a distinction between a General Taste and a Taste of All, by analogy with the political theory. Yet he does not actually push it to this conclusion, because his sense of reality warns him that the cases are not quite comparable. The *amour du beau*, unlike *amour de soi*, does not include the principle of actual self-preservation; and aesthetic experience is not a universal necessity. It is, moreover, so individual in certain aspects, that Good Taste can never really be thought of as having the absolute authority of the General Will. And so, Rousseau draws a line at a point corresponding to the provisional acceptance of majority opinion in the politics of the new state, and accepts, as the nearest approximation to authority in aesthetic judgment, a majority opinion conditional upon an appropriate degree and form of enlightenment, deriving in this case from *volupté*.

There is, therefore—*mutatis mutandis*—a remarkable correlation between his aesthetics and his political thought; and one is hardly surprised to encounter now a familiar kind of problem: namely, that of ensuring the predominance of *volupté* over *vanité*, and of Good Taste over Fashion. This is undoubtedly a danger-point in the scheme, offering the temptation to invoke a censorship, or establish some kind of party-line or aesthetic dictatorship; but Rousseau avoids the trap, as indeed he must, since his own criticisms are directed largely against 'official culture'. He holds, certainly, that as far as the public is concerned, Good Taste can only be maintained through education—but it must be remembered that by education he means, not mass indoctrination, but a process of natural development. He clings, therefore, to the optimistic belief that in a normally intelligent and sensitive individual brought up on the principles of *Emile* and preserved from the social vanities, the *goût naturel* will develop smoothly into *bon goût*, through a sort of aesthetic conscience, more or less as innocence develops into virtue. In short, if there is no tyrannizing of taste, the truly valuable will in practice receive a valid majority vote made up of authentic *personal* judgments; and public opinion can be deemed to possess the greatest degree of authority compatible with the freedom of art.

This is very important because, although Rousseau does not make the point explicitly in *Emile*, what is implied here is the public contribution to a kind of tacit convention which the artist could respect without any sacrifice of real liberty or integrity. We have once more, in fact, a glimpse of the contract idea, even in aesthetics. It may be protested, of course, that any convention is offensive to the 'free' artist; but on Rousseau's premises this would be countered by saying that even the artist is a citizen, with certain social obligations concerning, for example, morality; and that in any case, an artist who refuses any concession to public Good Taste is limiting the possibilities of communication, and so destroying for himself some part of the pleasure of art. We are not under any obligation to think like Rousseau; but whether we sympathize or not, one thing is now clear: that in aesthetics as in other fields, he is preaching a New Order, the authenticity of which is expressed, from the public standpoint, in the replacement of Fashion by Good Taste.

A number of comments can be made here, by way of evaluation of his thought. First, the tendency of this part of his doctrine is to 'democratize' art; secondly, although there is a certain extravagance in his critical doctrine, this phase of his constructive thought is expressed with considerable delicacy, and in a liberal spirit which deserves to be remembered as a counterweight to the more unfavourable interpretations of Rousseauism. And a third point, arising from this, is that the doctrine is not, after all, incompatible with the traditions of classicism. Where it differs, as in the attempt to qualify the principle of universal consent, it is in the direction of refinement rather than violent revolution. Yet Rousseau is thought of as a father of Romanticism, and as the operator of great changes in literature. This seeming paradox is, of course, explainable partly by his own creative writing, and partly through the other side of his doctrines concerning art—the aspect which relates to Genius.

The word *génie* is used by Rousseau in various ways; and often to express individuality, or the fundamental integrity of the Self. In relation to the arts, its use is determined partly by this interpretation, partly by the need to describe a new kind of artist, and partly by the desire to explore the creative aspect of art, where the writ of mere taste is obviously inadequate. He observes that taste is a faculty of discrimination, necessary and legitimate enough as the most liberal form of social sanction where art is concerned, but that it has nothing to do with creation. The creative gift is quite special and personal; and there is nothing in his theory of good taste, apart from the vague principle of imitating nature, which could lead to actual 'rules' for the artist. On the contrary, if the validity of public taste depends ultimately on authentic individual judgments, the obvious complement to this is an equally personal experience or effort on the part of the artist. Public taste may condemn an artist's work retrospectively, but it is the essence of Rousseau's belief concerning the true artist, that he has not only the right, but the obligation to express his personal response to nature, and experiment along the lines of his own sensibility. If he does not, he is merely reflecting other men's experience; and it would seem that for Rousseau, no amount of technical skill can compensate for this lack of integrity in inspiration.

It is evident that his new order in the arts would involve, as a complement to the change in the public attitude from the rule of fashion to the rule of taste, some corresponding legitimization of the artist. He does not work this idea up into a formal theory; but the trend of his thought is clear enough, and can be expressed simply, for the sake of discussion, as a distinction between the Man of Talent and the Genius. There are some disturbing implications in this line of thought; it tends to suggest, for example (but quite consistently with the critical doctrine), that the Racines, the Molières and so on, must be thought of as no more than men of talent. Nevertheless, it does show one of the ways in which Rousseau is a herald of Romanticism. In all aspects of his thought, he postulates an ideal man of genius, and represents a vital stage in the process by which, during the eighteenth century, the Genius emerges as a new social ideal, replacing the *honnête homme*, the courtier, and other famous figures in this gallery, to become, in the next century, the object of a romantic cult. Rousseau is not the initiator of this movement, and he has, perhaps, less to say on the subject than some contemporaries—Diderot, for example; but his influence is very great because, like so much in his philosophy, this is an idea that he has lived.

It is useless to expect from Rousseau a rationalization of Genius on the lines of his theory of taste; and the simplest way to see why, is to read the short article 'Génie', in his *Dictionnaire de Musique*, which begins:

Ne cherche point, jeune artiste, ce que c'est que le génie. En as-tu, tu le sens en toi-même. N'en as-tu pas, tu ne le connaîtras jamais.

The most that can be done here is to pick out a few characteristics, as conceived by Rousseau's enthusiasm. One of them is the idea of leadership or guidance; the true Genius is, in general, a *précepteur du genre humain*,[46] supplied by nature (or Providence, according to the point of view) for the good of all. So far as art is concerned, this implies a power of initiation capable of leading public taste in the direction of nature, the eternal values, and *volupté*, in contrast to the tendency of talent, which is to *follow* the dictates of fashion. A second requirement to which Rousseau's system points, is a superiority of moral insight; and a third, more relevant to art, is sensibility, or the capacity for a strong emotional response to nature, and to life in all its aspects. This attribute is particularly important because, whereas taste operates, on the whole, as part of the public response to art, and usually at the level of 'small-scale' values such as subtlety of arrangement or elegance, sensibility is associated primarily with the 'large-scale' response of Genius to nature itself. This does not mean, however, that the ordinary man of taste has *no* sensibility, or that Genius can be oblivious to taste if he is to communicate effectively. For, as Rousseau observes in the article 'Goût':

> le génie crée, mais le goût choisit; et souvent le génie trop abondant a besoin d'un censeur qui l'empêche d'abuser de ses richesses. Sans goût, on peut faire de grandes choses, mais c'est lui qui les rend intéressantes.[47]

Although the relationship between taste and sensibility is not really clarified, it would seem that so far as Genius is concerned, sensibility is associated with the initial enlightenment and creative energy, and taste with matters of form and communication. Genius, in fact, must combine the two, and communicate a *volupté* to the greatest number, through *force* and *simplicity*. For simplicity is another quality attributed by Rousseau to the work of Genius; and one which may determine in part some of his own views on specific art-forms—for example, his preference of melody to harmony in music; or his feeling for line rather than chromatic subtlety in the visual arts.

None of this, however, *defines* the Genius; nor can it be expected to do so, since he is outside the ordinary human categories. He cannot be explained, or trained, or legislated into existence. He is a theoretical necessity in Rousseau's philosophy of art, standing in the same sort of relationship to the man of taste, as does the Lawgiver to the ordinary citizen; and, by the same analogy, the antithesis of the Man of Talent as the Lawgiver is the antithesis of the Despot. He is, in fact, brother to the Lawgiver and the Tutor, invoked to inaugurate a regeneration of art; and like those figures, must be regarded in the last analysis as a projection of Rousseau himself.

This being so, as the discussion of Rousseau and art reaches the point of transition from theory to practice, it becomes necessary to assume that he is the kind of Genius postulated in his philosophy; and while one may be inclined to demur at this prospect, it is at least a useful belief. It means, for example, that he can be seen once more as an outsider, nearer to Nature than is the public as a whole; and nearer to it, moreover, in two ways. The 'primitive' in him remains, as it were, *behind* the general movement towards sophistication and artifice, in that through physical sensation, he is more immediately and pleasurably aware of nature in the parts. On the other hand, as the highly 'evolved' Genius, he represents, through the collaboration of intellect, moral sentiment, emotion and imagination, an awareness of the whole system of nature, and man's relation to it. In this way, Rousseau the artist is *ahead* of society in aesthetic sensibility, as the Lawgiver is ahead of it in political enlightenment, or as the Tutor is ahead of the pupil in moral enlightenment; and his work must be thought of not merely in terms of self-expression, but in terms of a social, educative and even pastoral function.

Creative writing will, in fact, tend to appear as an exemplary act, an initiative like confessing, which, by evoking a response from the freely-developed good taste of the public, can lead to a general enlightenment in respect of the beauty and goodness of the natural order. And beyond this enlightenment, which is the only justification of art, it is possible, of course, to glimpse a meeting of aesthetic and religious experience; and a conception of the Genius not simply as an autonomous individualist, but as a mediator between Man and God, striving to bring the majority opinion of taste to the point of unanimity or 'unison', in praise of the greatest Artist of all—the Deity. It is hardly necessary to add that this too, in that it would make of the true artist a mixture of prophet and priest, shows a tendency which will culminate in well-known Romantic positions of the nineteenth century.

We can now look again at the works themselves, particularly the *Nouvelle Héloïse* and the autobiographical writings, to see what bearing his ideas have upon his achievements or failures as a writer; and the first point to note is that all these works have an obvious 'primitive' basis, of a sensuous, non-intellectual kind. In comparison with most of the classical writers of seventeenth-century France, for example, Rousseau demonstrates the increasing emphasis laid upon sensory experience as the raw material of art; and the importance accorded to the accumulation of such experience as the passive part of the artist's function. He is not, of course, unique in this respect, since it is a general tendency of the century, reflecting, amongst other things, the pervasive influence of Locke; but the *Nouvelle Héloïse* bears witness to exceptional sensitivity, not merely in the enrichment of descriptive writing, and the actual landscapes, but in the 'epicurean' elements such as Julie's addiction to relatively harmless sensual pleasures. Probably the best-known example of Rousseau's *sensualisme* in the *Nouvelle Héloïse* is the first kiss of Julie and Saint-Preux, which, in its day, seems to have set a standard in *volupté*.

It does not follow, however, that the various kinds of sensory experience have an equal importance in his work. The second book of *Emile*, dealing with the age of sensations, throws some light on this point,

by its suggestion of a hierarchy of the senses, particularly with regard
to the stimulation of the imagination. Taste, for example, is the most
completely 'physical' sense, offering little to the imagination; whereas
the sense of smell, slow to develop in the child, awakens the adult
imagination more than any other sense, especially in an erotic context.
There is a similar relationship between touch and sight. The first is sure
in operation, but limited in range, although as the incident of the kiss
shows, a great deal of emotion can be associated with it. Sight, on the
other hand, is expansive in operation but subject to error because of the
multiplicity of impressions involved. It calls for a greater degree of
intellectual judgment, and intrigues Rousseau on account of such things
as the illusions of perspective, which enter into his descriptions of
mountains, as, for example, in the twenty-third letter of the *Nouvelle
Héloïse*. Hearing, too, has a special interest for Rousseau because of the
connection with music and language; it is conceived as the most 'social'
of the senses, and exploited to create all kinds of moods, through sound,
and especially through rhythm.

But even more important for understanding of the sensuous element
in his writing is the description, in *Emile*, of a sixth sense; and the
postulation of a *raison sensitive*, which forms simple ideas through the
combination of several sensations, and of a *raison intellectuelle*, which
forms complex ideas through a combination of simple ideas. However
debatable this technical background may be as a theory of knowledge,
it is certainly relevant to Rousseau's art; for it means ultimately that
whereas everyone has the mere capacity for sensation, it is the business
of the artist to work on this raw material of sensation through the 'sixth
sense', if he is to fulfil his social function. In those parts of his work
which have a clear social aim, such as most of the *Nouvelle Héloïse*,
Rousseau carefully *organizes* sense-experience for the purpose of communication, and to stimulate the public imagination; and this fact must
be grasped at the outset, because it is a pointer to certain differences
between his 'public' and 'private' styles of writing.

Although Rousseau did much to revive the taste for nature and the
simple life, his art is by no means indiscriminate naturalism, nor is it in
any way naïve. The primitive in him may register impressions, but it is
the Genius who selects from them to convey essentials, concentrating
less upon accumulated details than upon proportions, relationships,
perspectives and the order of the whole. For this reason, his 'imitation
of nature' is apt to involve (contrary to common belief) an intellectual
technique of a fairly classical kind. This technique is, of course, intended

to stimulate emotion and imagination, in a way which is somewhat reminiscent of religious ritual; and can be associated with the idea of mediation which we have seen emerging from his philosophy of art.

This mediation calls for great skill; the Genius may, as we know, be considered to be far ahead of the public in sensibility, but his technique must not be too far ahead of taste, or communication breaks down. Rousseau's understanding of this problem of communication can be illustrated by an outstanding page of *Emile*, which emphasizes the great distance which separates raw sensation and evolved sensibility. It describes the beauty of the sunrise, with a brilliant ordering of sensory experience; and goes on to contrast the enthusiastic response of the Tutor's sensibility with the incomprehension of the pupil, who lacks the experience necessary for a full emotional response to the 'concert' of sense-impressions.

Une belle soirée on va se promener dans un lieu favorable, où l'horizon bien découvert laisse voir à plein le soleil couchant, et l'on observe les objets qui rendent reconnaissable le lieu de son coucher. Le lendemain, pour respirer le frais, on retourne au même lieu avant que le soleil se lève. On le voit s'annoncer de loin par les traits de feu qu'il lance au-devant de lui. L'incendie augmente, l'orient paraît tout en flammes; à leur éclat on attend l'astre longtemps avant qu'il se montre; à chaque instant on croit le voir paraître; on le voit enfin. Un point brillant part comme un éclair et remplit aussitôt tout l'espace; le voile des ténèbres s'efface et tombe. L'homme reconnaît son séjour et le trouve embelli. La verdure a pris durant la nuit une vigueur nouvelle; le jour naissant qui l'éclaire, les premiers rayons qui la dorent, la montrent couverte d'un brillant réseau de rosée, qui réfléchit à l'œil la lumière et les couleurs. Les oiseaux en chœur se réunissent et saluent de concert le père de la vie; en ce moment pas un seul ne se tait; leur gazouillement, faible encore, est plus lent et plus doux que dans le reste de la journée, il se sent de la langueur d'un paisible réveil. Le concours de tous ces objets porte aux sens une impression de fraîcheur qui semble pénétrer jusqu'à l'âme. Il y a là une demi-heure d'enchantement auquel nul homme ne résiste; un spectacle si grand, si beau, si délicieux, n'en laisse aucun de sang-froid.

Plein de l'enthousiasme qu'il éprouve, le maître veut le communiquer à l'enfant: il croit l'émouvoir en le rendant attentif aux sensations dont il est ému lui-même. Pure bêtise! c'est dans le cœur de l'homme qu'est la vie du spectacle de la nature; pour le voir, il faut le sentir. L'enfant aperçoit les objets, mais il ne peut apercevoir les rapports qui les lient, il ne peut entendre la douce harmonie de leur

concert. Il faut une expérience qu'il n'a point acquise, il faut des sentiments qu'il n'a point éprouvés, pour sentir l'impression composée
qui résulte à la fois de toutes ces sensations.[48]

With this passage in mind, it is interesting to remember that in a preface
to the *Nouvelle Héloïse*, Rousseau claims to be 'speaking to children'[49];
it would seem that this reflects not only upon the casting of a philosophy
into the form of a novel, but also upon certain stylistic procedures,
particularly in the descriptive elements, which fulfil the social function
of art in communicating enthusiasm through an *impression composée*.
To put it simply, he brings his writing into reasonable conformity with
public taste by processes of careful composition.

   Of all Rousseau's major works, it is in fact the *Nouvelle Héloïse* which
illustrates most clearly the aspects of individual sensibility and social
obligation in his conception of Genius; and this theoretical background
is undoubtedly a help in the evaluation of the book, both as an allegory
and as a novel. To begin with, it explains two specific defects: first, the
fact that almost all the characters are projections of Rousseau, in some
way and to some degree. The sensibility of Saint-Preux is that of
Rousseau; the conscience of Julie is that of Rousseau; the Epicurean side
of Julie is that of Rousseau; the Stoicism of Bomston is that of Rousseau;
and even the atheism of Wolmar is a reflection of part of Rousseau's
experience. This would not matter in the least if he had the true novelist's
gift of creating people with a real life of their own; but this, unfortunately, he lacks. The second defect of the novel as a product of hypothetical Genius is the excessive didacticism. Admittedly, this is a fault of
Rousseau's century in general; but the insistence in his theories on the
close relationship of ethical and aesthetic value holds risks which are
made only too patent by the direct preaching in parts of the *Nouvelle
Héloïse*.

   Against these defects, however, it is only just to point out two merits
connected with the social orientation of the book as a whole. The first
is Rousseau's handling of the group, and the sense of the modification
of behaviour and the creation of common sympathies through social
relations and the interaction of personalities. The second, is the relation
of the group to the natural Alpine setting, and the different responses
shown by various characters—emotional, in the case of Saint-Preux;
practical, in the case of Wolmar; and so on.

   Related to these social aspects of the work are some noteworthy
examples of the ritualistic element in Rousseau's art, marking by 'set
pieces' certain major stages in the movement of the allegory, such as the

marriage, the wine-harvest, or the last supper. These are of unequal merit, but are by no means to be despised. The handling of the marriage-ceremony, in particular, demonstrates excellently the operation of an *impression composée*, in Julie's response to the scene in the church, which begins with physical sensations and culminates in a moral gesture.

> Arrivée à l'église, je sentis en entrant une sorte d'émotion que je n'avais jamais éprouvée. Je ne sais quelle terreur vint saisir mon âme dans ce lieu simple et auguste, tout rempli de la majesté de celui qu'on y sert. Une frayeur soudaine me fit frissonner; tremblante et prête à tomber en défaillance, j'eus peine à me traîner jusqu'au pied de la chaire. Loin de me remettre, je sentis mon trouble augmenter durant la cérémonie, et s'il me laissait apercevoir les objets, c'était pour en être épouvantée. Le jour sombre de l'édifice, le profond silence des spectateurs, leur maintien modeste et recueilli, le cortège de tous mes parents, l'imposant aspect de mon vénéré père, tout donnait à ce qui s'allait passer un air de solennité qui m'excitait à l'attention et au respect, et qui m'eût fait frémir à la seule idée d'un parjure. Je crus voir l'organe de la Providence et entendre la voix de Dieu dans le ministre prononçant gravement la sainte liturgie. La pureté, la dignité, la sainteté du mariage, si vivement exposées dans les paroles de l'Ecriture, ses chastes et sublimes devoirs si importants au bonheur, à l'ordre, à la paix, à la durée du genre humain, si doux à remplir pour eux-mêmes; tout cela me fit une telle impression, que je crus sentir intérieurement une révolution subite. Une puissance inconnue sembla corriger tout à coup le désordre de mes affections et les rétablir selon la loi du devoir et de la nature.[50]

It can hardly be denied that this passage has a high artistic interest, bound up with its philosophical significance (and ambiguity); and a more sustained but less formal effort of the same kind is involved in the social climax of the wine-harvest. To recall the 'charms of the Golden Age', Rousseau here alternates between realistic detail and nostalgic appeals to the imagination, combining Old Testament echoes with a pagan and primitive atmosphere; and ends with the symbolic unison-singing of the women, and a ceremonial *feu d'artifice*, as a ritual of praise and thanksgiving.

These things are excellent in their way, but the rather obvious didacticism may prevent them from being rated as more than effective exercises at the level of 'good taste' as Rousseau understands it. There are, fortunately, more subtle and personal aspects of his genius, which give to the *Nouvelle Héloïse* a more lasting interest.

The importance of this novel in the history of literature has always been ascribed mainly to the subjective inspiration and the exploitation of the natural setting, both of which are clearly Romantic in tendency. The projection of Rousseau's aspirations and frustrations in Saint-Preux undoubtedly gave a great impetus to the *roman personnel* in France, and has an easily recognizable posterity in the writings of Senancour, Constant, Musset and others. Similarly, the exotic idyll of Bernardin de Saint-Pierre, or the virtuosity of Chateaubriand's descriptive style can be cited as stages in the line of influence leading to the Romantic presentation of external nature; and comparable currents can, of course, be detected in the literature of England and Germany (taking Goethe's *Werther* as a single example). But mere emotionalism or enthusiasm for nature, however important historically, are not necessarily good indications of lasting artistic interest; and Rousseau has perhaps suffered to some extent from a historical approach which has tended to stress potentialities rather than the intrinsic merits of his own achievements.

The landscape element is a good example of this, because it happens to be convenient, historically, as a mark of the transition from the false conventions of the Pastoral tradition to the 'ruggedness' of certain Romantic presentations of external nature. It is sometimes said that although Rousseau uses a mountainous setting of a more or less Romantic type, he has no real taste for nature in the raw, and is happy to settle for a comfortable and comforting rusticity. Now there may be some truth in this, but it is not the whole truth, and should certainly not be taken as a sign of a limited response on his part. The point is that his presentation of nature varies, often for philosophical reasons; and the reduction of it to terms of a mere sentimental idyll is a gross over-simplification.

The Alpine landscape is much more than a beautiful background or frame. Lake Geneva and its environs were not, in fact, Rousseau's first choice as a setting; and when he did decide upon it, he was influenced partly by personal associations and nostalgia, but also by the fact that he found it particularly adaptable to all the nuances of moral and sentimental life which he presents in his work. He exploits nature, indeed, in several ways, and at various levels of consciousness; and it is in this that much of the permanent artistic interest of the novel resides. There is obviously a level of simple 'realism', which does something (though not, perhaps, enough) to give the characters real existence. There is also the very Romantic enterprise of linking the mood of the characters with the mood of nature, seen in a number of passages, including, for example, Part I, letter 26, where the frustrated passion of Saint-Preux is associated with the harshness of winter in the mountains; or Part IV, letter 17, with the moonlit melancholy of the lake as an accompaniment to the crisis of resignation, displaying another remarkable selection and organization of sense-impressions. But beyond all this, there is a level of elusive symbolism which cannot always be felt without knowledge of Rousseau's whole philosophy.

It is at this level that the mountains cease to be mere scenery and become a 'presence' symbolizing eternal values, and implying, by their very grandeur, the necessity of human restraint, and sense of proportion. Peaks and isolated masses of rock stand out as symbols of genuinely primitive ruggedness, while the ice-fields suggest an unattainable purity which is almost certainly connected with the concept of Original Innocence. Conversely, it is the lower slopes which provide an accessible setting for the constructive social element. The domain of Clarens represents physically as well as morally the synthesis of nature and civilization; and it is surprising that even the most perceptive commentators have sometimes tended to criticize Rousseau for not taking us right up among the glaciers in his novel. In the general context of thought and symbolism, it would be quite inappropriate for him to do so.

Another aspect of his symbolic landscape is the lake itself. It is generally recognized that water, and feelings associated with it, have a special place in Rousseau's writing; and consideration of the related ideas of purity and transparency raises complex psychological problems which lie beyond the scope of a general introduction. Nevertheless, as part of the response to nature in the *Nouvelle Héloïse*, the water-theme is conspicuous enough to require some comment. It is used in various ways, sometimes to create special moods, as in Part IV, where the storm on the lake echoes and evokes the disturbances of emotional life. The careful irrigation of Julie's private garden or *Elysée*, and the contrast with the unnatural ostentation and luxury of fountains are fairly obvious pieces of symbolism, but other instances are more subtle, and leave the reader greater freedom of inference.

For example, Part II, letter 27, contains a simile comparing humanity and water, as the natural element which descends and seeks the level[51]— an isolated clue from which it is possible to glimpse a symbolic system reflecting something of Rousseau's egalitarian philosophy. In it, the lake itself seems to represent vaguely the new society, as a totality absorbing individual streams, while allowing some legitimate development on the periphery. The complement to this would seem to be a reflection of man's history in the streams and rivers which flow from the crystalline purity of the ice-fields, and in their descent collect impurities and débris which must be deposited before they flow into the lake.

These symbol-systems are loose and nebulous; and, one feels, more personal to the Genius than are the more obvious didactic elements in the book. It is not surprising, therefore, that the Genius-Lawgiver-Tutor figure also has a characteristic symbol or image—namely, that of the Navigator. From the *Discours sur les sciences et les arts* onwards, Rousseau tends to present human history as a voyage into the unknown, starting from the *beau rivage* of the state of nature,[52] and in which the destiny of the ship's company is in the hands of the genius-pilot. This theme is capable of a number of variations and associations, including Saint-Preux's voyage with Anson in the *Nouvelle Héloïse*, and even the use of *Robinson Crusoe* in the educational scheme of *Emile*. It occurs at the beginning of the *Profession de foi*, and can be traced right through to the *Rêveries*, where it links up with a cognate 'desert-island' theme, to create a last impression of Rousseau as a pilot who has been marooned by humanity at large. Such themes are seldom allowed to become obtrusive, but they are always there as recurring pointers to Rousseau's conception of his function as a Genius, and the ways in which his literary methods are affected by this aspect of his aesthetic doctrine.

The relationship between philosophy and art is fairly clear in the case of a 'public' work like the *Nouvelle Héloïse*, both at the moral and the technical level; but it is a matter which is bound also to enter into the appreciation of the more personal side of Rousseau's production. Since, in the autobiographical works, he presents himself directly, both as primitive and Genius, we shall naturally expect to find differences in literary techniques; but the earlier discussion of them is a warning not to expect a single set of characteristics in, say, the *Confessions* and the *Rêveries*.

The literary interest of the *Confessions* is bound up with the fact that they are intensely personal, and yet have an obviously social aim, both as a justification and as an initiative. They pose, indeed, a particularly interesting problem of facts, truth and art; and in spite of Rousseau's aspiration to 'tell all', it is evident that they are not a work of history, but a work of art, and social art into the bargain. It has been observed already that patient research tends to reveal inaccuracies in the *Confessions*; and some of these may be the result of forgetfulness, as Rousseau would claim. Others, however, must almost certainly be ascribed to an instinctive flinching from harsh reality; and to that *amour-propre* which he tries so hard to destroy. This must be borne in mind in connection with such a controversial matter as the presentation of the episode of Les Charmettes; or the treatment of Claude Anet and Winzenried. Rousseau undoubtedly slants his picture of Mme de Warens, and of circumstances relating to her, in a way consoling to his pride; and a vagueness as to the actual dates involved in this part of his life-story may also be in some degree the result of similar considerations. Yet it would not be fair to say that Rousseau has systematically distorted his life-story purely for reasons of self-esteem. We have to remember that he is defending a thesis involving the notion of the 'innocent fall'; and that this thesis will tend inevitably to lead to a whitening of the golden age in his life, and a corresponding blackening of the social hell into which he falls, and which is to be found in the presentation of the 'conspiracy' against him towards the end of the Confessions.

In short, the presentation of the Self, whether as primitive or as Genius, is a creative process, requiring a selective operation on the facts to produce what Rousseau would call a General Truth, and what we may think of more simply as a communicable image. The result may be—as he admits in the Rêveries—a 'profile',[53] but it is certainly a fascinating product of art; and the simplest way of appreciating it is to compare it with the process by which, in his descriptions of nature, Rousseau selects and organizes, to produce an impression composée. The figure whom we see in the Confessions is in a sense an impression composée of which the raw material is moral rather than physical. In this case, the Genius stands before the 'facts' of his own existence, responds to them emotionally through his highly-developed sensibility, and composes a picture which is doubtless consoling to himself, but which is also socially useful. And so, once again, the truth of the Confessions appears as a sentimental or pragmatic truth; and our attitude to the book must vary according to whether we judge it from a moral or aesthetic standpoint. There is certainly some imprecision as to fact, and in particular, some manipulation of perspectives, as in the case of Les Charmettes; but in so far as the Confessions have a social purpose, the inaccuracies seem to fall into the category of 'art' rather than that of 'lies'.

In general, all this can be said of the Dialogues as well. These quite exceptional writings contain remarkable self-portraiture; but because of the urgency of the defensive purpose, and the distressing circumstances in which they were composed, they are hardly a suitable basis for general judgments of Rousseau as an artist. They are, of course, fascinating in the actual degree of self-analysis, in the use of the device of *dédoublement*, and in the scale of the special pleading; but none of these things could be said to alter substantially the view of his art which is derived from the *Confessions*. This, however, is certainly not true of the *Rêveries*, a work which cannot but direct our attention back to the 'primitive' phase in his actual philosophy of art.

In view of the complexities of the philosophical and psychological background, it would be surprising if the art of the *Rêveries* did *not* differ markedly from that of the *Nouvelle Héloïse* or even the *Confessions*. The former, either as novel or as allegory, poses one set of problems of appreciation; and the latter, as autobiography, obviously raises different ones. Yet the change from autobiography to reverie is, if anything, even greater so far as artistic implications are concerned. In fact—and this is a curious irony connected with this very influential work—the fundamental question posed by the *Rêveries* is how far they can be thought of as *art* at all, according to any positive definition that could be provided by Rousseau's own philosophy.

The *Rêveries* involve, as we have seen in the previous chapter, a process of disengagement which could, and perhaps ought to, imply a liberation from art itself, if it is considered as a social activity. It is a matter of argument whether Rousseau goes this far or not; but it is clear that in the course of the work he does emancipate himself almost completely from the restraints of taste—even 'good taste'—or direct concern with public moral welfare. Theoretically, it could be argued that the *Rêveries* are not written to please or edify the public; and the fact that they have done both is a point on which it would be exceedingly interesting to have the opinions of their author! What happens, of course, is that following the general trend of the thought, the influential passages show the resignation and abstention of rejected Genius (corresponding to the withdrawal of the Lawgiver), and a deliberate return to the state of the primitive. In theory, this implies a drastic reduction in the scope of reverie; and in practice, it results in an attempt to abandon formal organization, in favour of the passive registration of sense-impressions derived from a strictly limited range of experience. Leaving aside the special circumstances in which the *Rêveries* were written, Rousseau sees this as being in any case the natural accompaniment of old age, and describes the actual process of restriction in a passage of the seventh Promenade.

> ... je ne puis plus, comme autrefois, me jeter tête baissée dans ce vaste océan de la nature, parce que mes facultés, affaiblies et relâchées, ne trouvent plus d'objets assez déterminés, assez fixes, assez à ma

portée, pour s'y attacher fortement, et que je ne me sens plus assez de vigueur pour nager dans le chaos de mes anciennes extases. Mes idées ne sont presque plus que des sensations, et la sphère de mon entende-ment ne passe pas les objets dont je suis immédiatement entouré.[54]

By acquiescing thus in the passing away of his former ecstasies (which are, of course, the most evolved form of *volupté*, the communication of which is the noblest aim of art), Rousseau seems to be renouncing in principle the status of Genius, although he continues to communicate a primitive and purely sensuous kind of *volupté*.

The effects of this particular aspect of disengagement upon his actual literary technique can be most easily grasped in the fifth Promenade, where he recalls his stay on the island of Saint-Pierre. Here, within the space of a few pages, are two remarkable and contrasting passages, the first of which is an 'organized' description with a strong social element in the conclusion, while the second is simply a record of sensations, of a purely personal and intimate kind. The description runs as follows.

Les rives du lac de Bienne sont plus sauvages et romantiques que celles du lac de Genève, parce que les rochers et les bois y bordent l'eau de plus près; mais elles ne sont pas moins riantes. S'il y a moins de culture de champs et de vignes, moins de villes et de maisons, il y a aussi plus de verdure naturelle, plus de prairies, d'asiles ombragés de bocages, des contrastes plus fréquents et des accidents plus rapprochés. Comme il n'y a pas sur ces heureux bords de grandes-routes commodes pour les voitures, le pays est peu fréquenté par les voyageurs; mais il est intéressant pour des contemplatifs solitaires qui aiment à s'enivrer à loisir des charmes de la nature, et à se recueillir dans un silence que ne trouble aucun autre bruit que le cri des aigles, le ramage entrecoupé de quelques oiseaux, et le roulement des torrents qui tombent de la montagne. Ce beau bassin, d'une forme presque ronde, enferme dans son milieu deux petites îles, l'une habitée et cultivée, d'environ une demi-lieue de tour; l'autre plus petite, déserte et en friche, et qui sera détruite à la fin par les transports de la terre qu'on en ôte sans cesse pour réparer les dégats que les vagues et les orages font à la grande. C'est ainsi que la substance du faible est toujours employée au profit du puissant.[55]

This is beautifully 'composed', and, with the moral twist of its symbolic conclusion, is a perfect example of the response of self-conscious Genius, conditioned socially, and attentive to considerations of 'taste'. In it, Rousseau is acting as a mediator, and almost, one might say, as a show-man of nature. The second passage, a famous one, records the hypnotic

effect of sense-impressions associated with water, and does not show the
detached point of view of the first.

> Quand le soir approchait, je descendais des cimes de l'île, et j'allais
> volontiers m'asseoir au bord du lac, sur la grève, dans quelque asile
> caché; là, le bruit des vagues et l'agitation de l'eau, fixant mes sens et
> chassant de mon âme toute autre agitation, la plongeaient dans une
> rêverie délicieuse, où la nuit me surprenait souvent sans que je m'en
> fusse aperçu. Le flux et le reflux de cette eau, son bruit continu, mais
> renflé par intervalles, frappant sans relâche mon oreille et mes yeux,
> suppléaient aux mouvements internes que la rêverie éteignait en moi,
> et suffisaient pour me faire sentir avec plaisir mon existence, sans
> prendre la peine de penser. De temps à autre naissait quelque faible
> et courte réflexion sur l'instabilité des choses de ce monde, dont la
> surface des eaux m'offrait l'image; mais bientôt ces impressions
> légères s'effaçaient dans l'uniformité du mouvement continu qui me
> berçait, et qui, sans aucun concours actif de mon âme, ne laissait pas
> de m'attacher au point qu'appelé par l'heure et par le signal convenu,
> je ne pouvais m'arracher de là sans effort.[56]

Examination of these two extracts from a single text reveals better than
volumes of vague discussion the two tendencies of Rousseau's writing—
the one active, organizing, social, moral; and expressing the responsibility of Genius; and the other which seeks to break through the barriers
of formal convention and return to the passivity of the primitive. And
the conclusions to be drawn from them can be reinforced by a further
comparison between the second passage and an earlier treatment of the
same subject in Book XII of the *Confessions*,[57] which leads to a silent
admiration of the Deity and not, as in the fifth Promenade, to a mere
sense of existence.

Now the first of the above-quoted passages is clearly the product of
'art', and would presumably be admitted to be so by Rousseau himself;
but would he concede as much in the case of the second? It certainly
involves *volupté* in the form of sensuous pleasure, but it is less certain
whether this could be described as aesthetic pleasure properly speaking.
Furthermore, the aspiration to complete passivity might well tempt us
to think of it as some kind of anti-art, and an attempt to break through
to an 'authentic' experience for which any kind of art is at best an inferior
substitute. Within Rousseau's own philosophy of art, the nearest
approach to a positive term with which to describe the experience recorded here, seems to be *occupation*, which occurs in the second Discourse
in the account of primitive dance and song. Otherwise, it could only be

described negatively, using a term to be found in the relevant section of the *Confessions*, as a refusal to perform an *acte développé*.[58]

Looking at it from outside the system, we can still, of course, regard such a passage as a work of art, because Rousseau is still creating a linguistic form in which to fix the experience. Moreover, the literary technique, with its subtleties of rhythm, alliteration, assonances and so on, is as refined or evolved as anything in Rousseau. For this reason, it becomes possible to assert that what we have here is not simply the renunciation of art, but the last use by Genius of the most refined techniques of art to communicate the most primitive kind of *volupté*.

Whichever way we choose to interpret the situation, it is clear that in his last work, Rousseau is coming to the end of the road, as artist as well as thinker. He does, it is true, attempt some further synthesis of the sensations of the primitive and the sensibility of the Genius, notably in the fragmentary tenth Promenade, where the fully-developed imagination and memory are used to recall the Golden Age with Mme de Warens, before his soul had, as he puts it, 'taken on any determined form'. But this effort cannot be sustained, because memory itself cannot avoid unhappiness, and because the act of writing is a developed act of a social nature, which tends to interfere with the *volupté* which he is trying to recapture. And so, in the final Promenade, Rousseau's last logical step, not only as a thinker dedicated to the principle of *amour de soi*, but as an artist dedicated to the *volupté* deriving from the *amour du beau*, is simply to *stop writing*, and cease from interposing forms of his own creating between himself and the enjoyment of sheer existence, which is all that is left to him.

Form, which is an imitation of natural beauty, is finally emptied out of Rousseau's private world, just as is morality, or the imitation of natural goodness; and when this happens, we can say that he has literally written himself out. As an artist, he has fulfilled the social obligations of Genius, and has been left free to indulge his sensibility outside the social context. But in the end, Art, like Thought and Life itself, is reduced to a pleasant consciousness of existence; and beyond that lies only non-existence—or, if his gestures of faith are justified, recognition and integration in the paradise to come.

Conclusion

*

EXAMINATION of both the thought and the art of the *Rêveries du promeneur solitaire* shows the last act of Rousseau's career being played out in a state of mental isolation which is partly, though not entirely, an illusion. In such circumstances, it is extremely difficult to draw a firm line between the play of the artist's imagination and sensibility and what might be thought of more crudely as the delusions of an eccentric philosopher. Nevertheless, one thing at least is clear: namely, that while, at first sight, the *Rêveries* seem to take us into a completely different world from that of a work like the *Contrat Social*, they represent the application to particular and private problems of the basic principle of the public philosophy, carried as far as the *pays des chimères* invoked by Julie in the *Nouvelle Héloïse*.

So far as his philosophical status is concerned, the imaginative content of this last work is undoubtedly dangerous; and parts of it could obviously be used to support the opinion that in his last years, Rousseau's conception of himself and his function in the world was tending to transcend the level of mere genius, and developing on specifically Messianic lines. From this, it is easy to go on and blame him for the emergence of new forms of political mysticism, and of social systems depending on infallible leaders and prophets. To this rather one-sided view, the 'primitive' aspect of his last mental evolution is a necessary corrective.

It is most improbable that this extraordinary man ever thought of himself literally as a new Messiah; and it is certain that at the end he did not rate very highly his chances of success even as a Navigator or pilot of humanity. In fact, the last fleeting glimpse that we have of him as an expedition-leader refers to the founding, not of a new society of men, but of a colony of rabbits, on the little island of the lake of Bienne! This occurs in the fascinating fifth Promenade of the *Rêveries*, and there is some doubt as to whether the passage should be interpreted as pure pathos, or savage irony, or simply as a saving gleam of humour in a world of darkness and distress.

We may infer from it, in any case, that Rousseau tended to think of himself as having failed in a mission of *bon sens* and sincerity; and yet, in the long run, the gesture of the *Confessions* can be said to have succeeded in that men have been brought by his writings to think and feel in new ways about their nature and potentialities. His influence, both for good and ill, has been extraordinarily pervasive and persistent; and when account is taken of the transformation of political thinking and his impact upon aristocratic society; of the changes of emphasis in education; of the exploration of the self in literature; of the preservation of poetic and religious sensibility; or the more technical influence in philosophy by way of Kant, it can be said of him that he does indeed measure up to his own conception of intervening Genius. He belongs, incontestably, to the select minority who have genuinely wrought radical changes of outlook among men; and it is doubtful whether this could be said of any of the contemporary French thinkers, even though they may have had better minds than his. Nobody is under any obligation to approve of him, but it is certainly impossible to ignore his presence in the stream of European thought and literature.

The degree of admiration or dislike with which he is regarded seems to be bound up with the image of him as a revolutionary philosopher; but even this depends on the perspective in which he is set. It is true that his thought assumes revolutionary forms, but he would doubtless claim to be working for the end of revolution, in the name of conservation, conciliation and reason. In fact, he brought, not peace, but a sword; and it is a characteristic paradox that precisely because of his conciliatory intentions, the sword is a two-edged one. This is why there is not a single major element in his doctrine which has not provoked conflicting interpretations, and why his influence in history has not always taken the direction he would have wished.

The pattern of such controversies is indicated very clearly by the hoary arguments as to whether the *Contrat Social* is a work of liberal or repressive tendency. It is claimed, not without some justification, that he is a liberal who betrayed the cause of liberty; and it could be argued in exactly the same way that he was an individualist who opened a way to the crushing of individualism; that he was a religious genius who sapped religion from the inside; that his aesthetic doctrine is Classical, and his performance and influence Romantic; and so on. Clearly, the interpretation varies according to the prejudices of the critics; and it also varies according to the fashions of intellectual life—a fact which he would probably have noted with devastating irony, could he have lived to reflect upon it. Thus, for the nineteenth century, he is, on the whole, a great Romantic; when Pragmatism is the fashion in philosophy, he is presented as a pragmatist; when Existentialism is in the news, he becomes an existentialist; to the Freudian, he is a collection of complexes; to the Catholic, he is simply a Reformer, or an old-fashioned heretic—a Pelagian, perhaps—unless it is decided that he is a Catholic after all, which is also a possible view.

There is no reason to be disturbed by these conflicts of opinion—and no point in trying to classify him with a single or narrow label. The fact that he continues to challenge critical opinion, and that succeeding generations tend to fashion a Rousseau in their own image, is one of the signs of his real greatness; and it may be said also that if he has been all things to all men, this seems to support his claim to be expressing principles of common sense. On the whole, the most interesting and perhaps the most disturbing aspect of the eternal controversy is that which concerns Rousseau and the spirit of the Enlightenment. For some, he is the undertaker of the *siècle des lumières*: the man who by spellbinding rhetoric ruined the age of reason and led the way to disastrous emotionalism; for others, on the contrary, Rousseau *is* the Enlightenment, and the most complete symbol of the particular form of humanism in his age. The co-existence of such contrasting opinions depends evidently upon the interpretation of the word *lumières*. If this is taken in a narrow sense to mean dependence upon processes of ratiocination alone, then Rousseau does not represent the Enlightenment; but if it is taken to mean the expansion and exploitation of all forms of our awareness, then he must certainly be put among the great figures of the movement. Once more, it seems that there is truth on both sides, but that neither view gives the whole truth.

The safest way out of the difficulty is to recall the eclectic nature of Rousseau's original inspirations, and his repeated claims to be following the middle course between the extremes of intolerant dogmatism. This suggests that he was trying courageously to do what somebody has to do in every age: namely, to work out for his own times a practical and acceptable synthesis of old traditions and new philosophies, in the belief that there is value in all of them. This is what he means by reason; and it is in the light of this that his philosophy can be seen to make sense in a particular historical context.

This raises, however, the question of the permanent value and relevance of his work, and the ways in which he can be appreciated today; and here, one thing which cannot be said too often, is that the surest way to kill Rousseau is to study him only in the parts. It is necessary and valuable, no doubt, to consider the *Contrat Social* in the context of Western political theory, or *Emile* in the perspective of pedagogical thought; but this analytical treatment needs to be supplemented by some effort of synthesis, if any just assessment is to be made possible. It is only by reference to the metaphysical and religious thought that the paradoxes of the politics can be understood; and if the parts are not related to the whole in this way, it is only too likely that the reader will conclude that his philosophy is jejune or derivative; that his religion is a disastrous compromise; that in his literary work there is more promise than achievement, and so on.

All real communication must involve a sense of the uniqueness of the total phenomenon which is Rousseau, and which is more than a sum of parts; and this can only take place through what he himself would call an *impression composée*, in which the arbitrary distinctions between the philosopher, the man and the artist are effaced as much as possible. These aspects may have to be considered separately up to a point, because, as he observes in the *Contrat Social*, one cannot say everything simultaneously; but in the long run, the man's life is seen to be a philosophy in action, and both are works of art.

What finally emerges—and this is the real reason why Rousseau is still worth reading—is his artist's sense of the sheer richness of life; and the radical protest against anything which impairs or lessens our experience of it at any level, whether sensuous, intellectual, moral or spiritual. This, after all, is what is involved in the doctrine of Self-Interest, and it is in exploring the range of possible satisfactions—even the satisfaction of suffering—that his work remains creative and challenging.

Chronological Outline of the Life of Rousseau

CHILDHOOD

1712	28 June	Birth of Jean-Jacques Rousseau, son of Isaac Rousseau, Citizen of Geneva, and of Suzanne Bernard.
	7 July	Death of Rousseau's mother. He is brought up by an aunt, Suzanne Rousseau.
1719-1720		First records of his literary formation. He reads novels with his father, but also encounters historians and moralists, notably Plutarch.
1722	October	Isaac Rousseau leaves Geneva, after a dispute with a retired officer, and settles at Nyon. Jean-Jacques is installed with his cousin in the house of Lambercier, pastor of Bossey, near Geneva.
1724		Returns to Geneva.
1725	26 April	Articled for five years as apprentice to Abel Du Commun, engraver.

THE YEARS OF ADVENTURE

1728	14 March	Rousseau finds the gates of Geneva closed, on returning from a walk; and leaves his native city.
	21 March	Arrives at Annecy. First encounter with Mme de Warens.
	12 April	He enters the Hospice of the Holy Ghost at Turin.
	21 April	He abjures the Protestant faith, and is subsequently baptized.
	Summer-Autumn	Rousseau employed as lackey by Mme de Vercellis, and is the cause of the unjust dismissal of a servant-girl. Appointed secretary to the son of the Comte de Gouvon.
1729	June	He is dismissed, and returns to Annecy and Mme de Warens.
1730-1731		Mme de Warens departs for Paris. Travels and adventures in Lyons, Fribourg, Lausanne, Vevey, Neuchâtel, Bern, Soleure, Paris, Lyons again, and Chambéry. He lives by giving music-lessons, and other expedients. In Paris, he becomes a servant, but on hearing that Mme de Warens has left the city, follows her back to Savoy.

1731	October	He takes a post in the survey-office of Savoy.
1732	June	Gives up his post and returns to music-teaching in Chambéry.
1733		Becomes the lover of Mme de Warens.
1734	13 March	Death of Claude Anet, supplanted by Rousseau.
1735 or 1736	Summer–Autumn	First stay with Mme de Warens at Les Charmettes. The 'idyll'.
1737	September	His sight having been endangered by an accident, he travels to Montpellier for treatment. Amorous adventure with Mme de Larnage, and masquerade as an English Jacobite.
1738	February–March	Return to Chambéry, and discovery that his relationship with Mme de Warens has been destroyed by her factotum Winzenried.
1739	Spring	Rousseau, living alone at Les Charmettes, devotes himself to study.
1740	April	He leaves Chambéry for Lyons, where he becomes tutor to the sons of M. de Mably.
	November–December	He composes his first work on education: *Projet pour l'éducation de M. de Sainte-Marie.*
1741	Spring	Return to Chambéry, followed (probably) by another stay in Lyons.

THE YEARS OF AMBITION

1742	January (?)	Last stay at Les Charmettes. Further studies, and work on a new system of musical notation.
	July	Rousseau departs for Paris.
	22 August	He communicates his musical system to the Académie des Sciences.
1743	Spring	Introduced to the Dupin family, and to Francueil. Begins work on his opera *Les Muses galantes.*
	June	Accepts appointment as secretary to the Comte de Montaigu, ambassador-designate in Venice.
	4 September	Arrival of Rousseau in Venice.
1744	22 August	Departure from Venice, after quarrelling with Montaigu. On his return to Paris, Rousseau is introduced to the financier La Pouplinière.
1745	March	Beginning of the liaison with Thérèse Levasseur.
	September	Performances of *Les Muses galantes* before La Pouplinière and the Duc de Richelieu. Relations with Condillac and Diderot.
	December	First exchange of letters with Voltaire.

1746	Autumn	He becomes secretary to Mme Dupin and her son-in-law Francueil. His first child abandoned at the *Enfants-Trouvés*.
1747		He makes the acquaintance of Mme d'Epinay.
	Autumn	Composes a comedy, *L'Engagement téméraire*, during a stay at Chenonceaux.
1748	February	Rousseau's first meeting with Mlle de Bellegarde, later to become Mme d'Houdetot.
		Abandonment of a second child by Thérèse.
1749	January	He begins to write articles on music for the *Encyclopédie*.
	24 July	Arrest of Diderot, and his imprisonment at Vincennes.
	August	Rousseau meets Grimm, to be much involved in later quarrels.
	October	The visit to Diderot, and the 'revelation' on the road to Vincennes. Rousseau begins work on the *Discours sur les sciences et les arts*.
1750	9 July	The *Discours* awarded the prize by the Academy of Dijon. Published towards the end of the year.

THE YEARS OF ACHIEVEMENT

1751	February	Rousseau's *réforme*. He resigns his post with Francueil, and takes up music-copying as a livelihood.
	Spring	Birth of a third child.
	Autumn	Refutations of the *Discours sur les sciences et les arts* by the King of Poland, Gautier, Bordes etc.
1752	April	Publication of Rousseau's *Réponse à M. Borde*.
	August	He visits Mme d'Epinay at La Chevrette.
	18 October	Successful performance of his opera *Le Devin du Village* before the King at Fontainebleau. Rousseau lets pass an opportunity of gaining a royal pension.
	18 December	Performance of his early play *Narcisse*. He replies to his critics in a new Preface.
1753	November	The Academy of Dijon proposes a new essay competition on the subject of Inequality.
		The publication of the *Lettre sur la Musique française*, written in 1752, embroils Rousseau with the Paris Opera.
1754	1 June	Rousseau and Thérèse leave Paris for Geneva, with Rousseau's friend Gauffecourt.
		Last meeting with Mme de Warens at Chambéry. Later, he will reproach himself with having abandoned her in low circumstances.

	August	He regains his citizenship of Geneva, and returns to the Protestant faith.
		Composition of the *Discours sur l'origine de l'inégalité*.
1755	Summer	Publication of the *Discours*, and of the fifth volume of the *Encyclopédie*, containing Rousseau's article *Economie Politique*.
	September	He visits La Chevrette. Mme d'Epinay proposes that he should install himself at l'Ermitage, a house in her park.
1756	April	Rousseau, Thérèse and Mme Levasseur move to l'Ermitage.
	August	The *Lettre sur la Providence*—a reply to Voltaire's *Poème sur le désastre de Lisbonne*.
	Summer–Autumn	Rousseau's first conception of the *Nouvelle Héloïse*, and composition of a few letters.
1757	January	First visit to l'Ermitage by Mme d'Houdetot.
	March	Quarrel between Rousseau and Diderot, occasioned by a passage in the latter's *Fils naturel*.
	Spring–Summer	Rousseau's passion for Mme d'Houdetot.
	Autumn	Quarrels with Mme d'Epinay and Grimm, arising from the liaison between Mme d'Houdetot and Saint-Lambert.
	December	Rousseau and Thérèse move to Montmorency.
1758	2 March	He attempts a reconciliation with Diderot.
	6 May	Mme d'Houdetot severs relations with him.
	Summer	Publication of the *Lettre à d'Alembert sur les spectacles*.
1759	May	Rousseau is installed at Montmorency by the Maréchal de Luxembourg; and works simultaneously on the *Nouvelle Héloïse*, *Emile* and the *Contrat Social*.
1760		Work continues on *Emile* and the *Contrat Social*, while the *Nouvelle Héloïse* is printing.
	December	The *Nouvelle Héloïse* on sale in London.
1761	January	Appearance and success of the novel in Paris.
	February	Publication of the Preface to the *Nouvelle Héloïse*.
	August	Revision of the MS of the *Contrat Social*.
	September	Rousseau sends to Malesherbes his *Essai sur l'origine des langues*.
	31 December	The publisher Marc-Michel Rey asks Rousseau for an autobiography, to accompany an edition of his works.
1762	January	In a state of depression, Rousseau writes the four autobiographical *Lettres à Malesherbes*.
	April–May	Publication of *Emile*, followed by the *Contrat Social*.

| | 9 June | *Emile* condemned by the Parlement of Paris. Rousseau flees from France to avoid arrest. |

THE YEARS OF ATONEMENT

1762	14 June	Arrival of Rousseau at Yverdon, in the territory of Bern.
	19 June	*Emile* and the *Contrat Social* burned by the authorities in Geneva; and the arrest of Rousseau is ordered.
	1 July	The Bernese authorities decree his expulsion.
	10 July	Arrival of Rousseau at Môtiers, in the Val-de-Travers (in the Prussian principality of Neuchâtel).
	29 July	Death of Mme de Warens at Chambéry.
	28 August	Publication of the *Mandement* of Christophe de Beaumont, Archbishop of Paris, condemning *Emile*.
1763	March	Publication of the *Lettre à Christophe de Beaumont*, in defence of *Emile*.
	16 April	Rousseau naturalized in the territory of Neuchâtel.
	12 May	He renounces citizenship of Geneva.
1764		He is involved in the politics of Geneva, and publishes his *Lettres écrites de la Montagne*.
	December	Final decision to write the *Confessions*, and composition of the preamble.
1765	Spring	Rousseau involved in a dispute with Montmollin, pastor of Môtiers.
	July	First stay of ten days on the island of Sainte-Pierre, on the lake of Bienne.
	1-3 September	Visit of Mme de Verdelin, and suggestion that he should go to England under the auspices of David Hume.
	6 September	Stoning of Rousseau's house at Môtiers.
	September–October	Second stay of six weeks on the island of Saint-Pierre, ending with his expulsion by the Bernese authorities.
	29 October	He leaves Bienne for Berlin, but is received with enthusiasm at Strasbourg.
	November	He is given a passport for France, but decides to go to England.
	16 December	He arrives in Paris, and is the guest of the Prince de Conti.
1766	4 January	Departure from Paris with Hume.
	January–March	Rousseau is installed at Chiswick, and joined by Thérèse.
	22 March	He arrives at Wootton, in Staffordshire.
	Summer–Autumn	Public quarrel with Hume, whom Rousseau suspects of plotting to discredit him.
		Composition of the first books of the *Confessions*.

1767	18 March	Rousseau is granted a pension by George III.
	1 May	Departure from Wootton with Thérèse.
	21 May	Departure from England.
	21 June	Back in France, he arrives at Trye, under the protection of the Prince de Conti, using the pseudonym of Renou.
	November	Publication of the *Dictionnaire de musique*.
1768	14 June	Departure from Trye.
	11 July	Arrives at Grenoble. Preoccupied with botany.
	25 July	Pilgrimage to the tomb of Mme de Warens at Chambéry.
	13 August	He takes up residence at Bourgoin (Dauphiné).
	30 August	'Marriage' of Rousseau and Thérèse at Bourgoin.
1769	27 April	He tells his publisher Rey that he wishes to abandon the *Confessions*.
	November	Resumption of work on the second part of the *Confessions*.
1770	10 April	Departure for Lyons.
	June	Return of Rousseau to Paris. He settles in the rue Plâtrière, and resumes music-copying as a profession.
	November	His obsession with the 'plot' against him plunges him into great agitation.
	December	Approximate date of the completion of the *Confessions*, from which he gives readings in the house of the Marquis de Pezay.
1771	Spring	Further readings of the *Confessions*, e.g. before the Comtesse d'Egmont.
	10 May	Mme d'Epinay seeks a police ban on these readings.
1772	April	Completion of the political work *Considérations sur le gouvernement de Pologne*.
		Rousseau begins to write the *Dialogues* or *Rousseau juge de Jean-Jacques*.
1773		Continuation of the *Dialogues*. Music-copying and botany.
1774		New preoccupation with music. Relations with Gluck. Composition of part of *Daphnis et Chloé*, and of a new score of *Le Devin du village*.
1775	31 October	Successful performance of Rousseau's *Pygmalion* at the Comédie-Française.
1776		Completion of the *Dialogues*.
	24 February	Unsuccessful attempt to place the MS on the altar of Notre-Dame.
	25 February	He places the MS in the hands of Condillac.

	6 April	Convinced that he has made a mistake, he entrusts a copy of the first *Dialogue* to Brooke Boothby.
	April	He distributes in the street his circular *A tout Français aimant la justice et la vérité.*
	Summer	He writes the *Histoire du précédent écrit.*
	Autumn	Composition of the first Promenade of the *Rêveries.*
	24 October	Date of the accident recounted in the second Promenade.
	December	Composition of the second Promenade.
1777	Spring-Summer	Composition of Promenades nos. 3-7.
	August	He gives up music-copying.
1778	Late Winter	Composition of the eighth Promenade.
	March	Ninth Promenade.
	12 April	Tenth Promenade begun and abandoned.
	2 May	He entrusts MSS, including copies of the *Confessions* and *Dialogues*, to his friend Paul Moultou.
	20 May	He accepts the hospitality of the Marquis de Girardin at Ermenonville, and is joined by Thérèse.
	2 July	Death of Rousseau.
	4 July	Burial of Rousseau on the Ile des Peupliers, Ermenonville.
1794	October	Rousseau's remains transferred to the Panthéon in Paris.

APPENDIX II

Bibliography

COLLECTED WORKS

Œuvres, Paris, H. Féret, 25 vols., 1826.
Œuvres, ed. Lahure. Paris, Hachette, 13 vols., 1865.
Œuvres, ed. B. Gagnebin and M. Raymond. Paris, Gallimard, Bibliothèque de la Pléiade, 1959-. The volumes so far published are
Vol. I *Confessions; autres textes autobiographiques.*
Vol. II *La Nouvelle Héloïse; théâtre; essais littéraires.*
Correspondance Générale, ed. T. Dufour and P. Plan. Paris, Colin, 1924-34, 20 vols.

INDIVIDUAL WORKS AND GROUPS OF TEXTS

Discours sur les sciences et les arts, ed. G. R. Havens. New York, Mod. Lang. Association, 1946.
The Political Writings of Jean-Jacques Rousseau, ed. C. E. Vaughan. Cambridge, 1915.
Du Contrat Social (with the *Discours* and the *Lettre à d'Alembert sur les spectacles*). Paris, Garnier, 1959.
Emile, ed. F. and P. Richard. Paris, Garnier, 1951.
La Profession de foi du vicaire savoyard, ed. P. M. Masson. Paris, Hachette, 1914.
La Nouvelle Héloïse, ed. D. Mornet. Paris, Hachette, 1925, 4 vols.
La Nouvelle Héloïse, ed. R. Pomeau. Paris, Garnier, 1960.
Les Rêveries du promeneur solitaire, ed. M. Raymond. Geneva, Droz, 1948.
Les Rêveries du promeneur solitaire, ed. J. S. Spink. Paris, Didier, 1948.
Les Rêveries du promeneur solitaire, ed. H. Roddier. Paris, Garnier, 1960.

ENGLISH TRANSLATIONS

The Social Contract and Discourses, with introduction by G. D. H. Cole. Everyman, no. 660.
Political Writings, transl. and ed. F. Watkins. Edinburgh, Nelson, 1953.
Emile (including the *Profession de foi*), transl. B. Foxley. Everyman, no. 518.
Confessions, with introduction by R. Niklaus. Everyman, nos. 859-860.
Reveries of a Solitary, transl. J. G. Fletcher. Routledge, 1927, Broadway Library of Eighteenth-Century French Literature.

A REPRESENTATIVE SELECTION OF STUDIES AND CRITICISM

Annales de la Société Jean-Jacques Rousseau. Geneva (34 vols. since 1905).

Babbitt, Irving, *Rousseau and Romanticism.* Boston, Houghton Mifflin, 1919.

Boyd, W., *Emile for Today.* London, Heinemann, 1956.

Burgelin, P., *La Philosophie de l'existence de Jean-Jacques Rousseau.* Paris, Presses Universitaires Françaises, 1952.

Cassirer, E., *The Problem of Jean-Jacques Rousseau* (transl. P. Gay). New York, Columbia University Press, 1954.

Chapman, J. W., *Rousseau, Totalitarian or Liberal?* New York, Columbia University Press, 1956.

Cobban, A., *Rousseau and the Modern State.* London, George Allen and Unwin, 1934.

Derathé, A., *Jean-Jacques Rousseau et la science politique de son temps.* Paris, Presses Universitaires de France, 1950.

Derathé, A., *Le Rationalisme de Jean-Jacques Rousseau.* Paris, Presses Universitaires de France, 1948.

Ducros, L., *Jean-Jacques Rousseau.* Fontemoing, De Boccard, 1908-1918.

Ellis, M. B., *Julie ou la Nouvelle Héloïse. A Synthesis of Rousseau's Thought, 1749-1759.* University of Toronto Press, 1949.

Green, F. C., *Jean-Jacques Rousseau.* Cambridge University Press, 1955.

Grimsley, R., *Jean-Jacques Rousseau. A Study in Self-Awareness.* Cardiff, University of Wales Press, 1961.

Hendel, C. W., *Jean-Jacques Rousseau, Moralist.* London and New York, Oxford University Press, 1934.

Jimack, P. D., *La Genèse et la rédaction de l'Emile* (Studies on Voltaire and the Eighteenth Century, Vol. XIII). Geneva, Institut et Musée Voltaire, 1960.

Maritain, J., *Trois Réformateurs.* Paris, Plon, 1925.

Masson, P. M., *La Religion de Jean-Jacques Rousseau.* Paris, Hachette, 1914, 3 vols.

May, G., *Rousseau par lui-même.* Paris, Editions du Seuil, 1961.

Morley, J., *Rousseau and his Era.* London, Macmillan, 1923 etc.

Ravier, A., *L'Education de l'homme nouveau; essai historique et critique sur le livre de l'Emile de J.-J. Rousseau.* Issoudun, 1941.

Schinz, A., *La Pensée de Jean-Jacques Rousseau.* Paris, Alcan, 1929.

Starobinski, J., *Jean-Jacques Rousseau. La transparence et l'obstacle.* Paris, Plon, 1957.

Wright, E. H., *The Meaning of Rousseau.* Oxford University Press, 1929.

References

(1) *Confessions* VIII, Pléiade ed., Gallimard, 1959, p. 351.
(2) *Disc. sur les sciences et les arts* (with *Contrat Social*), Garnier, 1960, p. 5.
(3) *Œuvres*, Pléiade ed., Gallimard, 1961, Vol. II, p. 970.
(4) ibid., p. 969.
(5) *Disc. sur l'origine de l'inégalité* (with *Contrat Social*), Garnier, 1960, p. 76.
(6) ibid., p. 79.
(7) *Emile*, Garnier, 1951, p. 279.
(8) *Contrat Social*, Garnier, 1960, p. 235.
(9) ibid., p. 247.
(10) *Emile*, Garnier, 1951, p. 5.
(11) ibid., p. 13.
(12) ibid., p. 12.
(13) ibid., pp. 70-71.
(14) ibid., p. 237.
(15) ibid., p. 404.
(16) *Confessions* etc., Pléiade ed., Gallimard, 1959, p. 1018.
(17) *Emile*, Garnier, 1951, p. 343.
(18) ibid., p. 354.
(19) ibid., p. 359.
(20) *Julie ou la Nouvelle Héloïse*, Garnier, 1960, IV, 10, p. 428.
(21) ibid., IV, 11, pp. 453-472.
(22) *Confessions*, Pléiade ed., Gallimard, 1959, p. 5.
(23) ibid., p. 3.
(24) ibid., p. 5.
(25) ibid., p. 229.
(26) ibid., pp. 977-989.
(27) ibid., p. 858ff. Dialogue II.
(28) ibid., pp. 765-6.
(29) *Emile*, Garnier, 1951, pp. 46-47.
(30) *Confessions* etc., Pléiade ed., Gallimard, 1959, pp. 1062-3.
(31) *Julie ou la Nouvelle Héloïse*, Garnier, 1960, I, 12, pp. 32-33.
(32) *Emile*, Garnier, 1951, p. 425.
(33) *Œuvres*, Féret, 1826, Vol. XI, p. 264.
(34) ibid., p. 288.
(35) *Contrat Social* etc., Garnier, 1960, p. 71.
(36) *Emile*, Garnier, 1951, p. 213ff.
(37) *Contrat Social* etc., Garnier, 1960, p. 4.
(38) ibid., p. 19.

(39) *Œuvres*, Féret, 1826, Vol. XI, pp. 278-282.

(40) *Julie ou la Nouvelle Héloïse*, Garnier, 1960, II, 23, pp. 259-268.

(41) *Emile*, Garnier, 1951, p. 425.

(42) *Contrat Social* etc., Garnier, 1960, pp. 150-158, 164-166.

(43) ibid., p. 16.

(44) *Emile*, Garnier, 1951, p. 226ff.

(45) ibid., p. 425.

(46) *Contrat Social* etc., Garnier, 1960, p. 22.

(47) *Œuvres*, Féret, 1826, Vol. XII, p. 420.

(48) *Emile*, Garnier, 1951, pp. 186-187.

(49) *Julie ou la Nouvelle Héloïse*, Garnier, 1960, p. 743.

(50) ibid. pp. 332-333.

(51) ibid., p. 283.

(52) *Contrat Social* etc., Garnier, 1960, p. 16.

(53) *Confessions* etc., Pléiade ed., Gallimard, 1959, p. 1036.

(54) ibid., p. 1066.

(55) ibid., pp. 1040-1.

(56) ibid., p. 1045.

(57) ibid., p. 642.

(58) ibid., p. 642.

Index

225